LEGAL CONCEPTS OF CHILDHOOD

Legal Concepts of Childhood

Edited by

JULIA FIONDA
University of Southampton

·H A R T·
PUBLISHING

OXFORD – PORTLAND OREGON
2001

Hart Publishing
Oxford and Portland, Oregon

Published in North America (US and Canada) by
Hart Publishing c/o
International Specialized Book Services
5804 NE Hassalo Street
Portland, Oregon
97213-3644
USA

Distributed in the Netherlands, Belgium and Luxembourg by
Intersentia, Churchillaan 108
B2900 Schoten
Antwerpen
Belgium

Hart Publishing is a specialist legal publisher based in Oxford, England.
To order further copies of this book or to request a list of other
publications please write to:

Hart Publishing, Salter's Boatyard, Folly Bridge,
Abingdon Road, Oxford OX1 4LB
Telephone: +44 (0)1865 245533 or Fax: +44 (0)1865 794882
e-mail: mail@hartpub.co.uk
WEBSITE: http//www.hartpub.co.uk

British Library Cataloguing in Publication Data
Data Available
ISBN 1–84113–150–4

Typeset by Hope Services (Abingdon) Ltd.
Printed and bound in Great Britain on acid-free paper by
Biddles Ltd, www.biddles.co.uk

For Dr Vera Harsanyi

Contents

viii   *Contents*

List of Contributors

David Archard was educated at Oxford and the London School of Economics. He taught for a number of years at the University of Ulster but is currently Reader in Moral Philosophy at the University of St Andrews. He is the author of a number of books including *Children: Rights and Childhood* (London, Routledge, 1993), and many articles and chapters in social, political, moral and legal philosophy. He is the co-editor of and contributor to the forthcoming *The Moral and Political Status of Children: New Essays*.

Roderick Bagshaw is Tutor and Fellow in Law at Mansfield College, University of Oxford. He is co-author of McBride and Bagshaw, *Textbook on Tort* (London, Longman, 2001) and an editor of *Phipson on Evidence* (15th ed, London, Sweet and Maxwell, 2000) and *Cross and Wilkins' Outline of the Law of Evidence* (7th ed, London, Butterworths, 1996). He lives in Oxford with his wife, who is also a law academic.

Dave Cowan is a lecturer at the University of Bristol. He is author of *Homelessness: The (In-)Appropriate Applicant* (Aldershot, Dartmouth, 1997) and *Housing Law and Policy* (Basingstoke, Macmillan, 1999), as well as editor of several collections and journal articles on housing and related issues.

Nick Dearden is a solicitor and Senior Lecturer in Law at Manchester Metropolitan University. He is a Trustee of the Albert Kennedy Trust, a voluntary agency committed to addressing the problems faced by homeless lesbian and gay teenagers.

Julia Fionda is a lecturer and Director of the Institute of Criminal Justice in the Law Faculty at Southampton University. Her teaching and research interests include youth justice, criminal justice and criminology. She has published a number of articles in these fields and is author of *Public Prosecutors and Discretion: A Comparative Study* (Oxford, OUP, 1995).

Michael Freeman is Professor of English Law at University College London. He is the editor of the *International Journal of Children's Rights*, was formerly editor of the *Annual Survey of Family Law* and is Vice-President of the International Society of Family Law. He is the author of *The Rights and Wrongs of Children* (Pinter, 1983); *Children, Their Families and the Law* (Macmillan, 1992) and *The Moral Status of Children* (Nijhoff, 1997). His current research is into cultural pluralism and the rights of children.

Chris Jenks is Professor of Sociology and Pro-Warden (Research) at Goldsmiths College, University of London. He has worked in the area of childhood studies for a number of years his major works being *The Sociology of Childhood* (London, Batsford 1982); *Childhood* (London, Routledge 1996) and *Theorizing Childhood* (with A James and A Prout) (Cambridge, Polity 1999). His most recent books are *Aspects of Urban Culture* (London, Sineca 2001) and *Images of Community:Towards a Sociology of Art* (with J Smith) (Aldershot, Ashgate, 2001).

Alexandra John qualified as a clinical psychologist in the early 1980s. Following her generic training she chose to work with children and families presenting with both physical and mental health difficulties. This career choice has resulted in her working in a number of service contexts: rural and urban departments; independent clinical psychology services; and more recently in an integrated mental health team in which a variety of disciplines meet the needs of the clients. After gaining experience in a single-handed speciality working across all areas of child psychology in Northampton, she took a post to develop and run a paediatric service at St George's Hospital. This was followed by a period of managing a child psychology service. Her most recent post has been a joint appointment with the University of Surrey and Sussex Weald and Downs NHS Trust. The main emphasis is to train clinical psychologists to be able to work within the National Health Service in any of the specialities currently available. This opportunity has enabled her to develop her research interests in health psychology and to consider the applicability of psychological research to both clinical and forensic practice. Her publications have addressed paediatric-related issues.

Allan Levy QC is a barrister specialising in child law and human rights law. He is an author, lecturer and broadcaster. He chaired the Pindown Inquiry in Staffordshire in 1990/91 and is a Fellow of the Society for Advanced Legal Studies.

Penney Lewis is a lecturer at the School of Law and Centre of Medical Law and Ethics, King's College London. She is the author of articles and case-notes on patients and proxies who refuse treatment, including anorexic patients, children, and pregnant women. Her research interests also focus on the evolution of legal responses to the issue the legalisation of euthanasia and assisted suicide, which she has examined in various jurisdictions including the United Kingdom, Canada, the United States, and the Netherlands.

Paul Meredith is Reader in Education Law at the University of Southampton. He is co-editor of Education and the Law and a member of the editorial board of the European Journal for Education Law and Policy. He is a member of the executive board of the European Association for Education Law and Policy.

Dr Quentin Spender qualified in medicine in 1979, and trained initially as a paediatrician, before specialising in child and adolescent psychiatry. He currently holds a joint clinical and academic post in Chichester, West Sussex and St George's Hospital Medical School in Tooting, south west London. His clinical interests include child abuse, Asperger's disorder and systemic family therapy: he is a registered family therapist. His research interests include the management of antisocial behaviour. He does a variety of expert assessments for the courts. He is currently working on a textbook on the management of child mental health problems for general practitioners and health visitors.

Ian Ward is Professor of Law at Newcastle Law School. His research interests are concentrated in various aspects of legal theory and interdisciplinary legal studies. His published work in the particular field of law and literature include *Law and Literature: Possibilities and Perspectives* (Cambridge, Cambridge University Press, 1995) and most recently *Shakespeare and the Legal Imagination* (London, Butterworths, 1999). He is presently engaged in a study of legal humanism.

Nick Wikeley holds the John Wilson Chair in Law at the University of Southampton. He was Dean of the Faculty of Law between 1996 and 1999. He is general editor of *The Law of Social Security* (London, Butterworths, 1995), author of *Compensation for Industrial Disease* (Aldershot, Dartmouth, 1993) and co-editor (with Professor Neville Harris) of the *Journal of Social Security Law*. His co-authored work includes *Judging Social Security* (with John Baldwin and Richard Young, Oxford, OUP, 1992) and *Child Support in Action* (with Gwynn Davis and Richard Young, Oxford, Hart Publishing, 1998).

Table of Cases

Table of Legislation

PART I

Perspectives on Childhood

1

Legal Concepts of Childhood: An Introduction

JULIA FIONDA*

"We claim to be a child-centred society, but in reality there is little evidence that we are. In many ways we are a ruthlessly adult-centred society where children are defined almost exclusively in terms of their impact on adult lives . . . Our adult-centred society has tried to contain and limit the impact of children on adult life by either excluding them from much of it, blaming them for disturbing it or by admitting them only as designer accessories or treating them like pampered pets".[1]

WE ALL IMAGINE we know what childhood is and who children are. In basic terms it may be seen as a biological or psychological phase of life somewhere between infancy and adulthood. However, the fact that there is constant disagreement even at the level of public discourse over where childhood begins and ends illustrates that childhood is not a concrete or objectively defined "truth" and is in fact a complex social construct. Or indeed a series of them. Neil Postman argues there is a clear distinction between biological and social childhood:

"Children are the living messages we send to a time we will not see. From a biological point of view it is inconceivable that any culture will forget that it needs to reproduce itself. But it is quite possible for a culture to exist without a social idea of children. Unlike infancy, childhood is a social artifact, not a biological category. Our genes contain no clear instructions about who is and is not a child and the laws of survival do not require that a distinction be made between the world of an adult and the world of a child".[2]

Concepts of who and what children are and what childhood consists of are therefore constructed artificially in and by the adult world to define a discrete social group.

Historians have shown that the construction of children as such a social group is a modern phenomenon and that childhood in this sense was non-existent until

---

* Many thanks to Nick Wikeley for his helpful comments on an earlier draft of this chapter.
[1] Mental Health Foundation, *The Big Picture* (London, Mental Health Foundation, 1999), p 4.
[2] N Postman, *The Disappearance of Childhood* (London, Vintage, 1994), p xi.

at least the seventeenth century in (largely middle class) Europe.[3] Since then concepts have changed over time but also vary according to the context in which they are constructed. Over the centuries we can trace society's notions of childhood through, *inter alia*, the way that children are educated, the way they are dressed, the age at which they are expected to work and fend for themselves and through common notions of the responsibilities of parents and the state towards them.[4] We can also derive fluctuating contemporary concepts of childhood from the various social or academic disciplines creating them.

The concepts may be differently constructed both within and between such disciplines and dichotomous or even contradictory perceptions of a child's capacities or social roles may emerge. In the media, for example, the reporting of news stories involving children has produced a "good child/bad child" dichotomy. This is particularly pronounced in relation to the media reporting of crime and victimisation. The careful editorial selection of stories and development of certain "angles" within those stories[5] can perpetuate stereotypical images of youths and children. Such images are further manipulated by the use of pictures, again selected to portray certain facial expressions conveying evil or angelicism. The reporting of the murder of James Bulger epitomised the paradigms of the "good" and "bad" child:

> "James Bulger was represented as the quintessential child: small, affectionate, trusting, dependent, vulnerable, high-spirited . . . Robert Thompson and Jon Venables are portrayed as aberrations of children, approximations of what a child might be or fraudulent impostors. Venables and Thompson appear to be children but are not: they are more like evil adults or monsters in disguise".[6]

Photographs of young victims such as Sarah Payne or Josie Russell become media symbols of the innocence and cuteness of the "good" child. Those who have injured or harmed them symbolise the "bad" child seeking to destroy childhood. The media becomes a symbolic parent expressing affection and approval towards the former and chastisement and rebuke towards the latter. This parenting style, even where symbolic, is often indicative of contradictory expectations of the appropriate behaviour of children. Blake Morrison expresses this exquisitely in describing the media hatred towards Venables and Thompson as: ". . . wanting to kill the kids who'd killed the kid, because there's nothing worse than killing a kid".[7]

---

[3] P Ariès, *Centuries of Childhood* trans R Baldick (London, Jonathan Cape, 1962); H Cunningham *Children and Childhood in Western Society since 1500* (London, Longman, 1995).

[4] See M D A Freeman, *The Rights and Wrongs of Children* (London, Frances Pinter, 1983), pp 8–18.

[5] See for example, S Chibnall, *Law and Order News: an analysis of crime reporting in the British press* (London, Tavistock, 1977).

[6] A Young, *Imagining Crime* (London, Sage, 1996), pp 114–15. See also B Franklin and J Petley, "Killing the Age of Innocence: Newspaper Reporting of the Death of James Bulger" in J Pilcher and S Wagg, *Thatcher's Children? Politics, Childhood and Society in the 1980s and 1990s* (London, Falmer, 1996).

[7] B Morrison, *As If* (London, Granta, 1997), p 27.

Similar dichotomies emerge from depictions of childhood in other disciplines. In children's literature we are presented with "good" children such as Harry Potter or the Famous Five. In contrast with the media stereotype, the "good" child in literature is often the one with adult-like qualities of competence, maturity and social awareness. They are often depicted fighting forces of evil (either in other "bad" children or in adults) using cunning and ingenuity. In some cases depictions of childhood in literature may be linked to class—the middle class child being represented as more knowing, articulate and "sensible".[8] Chris Jenks, David Archard, Quentin Spender and Mary John in chapters two, three and four respectively explore the multiplicity of constructions of childhood in the disciplines of sociology, history, philosophy and psychology.

The thesis of this book rests on the assumption that our historical and contemporary notions of childhood also change according to the context of the interaction between the child and the state. In particular, the book is concerned with the various ideas of what childhood consists of where the child is involved with the legal system. An identification of legal concepts of childhood can offer many insights into our treatment of children, the capacities which we expect them (possibly unfairly) to possess and the extent of any protection which they deserve or can expect from those charged with the responsibility for their welfare. The essays focus on a number of individual legal disciplines which centrally involve children whether as litigants, victims or perpetrators of crimes, owners of property, recipients of welfare services, education or medical treatment. The analysis in each chapter assesses how children are regarded by lawyers in each discipline. The discussion of these legal concepts is informed by the perspectives on childhood at the core of the non-legal disciplines mentioned above.

In chapter two Jenks reviews the proliferation of explanatory and theoretical models of childhood. These he identifies as falling into two broad groups—the pre-sociological and the sociological. The former inform everyday understandings and media representations of children and childhood and include the perception of children as evil, innocent, immanent, naturally developing and unconscious. The latter represent the awakening of social theory's concerns with childhood through the concept of socialisation. Jenks constructs four contemporary sociological models: the socially constructed child, the tribal child, the minority group child, and the social structural child. These new models, he argues, help us to locate the interests, traditions and ideologies that articulate different approaches to the study of the child.

Archard, in chapter three, examines the extent to which philosophers have analysed children and childhood. Childhood provides a subject area within which philosophers have been able to discuss more general ideas of rights, duty and authority. Archard demonstrates how moral philosophers should be interested in

---

[8] The children depicted by Enid Blyton or E Nesbitt can be sharply contrasted with the innocent, vulnerable and rather pathetic images of Oliver Twist or Frank McCourt's own memories of childhood in *Angela's Ashes*.

what is permitted and forbidden in the treatment of children. Further, social and political philosophers need to address the question of the appropriate balance between the roles of the state and the family in the care of children. What has not been addressed however, according to Archard, is the fundamental philosophical question of what the essential nature of childhood is. He therefore argues that there is a need for a specific "philosophy of childhood".

Spender and John consider childhood from the psychological and psychiatric perspectives. They discuss various psychological theories which aim not only to explain the phenomenon of childhood but also to account for childhood and adolescent anti-social behaviour. Of particular importance is the developmental perspective, including attachment theory. They argue that childhood may be seen as beginning from birth at which point human rights are conferred, but tracing the end of childhood is more complex. Neither childhood nor adolescence has a clear endpoint. Instead the developmental perspective suggests that psychological processes such as cognitive capacity, memory and language skills have a time course. An important part of this development is attachment as childhood experiences of attachment have a profound impact on emotional development and the ability to form and sustain relationships.

In chapter five Fionda argues that the conception of childhood at the heart of the youth justice system has fundamentally changed over the last decade in particular relation to those aged between ten and fourteen. Policy changes and recent legislation have increasingly treated this age group as fully competent, aware of the significance and repercussions of their actions and mature enough to accept responsibility for them. Concomitant with the erosion in the recognition of children's incapacity and lack of awareness is a trend towards punitive treatment and Fionda argues that many of these policy changes are politically motivated rather than based on any real change in the nature of childhood or the competence of children.

The child who gives evidence in court has only recently been afforded protections. Until the 1980s it was feared that such protections would undermine the due process rights of the defendant. In chapter six Levy traces recent developments in the law arising from both the *Pigot Report* in 1989 and the European decision on the trial of Venables and Thompson in 2000 which have resulted in a re-assessment of the criminal trial procedures for children and the application of international human rights standards. Children are now regarded as "vulnerable" in court whether they are victims or offenders and recent legislation has brought forward a more child-orientated procedure within adult focused adversarial proceedings.

Ward examines the situation of children and the law within literature in chapter seven. In particular he examines children and the law within the works of William Shakespeare. In doing so he analyses the ability of literature to both describe and constitute imagined conceptions of ideality. He argues that these literary images play a crucial role in the process of constructing individual identities within political communities which is especially pertinent to the education of children. The liberating potential of self-identity is released by our participation in the dialogues which describe our situations within established political communities. Accordingly, individuals, and communities, can only refashion themselves if they enjoy a proper appreciation of the historical and literary formation of central social conceptions, such as the "law" or the "child".

In chapter eight Bagshaw examines the legal duties owed by and to children through the law of torts. Much of the law in this area hinges on an assumption of "youthful inexperience" and the risks of "children behaving like children". On this assumption the law tends to view children as requiring control by others and imposes duties on parents and others to reduce the risk posed by children's behaviour. As litigants themselves children are viewed as dependent on the care and support of a parental figure, the loss of which is a material privation giving rise to a claim for compensation.

Lewis observes, in chapter nine, that the law governing the medical treatment of children is characterised by an "ostensible respect" for the autonomy for the "primary decision-maker". The law here is largely concerned with who that primary decision-maker can be. Children who pass a test of competence can make their own decisions on medical treatment, but as in family law discussed in chapter eleven, this requires remarkably high degrees of intelligence and maturity. The courts have, according to Lewis, been reluctant to give the child or the parent complete autonomy and have retained an absolute power to override any decision involving medical treatment on the grounds of the child's "best interests".

The conception of children or minors as housing applicants according to Cowan and Dearden in chapter ten, rests on a fundamental assumption of the incapacity of a minor to hold an estate in land. This rule is used to justify the exclusion of the minor from accessing social and other types of housing on the grounds that they pose an undue risk either as a social group in the creation of "tipped" estates or individually in housing management terms through not paying their rent or maintaining the property. The housing allocations process thereby marginalises young people and reinforces the power of the state to discipline and punish its subjects in terms of who is rewarded and recognised and who is disciplined. Consequently those under twenty-five's who can, are encouraged to remain dependent on their parents for accommodation. Those who cannot are socially excluded.

In chapter eleven Freeman traces the emergence of the concept of a child as an autonomous legal personality. Family law no longer regards children as the property of their parents. There is now an increasing recognition of the developmental process of childhood and the need to be sensitive to children's individual diversity and growing capacity to make reasoned decisions as they age. Courtesy of the Children Act 1989 the child now has rights of their own and the parent child relationship has, according to Freeman, been transformed to one based on parental responsibility rather than traditional parental rights.

Meredith concludes in chapter twelve that the child is rather more the object of education law than the subject of it. Any rights within this area of law (whether in the context of choice of school, school attendance, the disciplinary process or sex education) are vested in the parents rather than in the child. The law here rests in the assumption that the rights of parent and child vis à vis the education system coincide and do not conflict. Meredith argues this may often not be the case and the result of this assumption is that the voice of the child and the opportunity for him to express his own views and wishes may be lost when decisions regarding his education are made.

In chapter thirteen Wikeley notes the significant increase in child poverty since 1979 and rising number of children dependent on income support. New Labour have announced a long-term strategy to alleviate child poverty, but their legislation on welfare reform has focused on "making work pay"—being more generous in the allocation of benefits to working parents through the working families' tax credit and the New Deal for Lone Parents. Notwithstanding the rights of children to a standard of living conducive to healthy development under the UN Convention on the Rights of the Child, Wikeley argues that the political strategy is to see children's entitlement as "parasitical to those of their parents", including since 1988 that of sixteen and seventeen-year-olds.

A number of concepts of childhood emerge from these assessments of the child in various legal and other disciplines. To some extent these concepts may overlap or contradict each other. There may, of course, be many other interpretations of the childhoods presented in this book.

THE DEPENDENT CHILD

This construction views the child as a subsidiary of their parents or as Wikeley states in chapter thirteen "parasitical to their parents". It does not necessarily impute an incompetence and should not be confused with the concept of the incompetent child described below. Rather, the dependent child takes a submissive role in relation to either the parents or the state. Both Wikeley and Cowan and Dearden[9] refer to a political agenda in place in the welfare system which seeks to reinforce the dependence of the child or young person in relation to those aged under twenty-five. Their claim is that welfare agencies contrive such a construction either in order to restrict access to declining resources or, according to Cowan and Dearden, to reinforce the power of the state to discipline and punish those who cannot or will not fit within this prescribed norm.

Meredith[10] similarly notes how the child is the object of rights in education law but not the possessor. The parents are the "clients" of the education system and not the child. The child is dependent here on the parents ensuring that their wishes and needs are appropriately met and that they are not unfairly treated. Where the child's and the parent's wishes conflict it is only in exceptional cases,

---

[9] Chs 13 and 10 in this volume respectively.
[10] Ch 12 in this volume.

according to Meredith, that the child's wishes will be formally ascertained and taken into account. Paradoxically a child with special educational needs has greater curricular rights in seeing that special provision is made to meet their particular needs and may, in this respect at least, be less dependent.

The child's dependence is recognised in tort where a child may claim financially for the loss of a supporting parent. This recognition of dependence however is entirely material—the claim may not include compensation for the loss of emotional dependence but only for substituting financial support. Although the child himself is entitled to bring this claim, this is more a functional autonomy. Where the parent is injured rather than killed it is up to the parent to claim for a substitute carer and the child again becomes a passive recipient.

Children who are dependent are seen as vulnerable and in need of special protection. Levy[11] notes how children in the courtroom (as victims or witnesses) have been grouped together with other "vulnerable witnesses" under the Youth Justice and Criminal Evidence Act 1999 and afforded special protection from exposure to official processes and adult defendants, both of which may exert undue trauma. In court they may be literally physically cosseted behind screens or videotapes. Archard[12] further notes how society's moral code contains more wrongs against children than adults because of their inability to make their own choices and protect themselves. The need for special protection derives from a perception of children as defenceless, unable to protect themselves and therefore dependent on the benevolent guardianship of the state or their carers.

THE AUTONOMOUS CHILD

This concept acknowledges a child's independence and allows a child to exercise it. It recognises that the child has a legal and social persona which is not derivative of a more enfranchised or powerful body such as the parent or the state. Jenks identifies this child sociologically as "tribal", a model which witnesses "a moral reappraisal of the stratification system and power relation that conventionally exists between adults and children".[13] Hence we view the child almost anthropologically within his own social world, according to his own views and perceptions: ". . . we honour children's difference and celebrate their relative autonomy".[14] This is what Archard perceives as a "philosophy of childhood": ". . . a view that treats childhood as a distinctive, *sui generis* and self-contained state, one whose particular and uniquely defining features merit consideration in their own right".[15]

---

[11] Ch 6 in this volume.
[12] Ch 3 in this volume.
[13] Ch 2 in this volume at p 38.
[14] *Ibid*, p 38.
[15] Ch 3 in this volume at p 45.

In legal terms we see this child most clearly in family law, but relatively infrequently perceive of childhood in this way elsewhere. Internationally the children's rights movement, and in particular the UN Convention on the Rights of the Child, regards children as a specific social group meriting the assignment of human rights not just as human beings but additionally as children. However, in domestic law this view is less often articulated and incorporated into national legislation. Wikeley notes this paradox particularly in relation to social welfare law.[16] However, Freeman[17] has traced the development of family law in the twentieth century and detects a move away from the view of the child as dependent. The pinnacle of this movement can be seen in *Gillick*[18] where the House of Lords acknowledged a child's capacity to develop autonomy as he develops greater understanding of the world around him and a capacity to reason. Freeman also notes how this view was expressed in the Children Act 1989 which gives children greater opportunities to initiate proceedings in order to serve their own interests and "emphasises the importance of a child's wishes and feelings".[19] The Act also emphasises parental responsibility and a partnership approach to parenting between state and parent but does not do so in terms of parental *rights* which necessarily supersede those of the child. Nevertheless Freeman notes how despite this legislative paradigm, in practice there is still a degree of conservatism towards the "tribal child":

> "There is a . . . framework if not for cultural revolution, at least for a rethinking of childhood. But, as we have seen, the opportunities thus presented have been scorned by judges".[20]

THE INCOMPETENT CHILD

Lewis[21] has also noted how the inclination to allow children the autonomy to make decisions about their own medical treatment has been tempered by judicial reluctance to implement it in practice. The child in medical law as well as in family law can only be regarded as autonomous if they are also judged to be competent. In other words their autonomy is not so much derived from their conception as "tribal" but rather from an assessment of their ability to mimic adult reasoning. Indeed Freeman suggests that the judges' reluctance to assign autonomy is such that the test of (in)competence requires of children a level of understanding, knowledge and emotional stability that many average adults would not possess.

---

[16] Ch 13 in this volume at p 242.
[17] Ch 11 in this volume.
[18] *Gillick* v. *West Norfolk and Wisbech AHA* [1986] AC 112.
[19] Ch 11 in this volume at p 197.
[20] *Ibid*, p 200.
[21] Ch 9 in this volume.

Lewis similarly argues that the test is rigorous but also notes that the courts have "retained an absolute power to override any decision involving the medical treatment on the grounds of the child's 'best interests' ".[22] This paternalistic power is curious as it suggests that although we may acknowledge that the child (or even the parent) is competent, they may still be unable to judge for themselves how their own best interests can be served. Lewis specifically does not consider that the perception of the child as incompetent, and the invoking of this residual power, is a smokescreen to disguise public policy judgements being made by the courts. Cowan and Dearden, however, take a contrary view in relation to the allocation of housing. There they suggest that the ancient rule that a minor is unable to hold a legal estate in land, due to incompetence,[23] is used to justify decisions not to house young persons where those decisions are really part of the wider political agenda discussed above.

The law of torts takes an approach to negligence which clearly recognises children as incompetent. Bagshaw illustrates how childishness or "the irresponsibility of childhood"[24] renders the child less prone to accusations of contributory negligence as they may be assumed to inherently pose risks towards themselves. Also while they are recognised as a hazard to others they are less often sued in their own right when they injure others. Hence ". . . everyone must take the risk of being injured by children behaving like children".[25] Bagshaw has demonstrated how children are liable in the same way as adults but in practice greater allowance is made for their negligent behaviour in view of their lesser ability to foresee risk and exercise self-restraint and skill.

Levy and Fionda[26] take a more positive view of the relatively new perception of children as incompetent in court. Levy shows how it was as late as the 1980s that concern emerged over children being competent to give evidence in court where they had been victims of abuse. Only very recently has this concern spread to other children who give evidence as victims and offenders. Both Levy and Fionda take the view that while these developments may in part be due to a concern to ensure that the child is given sufficient support to give evidence which is useful and complete, there is nonetheless a tone of benevolence in these reforms which stems from genuine misgivings over children's lack of competence to withstand the rigours of the adversarial process, whichever side they are on.

[22] *Ibid*, p 157.
[23] The authors cite Birks who argues the rationale for this rule was that the incompetence of the child rendered them "easily exploited". P Birks, *An Introduction to the Law of Restitution* (Oxford, OUP, 1989) cited in ch 10 in this volume at p 165.
[24] Ch 8 in this volume at p 149.
[25] *Ibid*, p 149.
[26] Ch 5 in this volume.

THE UNDEVELOPED ADULT

This concept views the child as incomplete, lacking full maturity or "unfinished".[27] The expectation is that the child will grow and develop into adulthood but childhood is the period between birth and adulthood where the developmental process takes place. For psychologists this is an important model.[28] Psychological growth mirrors physiological growth where a child, after birth, grows into reproductive maturity or biological adulthood. Alongside this biological development, the child develops cognitive capacity, memory, language skills, self-esteem and other emotional factors and psychologists assess a child according to how far along the continuum between birth and adulthood they have reached. This is not always easy to judge however:

"The ending of adolescence is not clear, because the psychological changes and resultant behaviours persist into adulthood. The threshold of adulthood has become steadily more diffuse through the twentieth century because of the prolongation of education for many. Resulting in postponement of work choices and the need for continued financial dependence".[29]

Archard also suggests that this view of childhood is the cornerstone of traditional philosophy: "Philosophy is principally if not solely interested in childhood in so far as it may be understood as that which is not adulthood but is at the same time a necessary preparation for and indicator of what will follow as adulthood".[30]

For Jenks this is the "Immanent child"[31] an epistemological conceptual view of the child as a "no-thing"—that is without "in-built, or *a priori*, categories of understanding nor a general facility to reason". This child may be incompetent also, but Jenks sees the roots of this view in Locke's suggestion that the child is like a blank canvass—yet to have the experience which constructs their character and gives them knowledge. It is their lack of experience which renders them as yet not complete.

On this theme Ward has argued that literature plays a key role in this developmental process: "Literature plays a critical role in equipping the child to develop their own sense of moral obligation in terms of an obligation to the community, rather than merely to parents . . . the kinds of literature encountered by children varies in line with their stage of development".[32] He cites Tucker[33] who applied the theories of Jean Piaget on developmental psychology to the interpretation of children's literature and found that texts written for

---

[27] Archard, ch 3 in this volume at p 43.
[28] See Spender and John, ch 4 in this volume.
[29] *Ibid*, p 57.
[30] Ch 3 in this volume at p 43.
[31] Ch 2 in this volume at p 28.
[32] Ch 7 in this volume at p 124.
[33] N Tucker, *The Child and the Book: A psychological and literary exploration* (Cambridge, Cambridge University Press, 1981).

older children gradually begin to demand more in the way of moral judgements to be made by the reader.

Jenks outlines an alternative concept of childhood which may be seen as an interesting extension of the idea of the undeveloped. This concept is the Freudian or "unconscious" child.[34] Here childhood is the unconscious self, "a state of unfinished business or becoming". This notion of childhood may well extend beyond physiological adolescence and into adulthood. So rather than the child being an unfinished adult we may say that the adult has not yet finished being a child. Childhood, according to this psychological model, is divorced from biology as adults "transport their childhood like a previous incarnation from action to action".[35]

Hence outside the law the child as an incomplete or undeveloped adult is commonly understood. In law it is also evident, but in its own sense. There is commonly an assumption, in places linked to an assessment of incompetence, that the child will become "complete" and will then have autonomy or will be non-dependent, but has not yet reached that stage. The principle laid down in *Gillick* is central to this notion in both family law and medical law, as it is essentially a developmental principle. In practice, its application to later cases has been complicated by a rather different question about competence as discussed above.

However, in many areas of law the developmental idea is rather artificial as strict inflexible boundaries between childhood and adulthood are applied. These, unlike the *Gillick* principle, appear to take little account of the developmental process in reality and are in fact more regulatory than authentic. For example, laws which state that a young person can legally have sex at sixteen, vote at eighteen, drink alcohol at home at five but not purchase it until eighteen, marry (with parental consent) at sixteen but not have a homosexual relationship until eighteen, apply arbitrarily and take little account of the extent to which that person is actually "adult" enough to indulge in such activities. Indeed, to many these age limits are contradictory in that sense and therefore meaningless. Fionda[36] notes that in the criminal justice system strict cut off points between criminal competence and incompetence are problematic and unrealistic. The same may be said of social security benefits where age limits are rather more designed to be restrictive than to be an assessment of financial independence and therefore maturity. Hence in law there is evidence that children are thought of as undeveloped adults but the rigid adherence to rules about age and capacity suggest, in a literal interpretation, a developmental process which is fixed, certain and occurs in identifiable key stages. A child aged fifteen is not "adult" enough to smoke but a child of sixteen is.

[34] Ch 2 in this volume at p 32.
[35] *Ibid*, p 33.
[36] Ch 5 in this volume.

THE UNRULY CHILD

This child is perceived as a savage, untrained child who is out of control. The response of the law to this view of childhood reflects an apocalyptic fear of such children and the dangers they pose to the adult world. Jenks has likened this concept of childhood to Dionysian mythology:

> "The child is Dionysian in as much as it loves pleasure, it celebrates self-gratification, and it is wholly demanding in relation to any object, or indeed subject, that prevents its satiation. The intrusive noise that is childhood is expressive of a single-minded solipsistic array of demands in relation to which all other interests become peripheral and all other presences become satellites to enable this goal".[37]

Pearson[38] identifies this child as the "hooligan" and importantly suggests that yobbery is not a modern, twentieth century phenomenon. Indeed Ward[39] cites a number of examples from sixteenth and seventeenth century literature which express social disquiet and alarm at children's misbehaviour:

> "During the 1590s it was repeatedly reported that children played in the yard of St Paul's broke windows and disturbed services. At Wimborne in 1629 churchwardens lamented that 'our church and the seats thereof have often been beastly abused and profaned by uncivil children'. At Exeter cathedral, in 1658, a cage was erected in which unruly children could be placed during services".[40]

This is the "bad" or "evil" child which the media have, as discussed above, hysterically decried. The criminal justice system is one, obvious, way in which the legal system responds to such children. Fionda suggests that "The commission of a (very) serious offence can mean that a child essentially transcends their own childhood—they have committed an adult act and are therefore treated as an adult on that basis. This may alternatively be seen in more emotive terms as the withdrawal of the privilege of childhood for the most serious offenders".[41] Indeed Fionda's thesis is that the perception of children who commit any crime as unruly or out of control can be politically useful and can facilitate a hard line policy on youth crime.

Elsewhere the unruly child may be similarly harshly treated by the legal system. Cowan and Dearden argue that the minor is perceived by social housing professionals as unruly and therefore a "risk" in housing terms. They are thought to be responsible for the decline of some estates as well as more likely to not pay rent, for failure to maintain the property or to be evicted for some other reason: "The cost of letting to a minor would be assessed in terms of the

---

[37] C Jenks, "Decoding Childhood" in P Atkinson, B Davies and S Delamont (eds), *Discourse and Reproduction: Essays in Honor of Basil Bernstein* (Cresskill NJ, Hampton, 1995), p 182.

[38] G Pearson, *Hooligan: A History of Respectable Fears* (London, Macmillan, 1983).

[39] Ch 7 in this volume.

[40] *Ibid*, p 116.

[41] Ch 5 in this volume at p 88.

minor's ability to assume responsibilities against the risk of not meeting them".[42] So their perceived unruliness either denies them allocation of housing in the first place or, if successful, they are more likely, because of the risk they pose of disorder, to be housed on "tipped" estates which are thought to be too undesirable a location for other, more vulnerable, applicants. They therefore find themselves socially excluded either way and their unruliness renders them undeserving.

The law of torts is less retributive in its recognition of the dangers posed by unruly children. It has already been seen how childishness is readily recognised as hazardous and irresponsible. However, rather than impose liability on the children themselves, the law has rather seen the legal duties for preventing harm caused by children as falling on the parents:

> "The risk of children behaving like children is reduced to some extent by the imposition of duties on those who control children, principally parents, and those who control the accessibility to children of dangerous things. These duties are most easily imposed where there are grounds for believing that a child cannot prevent itself from being a risk to others or cannot be trusted to use a dangerous thing safely or leave it alone. The duties are long-established and relatively uncontroversial".[43]

This is perhaps not so surprising a view in private law. It is in public law where a more punitive attitude is taken towards the bad, undeserving child where it is seen as taking away, either literally as a recipient of a service or more esoterically in terms of damaging society through their disorder.

Ward finds depictions of rebellious children in Shakespeare, with allegorical tales of what becomes of them: "Rebellious children in Shakespeare either conform, such as Hermia and Lysander, or Hal, or die, such as Romeo and Juliet or Cordelia. Happy endings require conformity . . . Romeo and Juliet's Verona, like Cordelia's England, are communities entirely destroyed by filial disobedience, no matter how morally justified it might have been".[44] Concomitantly a virtuous child in law as well as in literature is one who "obeys the law and obeys their parent, because such obedience is the mark of an individual equipped to enter society and to act as a good citizen in the common cause of the common good".[45] The dichotomy is seen clearly in the criminal justice system where the good child is rewarded handsomely with wide reaching protections in the courtroom whereas the bad child, although now protected to some extent, is not excluded from the adult courts and is afforded only a proportion of the protections offered to child victims.

---

[42] Ch 10 in this volume at p 168.
[43] Ch 8 in this volume at p 149.
[44] Ch 7 in this volume at p 126.
[45] *Ibid*, p 126.

THE MARGINALISED CHILD

This child is an "outsider" or in Jenks' terms a member of a minority group.[46] They are socially marginalised or even excluded and have faced the same struggle for recognition and emancipation as other "minority" groups such as women and ethnic minorities in a society which discriminates against them: "[this model's] binding feature is its politicization of childhood in line with previously established agendas concerning an unequal and structurally discriminatory society".[47] The child in these terms can be seen throughout the legal system. Note how in family law the child was barely recognised at all until later in the twentieth century.[48]

Fionda[49] describes how young offenders have been the subject of moral panics and consequently cast as "social others" or scapegoats, a marginalised group sacrificed as a focus for society's hatred. They have this in common with, among others, dangerous dogs, gun owners, beggars, squeegee merchants and joints of beef. Cowan and Dearden view the minor as an outsider subject to control by the "insiders" of the housing market—housing professionals or their parents. They lack any enfranchisement in this respect which enables them to attain independence and recognition as citizens. Similarly Meredith shows that children are marginalised in terms of rights and "unheard" in relation to the provision of education. Ironically, given the central purpose of the education system, they are the treated as the least important players, the passive objects of law and policy. Being unheard makes them similarly unemancipated. Wikeley's chapter shows how children are largely marginalised in benefits terms, but this can result in double jeopardy: ". . . where particular groups within the community—for example, asylum seekers—are identified as appropriate targets for benefit cuts, their children are especially vulnerable".[50]

These legal concepts of childhood help us, on the one hand to understand the treatment of children within the legal system, but at the same time highlight contradictions and nonsensical paradoxes. The conception of childhood adopted within any area of law can, as has been demonstrated, impact significantly on the way that the child is treated or their needs or interests responded to. However, a cogent series of concepts within the legal system cannot be found and each discipline's policy and procedures reflect varying perceptions of the nature of childhood in relation to different legal actions or public services. Neither is it clear, from the constructions of childhood to be found in non-legal disciplines, that law's plurality of approach is unjustified. Socially, psychologically, philosophically and legally the child can also mean different things

---

[46] Ch 2 in this volume at p 39.
[47] *Ibid*, p 39.
[48] See Freeman, ch 11 in this volume.
[49] Ch 5 in this volume.
[50] Ch 13 in this volume at p 243.

in different contexts and at different times. This may, in part, be due to the fact that childhood is being defined and analysed in these contexts by adults, trying to make sense of children in an adult centred world. Hence children's conceptual malleability can be manipulated and exploited to fit the dominant interests in that adult world.

2

Sociological Perspectives and Media Representations of Childhood

CHRIS JENKS

INTRODUCTION

FOUR SUMMERS PAST I sat down to write the introduction to a book on childhood. I sat and looked around for inspiration or rather displacement, what I needed was doughnuts and a newspaper. When I returned to my desk with the displacement material they, or at least the newspaper, provided the inspiration to begin. The introduction I was to write was begun in a week marked out by its sustained assault on childhood. In the few days when the West, ironically, "celebrated" the fifty years that had elapsed since the Hiroshima bomb, an event which has mis-shaped the paranoia of a generation and provided a causal metaphor in the de-traditionalisation that has become the postmodern; here, in the UK, we had witnessed the murder of three boys, in two separate incidents, the rape and murder of a little girl and the successful first stage of the legal proceedings brought by parents to allow the death of their brain-damaged twenty-two-month old baby. This was serious and concentrated news. The only column inches on the front page of *The Independent* newspaper for 1 August 1995 not dedicated to childhood matters were advising us about the highest earners in this country or advertising Champagne. *The Independent* was not alone in this focus, television, radio and the press generally were alive with the issue of the modern child. In the wake of the then current disturbing events the overall media response was, predictably, somewhat apocalyptic: "we are at a crisis point"; "morality has collapsed"; "we are breeding a nation of child killers"; "childhood itself has come to an end" and so on. The original events had already transformed into the cliched "moral panic" and experts, like me, were being marshalled in broadcasting studios nationwide to allay the fears of parents (or perhaps to establish the grounds for a running debate) by stating, in good Durkheimian fashion, that the rates of criminality and abuse remain stable and that statistically children are no more under threat than they were ten, twenty, or even thirty years ago. This public response and the symbiotic upsurge of concern within the media were both utterly intelligible but also highly revealing processes. The clamouring of voices waiting to be heard on the issues surrounding childhood, both then and now, is instructive in both its breadth of interests and in its seeming magnitude. In the fifty years since the dropping of the atomic bomb more of the faces turning away from the blast appear to be gazing upon the child. Once childhood was a feature of parental (or maybe maternal) discourse, the currency of educators and the sole theoretical property of developmental psychology. Now the child has become popularised, politicised, scrutinised and analysed in a series of interlocking spaces, and from within the recently established arena of the sociology of childhood I continue to explore some of those spaces and map their emergence and their interconnections.

The aim of this chapter is to theorise a relatively new field of study and to embrace a variety of possible approaches to our shared phenomenon that will open up and also advise both extant and emergent debates about childhood. Although it will not produce an exhaustive taxonomy this chapter will both review and constitute the proliferation of explanatory and theoretical models of childhood. The first group I shall describe as those models that are *pre-sociological* in character and have become part of the conventional wisdom surrounding the child. This first group informs everyday understandings and media representations in a direct form. The second group I shall describe as *sociological* models, however this category sub-divides. The first instance provided, "the socially developing child", is really a transitional model in that it serves to demonstrate the awakening of social theory's concerns with the becoming character of young humankind through the concept of socialisation. Beyond this, I develop an exploratory typology of four contemporary *sociological* models. These four models are both original formulations[1] and, I anticipate, instructive of future study in this area of research. These models are: the *socially constructed child*; the *tribal child*; the *minority group child*; and the *social structural child*. Each of these new models should enable us to locate the interests, traditions and ideologies that articulate different approaches to the study of the child.

BACKGROUND

Rose[2], in a work concerned to chart the growth and proliferation of political strategies in late-modernity designed to govern the individual through a capture of the inside rather than a constraint of the outside, notes the dramatic increase in agencies and ideologies that claim estate over the child:

> "Childhood is the most intensively governed sector of personal existence. In different ways, at different times, and by many different routes varying from one section of society to another, the health, welfare, and rearing of children have been linked in thought and practice to the destiny of the nation and the responsibilities of the state.

---

[1] See A James, C Jenks and A Prout, *Theorizing Childhood* (Oxford, Polity, 1998).
[2] N Rose, *Governing the Soul* (London, Routledge, 1989).

The modern child has become the focus of innumerable projects that purport to safe-guard it from physical, sexual and moral danger, to ensure its 'normal' development, to actively promote certain capacities of attributes such as intelligence, educability and emotional stability".[3]

This is an illuminating thesis and one that highlights the subtleties of new forms of power-knowledge and accounts for the emergence of a whole series of voices, interests or discourses concerning the child. However, this is only part of the picture. The modern child has not come into being solely through a journey to the interior provided by the post-Freudian legacy. The pursuit of the secular soul through the twentieth century has, indeed, generated new provinces of meaning for the experience of and understanding of childhood. However, there is still an Enlightenment child who occupies a real concrete presence in our lives and in our thinking. A tangible, distinguishable and embodied status of person who has gained a popularity, perhaps even a celebrity, and whose parameters are even now being forcibly contested within the academic futures markets of economics, politics, law, medicine, social work, history, education, psychology, communications, criminology, cultural studies, women's studies, anthropology and sociology.

We must be cautious however, childhood is not a new phenomenon. It was, of course, the historian Ariès[4] who began the archaeology of childhood images that remains so influential in our thinking today. His breathtaking assertions that childhood has not always been the same thing established what Sennett referred to as: ". . . the study of the family as a historical form, rather than as a fixed biological form in history".[5] Ariès records the launching of childhood in Europe in the mid-eighteenth century. Adults in particular social classes, he told us, were steadily beginning to think of themselves as not quite of the same order of being as their children. An age based hierarchy and eventual dichotomy was becoming institutionalised in the relationship between adults and children and the defining characteristics of the differences were, by and large, oppositional. The obvious strengths of such an approach as Ariès pioneered lay in the rela-tivising of the concept of childhood and the provision of the grounds for an analysis of childhood in terms of its social context, rather than abandoning it to a naturalistic reduction. On the other hand, the poverty of such historicism is what Archard has referred to as its "presentism", that is, the way that it appears to lock childhood into the realm of modernity:

"Ariès understands by the concept of 'childhood' a peculiarly modern awareness of what distinguishes children from adults. This is manifested in morally appropriate forms of treatment, chiefly a certain separation of the worlds of child and adult. Previous societies, on Ariès's account, lacked this concept of childhood and whilst it does not follow that they treated children badly it is natural to think that they were

---

[3] *Ibid*, p 121.
[4] P Ariès, *Centuries of Childhood* (London, Cape, 1962).
[5] R Sennett, *The Fall of Public Man* (London, Faber & Faber, 1993), p 92.

disposed to do so. In reply it can be argued that the evidence fails to show that previous societies lacked a concept of childhood. At most it shows that they lacked our concept".[6]

I am not arguing here that childhood is something new, an invention of modernity or the product of a capitalist, industrialised division of labour. It is not my concern to challenge the historian's evidence for the "big bang" theory of the initiation of childhood. I do, however, remain preoccupied by the social and historical context that surrounds childhoods and I do begin from the pertinent observation that childhood is very much an issue of our time.

Another historian, Samuel, reflects somewhat caustically on one manifestation of the current obsession with the child:

> "Another genealogy which would repay attention would be the middle-class cult of childhood, with its celebration of the time-warped and its sentimentalization of the nursery. It is brilliantly represented in theatre by the annual revivals of *Treasure Island* and *Peter Pan*; in ethnography by the Opies' *Lore and Language of Schoolchildren* (1960), and in the auction rooms by the extraordinary prices paid for such vintage juvenilia as dolls' houses and toy theatres".[7]

But this sentimentalisation is only a particular mannerism, perhaps a trivialisation, certainly only a surface representation of our real object of attention. Indisputably, over the past two, or at most three, decades childhood has moved to the forefront of personal, political and academic agendas and not solely in the West. The moving spirit of this process is extremely complex and can be seen to involve an entanglement of factors such as: a structural re-adjustment to time and mortality in the face of quickening social change; a re-evaluation and a re-positioning of personhood given the disassembly of traditional categories of identity and difference; a search for a moral centre or at least an anchor for trust in response to popular routine cynicism; and an age-old desire to invest in futures now rendered urgent. I cannot begin, with any certainty, to offer a route through this imbroglio but I can provide an account of the various dimensions through which theorising about childhood has become articulate.

It would be easy to suppose that the conventional wisdom about childhood rests somewhere within the spectrum of what Galton originally described as "the convenient jingle of words",[8] nature and nurture. However, our imaginings about the child have not always set out from the same starting point, nor have they always had the same purpose in mind. Therefore despite the seemingly straightforward position espoused by Berger and Luckmann (1966) on this topic it remains highly contentious:

> "From the moment of birth, man's organismic development, and indeed a large part of his biological being as such, are subject to continuing socially determined interference.

[6] D Archard, *Children: Rights and Childhood* (London, Routledge, 1993), p 20.
[7] R Samuel, *Theatres of Memory: Past and Present in Contemporary Culture* (London, Verso, 1994), p 93.
[8] Galton, (1865).

> Despite the obvious physiological limits to the range of possible and different ways of becoming a man . . . the human organism manifests an immense plasticity in its response to the environmental forces at work . . . the ways of becoming and being human are as numerous as man's cultures".[9]

Childhood is conceived from different social, political and moral positions, many of which are utterly reductionist and the majority are certainly unreflexive in recovering their auspices. What, if anything, might the love and anxiety of a parent, the analytical demands of a sociologist and the journalist's desire to find a story with a high moral ground have in common? Let us begin our inventory of models.

THE PRE-SOCIOLOGICAL CHILD

This spacious category contains the dustbin of history, the realm of common sense, classical philosophy, the highly influential discipline of developmental psychology and the equally important and pervasive field of psychoanalysis. The gathering principle for the set of models assembled here is that they begin from a view of childhood outside of or uninformed by the social context within which the child resides. More specifically, these models are unimpressed by any concept of social structure.

The evil child

Such a model stems from an earlier historical period but is not without trace elements in contemporary moralising, criminology and debate over pedagogic practice. This image rests upon the assumption of an initial evil, corruption, baseness, disruption and incompetence as being primary elements in the constitution of the child. Childhood, then, is found in the exercise of restraint upon these dispositions or, more intrusively, in the exorcism of these dispositions by programmes of discipline and punishment. In the manner later analysed and extrapolated by Foucault[10] into a metaphor for the form of solidarity and social control within the *ancien regime*, correct training gave rise to docile bodies. And docile bodies are pliant members and good citizens—a utility emergent from docility. This resonates strongly with Durkheim's legal code of "retribution" as providing an external index of the condition of mechanical solidarity. Within this classical model, which contains no theory of the interior or inner life, the body became the site of childhood and its correction. As Foucault put it:

---

[9] P Berger and T Luckmann, *The Social Construction of Reality* (Harmondsworth, Penguin, 1966), pp 66–7.
[10] M Foucault, *Discipline and Punish* (Harmondsworth, Penguin, 1977).

"The classical age discovered the body as an object and target of power. It is easy enough to find signs of the attention then paid to the body—to the body that is manipulated, shaped, trained, which obeys, responds, becomes skilful and increases its forces".[11]

The image of the evil child found its lasting mythological foundation in the doctrine of Adamic original sin. Children, it was supposed, entered the world as a wilful material energy; but their wilfulness is both universal and held in an essentialism, to that degree it does not constitute a theory of intentionality. Children are demonic and harbour potentially dark forces. Such thinking has provided a powerful theme in contemporary literature and cinema, but also a useful media resource in explaining childhood transgression as, for example, in the murder of Jamie Bulger.[12] These primal forces, it was supposed, would be mobilised if, by dereliction or inattention, the adult world should allow them to veer away from the "straight and narrow" path that civilisation has bequeathed to them. Evil children must be made to avoid dangerous places. They will not, therefore: fall into bad company; establish bad habits; develop idle hands; and be heard rather than just seen. Such dangerous places are those contexts which will conspire in the liberation of the demonic forces within. Any such escape threatens the well-being of the child itself but, perhaps more significantly, it threatens the stability of the adult collectivity as well. Jenks has likened this model of the child to Dionysian mythology:

"The child is Dionysian in as much as it loves pleasure, it celebrates self-gratification, and it is wholly demanding in relation to any object, or indeed subject, that prevents its satiation. The intrusive noise that is childhood is expressive of a single-minded solipsistic array of demands in relation to which all other interests become peripheral and all other presences become satellites to enable this goal".[13]

The philosophical antecedent for the evil child is to be found in the work of Thomas Hobbes, not that he dedicated his time to accounting for the condition of childhood but he certainly produced an implicit specification of its content through his highly publicised conception of the human actor. Although not a Puritan himself Hobbes' initial scholarly education was within a puritan tradition and he shared some of their beliefs in terms of their bland materialism, an unostentatious minimalism that he extended into an empiricism, a reductionism that propelled his interest in geometry, and finally a commitment to the view that what is of most importance is good conduct. These elements combine in Hobbes' *Leviathan* which proffers a powerful advocacy of absolutism. The power of the monarch, and thus the power of parents, is absolute and stands over and above the populace or children who have no rights or power. The

[11] M Foucault, *Discipline and Punish* (Harmondsworth, Penguin, 1977) p 136.
[12] A James and C Jenks, "Public Perceptions of Childhood Criminality" (1996) 47 *British Journal of Sociology* 315–31.
[13] C Jenks, "Decoding Childhood" in P Atkinson, B Davies and S Delamont (eds), *Discourse and Reproduction: Essays in Honor of Basil Benstein* (Cresskill NJ, Hampton, 1995), p 182.

source of this power is knowledge which children could only attain by eventually becoming parents themselves. The powerful ogre of the state or the parent is omnipotent and the individual is saved from the worst excesses of him or herself by contracting into the society or the family. The life of the child without parental constraint is anarchistic; indeed, its childhood would surely be "solitary, poor, nasty, brutish and short" without such control. When Hobbes does call the child by name he is rather disparaging:

> "Likewise children, fools, and madmen that have no use of reason, may be personated by guardians, or curators, but can be no authors, during that time, of any action done by them, longer than, when they shall recover the use of reason, they shall judge the same reasonable. Yet during the folly, he that hath right of governing them, may give authority to the guardian".[14]

Old Testament Christianity provided perhaps the most significant contribution to the image of the evil child. Parental, God-parental and loco-parental guidance consisted in a forceful introduction of the young to the humourless ways of the Almighty. This sedimented a lasting tradition in child-rearing even though, as Shipman[15] has pointed out, the dramatic fall in infant mortality through modernity appears to have reduced our urgency and collective anxiety concerning the infant's state of grace, as has the inexorable process of secularization. Previously Ariès[16] had, in his discovery of the genesis of childhood, described its sixteenth century manifestation as a form of weakness. This weakness referred to the child's susceptibility, the fact that it had little resolve and was easily diverted and corrupted. Such belief gave rise to the widespread practice of "coddling", that is a binding and constraining of the child's body. Coddling can also be treated instructively as a metaphor for a style of parenting that is confining of the child's urges and desires; a distant, strict and physical direction of the young. With the formalisation of the evil child in the sixteenth century, the practice of socialisation most certainly took on the form of a contest. This combatorial relation between adult and child had close parallels with the way that people treated domestic animals and "broke" them or tamed them in order to integrate their naturalness into the adult human world of culturalness. This harshness and indeed brutality in childrearing gained a powerful ideological bedrock from the zeal for greater reformation that accompanied the religious puritanism of the sixteenth and seventeenth centuries. As with the most oppressive social movements, the control and constraint exercised on the subject (in this case the child) was for its own good. Puritanism was determined that rods should not be saved in order to save children and it was equally certain that the child should be grateful for the treatment it received. Though exhausted as a formal church elements of the Puritan morality extended with an

---

[14] T Hobbes, *Leviathan* (1651) (ed) M Oakeshott (New York, Collier, 1962).
[15] M Shipman, *Childhood: A Sociological Perspective* (Slough, National Foundation for Educational Research, 1972).
[16] P Ariès, *supra* n 4.

evangelical zeal into the nineteenth century creating the Poor Laws and the campaigns against drunkenness, while still regarding children as being in need of correction. Much of the literature of the period employs the evil child as a symbol of the outmoded and hypocritical morality that continues to buttress an anti-democratic state. Dickens' novels are a great source of reference for our institutionalised violence towards the young, and Coveney's later critical work gathers many of the ways in which children have been portrayed in literature setting such harsh treatment against the romantic images of Blake and Wordsworth.[17]

The innocent child

This model encapsulates far more of what we have come to imagine as the modern, Western, child. Such a conception has set the public standards for our demeanour towards the child, and for our expectations of policy and provision in relation to the child. Such infants are essentially pure in heart, angelic and uncorrupted by the world that they have entered. It is here that the media derives its moral stance towards the child be it in relation to welfare provision or sexual abuse. It would be cheering to believe that we had reached this view spontaneously as part of the civilising march of modernity but, like all significant steps forward in human civilisation, the idea has an architect in the person of Jean-Jacques Rousseau. Rousseau is properly understood as the apostle of individual liberty, and this was, indeed, a continuous theme in his work on both education and political theory. He began his *Social Contract* (1762) with the assertion that: "Man is born free; and everywhere he is in chains. One thinks he is the master of others, and still remains the greater slave than they" and opened *Emile* with a similar view, namely that: "God makes all things good; man meddles with them and they become evil". Children then, have a natural goodness and a clarity of vision. They are redolent with the reason that will form the society of tomorrow. These natural characteristics are those we can all learn from; they represent a condition lost or forgotten and thus one worthy of defence (and susceptible to sentimentalisation). Rousseau sought to banish all consideration of original sin. Rather than treat children to a punitive journey into grace we might, more profitably, idolise or worship the intrinsic values that they bring to bear on a world that threatens decay.

More than just instilling a sense of childhood innocence Rousseau, more significantly, opened up the question of the child's particularity; a question that still concerns contemporary theorists. The child, through *Emile*, had become promoted to the status of person in its own right, a specific class of being with needs and desires and even rights. As Robertson put it:

[17] P Coveney, *Poor Monkey* (London, Rockcliff, 1957).

"If the philosophy of the Enlightenment brought to eighteenth century Europe a new confidence in the possibility of human happiness, special credit must go to Rousseau for calling attention to the needs of children. For the first time in history, he made a large group of people believe that childhood was worth the attention of intelligent adults, encouraging an interest in the process of growing up rather than just the product. Education of children was part of the interest in progress which was so predominant in the intellectual trends of the time".[18]

Our legacy is the serious recognition that children are not bundles of our negative attributes, nor incompletely formed persons waiting to become adults; they are who they are. As parents and educators we are inevitably contracted to bring up our children in such a manner that their state of pristine innocence remains unspoilt by the violence and ugliness that surrounds them. What we also note being instilled in the adult-child relationship here is the notion of responsibility. Rousseau's advocacy of freedom ensures that he must consider and reconcile the problem of authority. Indeed, are freedom and authority incompatible ideas? If childhood innocence is to be nurtured at all cost then we must attain publicly recognisable standards in the treatment of children; all adults must assume responsibility for children, but a responsibility based on a recognition of the child's intentionality and competence. Children can no longer be routinely mistreated and neither can they be left to their own devices. They have become subject.

An educating society begins with Rousseau and a childhood that is recognisable through encouragement, assistance, support and facilitation. Jenks has likened this model to Apollonian mythology:

"What now of the Apollonian child, the heir to the sunshine and light, the espouser of poetry and beauty? . . . Such children play and chuckle, smile and laugh, both spontaneously but also with our sustained encouragement. We cannot abide their tears and tantrums, we want only the illumination from their halo. This is humankind before either Eve or the apple. It is within this model that we honour and celebrate the child and dedicate ourselves to reveal its newness and uniqueness. Gone are the strictures of uniformity, here, with romantic vision, we explore the particularity of the person. Such thinking has been instructive of all child-centred learning and special-needs education from Montessori, the Plowden Report, A S Neill and the Warnock Report, and indeed much of primary teaching in the last three decades. This Apollonian image lies at the heart of attempts to protect the unborn through legislation concerning voluntary termination of pregnancies and endeavours in the USA to criminalise certain 'unfit' states of motherhood such as drug-addiction or HIV infection".[19]

We see in the innocent child the foundations of child-centred education, of special needs provision, of nursery and kindergarten provision, of feeding on demand and of a whole host of adaptive child-rearing strategies that are tailored to the needs of the individual. We also see the seeds of the belief that children are everybody's concern and that they constitute an investment in the future.

[18] P Robertson, "Home as a nest: Middle class childhood in nineteenth century Europe" in L DeMause (ed), *The History of Childhood* (London, Souvenir, 1976), p 407.
[19] C Jenks, *supra* n 13, p 183.

Rousseau's child is touched by the *Geist*, he or she is clearly an idealist's creation and exemplifies the precedence of mind before matter. The combination
of intentionality and pure reason render this child a forceful creature with a high
priority in our scale of human significance. Growing out of the innocent child is,
then, a child imbued with a vitality and an immanence but we now need to construct another category for this immanence to inhabit.

The immanent child

This category is required because although the modern child is very much the
outcome of Rousseau's manifesto, his blueprint was established over half a century earlier by a philosopher from a radically different tradition. John Locke
concerned himself with the proper education of young citizens in a tract called
Some Thoughts on Education (1693), but he had previously established his
major thesis on cognition and the acquisition of knowledge in *An Essay on
Human Understanding* (1689).

We cannot place Locke within the model of the innocent child as he was quite
clear that no such idealised state of primitive kindness existed. Far from the free
and noble savage of Rousseau's dreams Locke is much more hard-headed and
even properly anthropological in his unsentimentalised views on the cruel, spite-
ful and incompatible dispositions of the child. He does not view childhood as an
Elysian paradise of goodness and reciprocity; which is not to say that he therefore regards it as intrinsically brutish either. For him, children are intrinsically
no-thing and this is an epistemological statement rather than a disregard.
Though he was from a Puritan family he appeared to share none of their fierce
attitudes towards the young; on the contrary, Locke is famous for his philosophical contribution to the tradition of empiricism and consequently, for him,
the matter of being precedes mind. Children do not possess in-built, or *a priori*,
categories of understanding nor a general facility to reason. The growing diver-
gencies with the idealist Rousseau are in danger of rendering the two philosophers utterly incompatible, however, despite their different starting points there
is a congruence over the learning process and hence their place within this ten-
tative category. Locke is somewhat unstable in his formulation of childhood
and although he appears quite unequivocal in his famous quotation:

> "Let us then suppose the mind to be, as we say, white paper, void of all characters,
> without any ideas; how comes it to be furnished? Whence comes that vast store, which
> the busy and boundless fancy of man has painted on it with an almost endless variety?
> Whence has it all the materials of reason and knowledge? To this I answer in one
> word, from experience: in that all our knowledge is founded, and from that it ulti-
> mately derives itself".[20]

[20] J Locke, *An Essay on Human Understanding* (1689) Book II, ch i, sec.2.

On the face of it that would appear to be most radical of assertions, the *tabula rasa*, but Locke's theory of mind is tempered by his anachronistic liberalism. He sees children as charged with a potential, as citizens of the future and as imperfect but latent reasoners. There are no innate capacities, no knowledge lodged in a universal human condition but the drives and dispositions that the child does possess are on a gradient of becoming, towards reason. Like Rousseau, Locke believed that they are what they are, they are not inadequate or partially formed adults, they have a set of interests and needs that are special and should be recognised as such. Children should always be reasoned with and parents, like pedagogues, have knowledge and experience and are in a position to exercise responsible control over them. Through education children will become rational, virtuous contracting members of society, and exercisers of self-control.

Although Locke's empiricism begins from the firm commitment to the view that knowledge is acquired through "experience" he begins to discover, though not acknowledge, inconsistencies in this belief. He distinguishes between primary and secondary qualities of mind and it is here that he exposes his crypto idealism. He begins to suggest that certain ideas are not simply reflections of objects but are created by the mind itself. In some circumstances, then, knowledge is the outcome of mental activity and thus perception, the gateway to "experience" is predisposed by our own mental processes.

Rousseau's child is immanent in as much as it is innately charged with reason and thus it will develop this reason given the appropriate environment. Locke's child is immanent in that it has mental processes and perception and if we provide the appropriate environment we can elicit the reason from it. Locke is therefore offering us: ". . . the earliest manifesto for 'child-centred' education"[21] and a delicate cocktail of idealist assumptions and empiricist stimuli and reinforcements comprise much early learning in schools and homes today. This model of the child has ensured a general view that children are motivated, if not anxious, to learn. We must note, however, that the media see this immanence as potentially diverted by video nasties, bad parenting and sex on TV before the watershed.

The naturally developing child

It is within this model that we encounter the unholy alliance between the human sciences and human nature, and we witness the triumph of positivism over the natural attitude. Psychology never made the mistake of questioning its own status as a science and in the guise of developmental psychology it formed a pact with medicine, education and government agencies—this has led, in turn, to enhanced prestige, authority and the power of persuasion, and a continued high level of public trust and funding. Developmental psychology capitalises,

[21] D Archard, *supra* n 6, p 1.

perhaps not artfully but effectively, on two everyday assumptions: first, that children are natural rather than social phenomena; and secondly that part of this naturalness extends to the inevitable process of their maturation. The belief in their naturalness derives from the universal experience of being a child and the persistent and commonplace experience of having children and having to relate to children; the belief in the inevitability and even "good" of their maturation emanates from a combination of post-Darwinian developmental cultural aspirations and, conflated with the these, the post-Enlightenment confusion of growth and progress.[22]

The single most influential figure in the construction, or should we say development, of the naturally developing child was Piaget. His work on genetic epistemology extended biology, quite successfully, into the vocabulary of the taken-for-granted and produced the most absolute, if materially reductive, image of childhood that we are likely to encounter. Perhaps ironically he sets out from an idealism more deeply founded than Rousseau's but this is tempered by a voracious empiricism—he sought to reconcile reason with fact.

Piaget's child, the poor biological creature that it is, is imbued with a grand potential to become not anything but quite specifically something, predicted. His work on the development of thought and bodily skills, the path to intelligence, lays out for us the inevitable and clearly defined stages of growth. These stages are well signposted, beginning immediately after birth with sensory-motor intelligence and progressing through pre-conceptual thought, intuitive thought and finally achieving the destiny of the "normal" person in formal operations. Beyond this, the stages are ordered temporally and arranged hierarchically along a continuum from infantile, "figurative" thought, which has relatively low status, up to adult, "operative" intelligence which has high status within the model. Figurative thought is realised in the form of very particularistic behaviour, an incapacity to transfer training and a concrete replication of objective states; such behaviour is summoned by emotional responses in specific situations; the child is understood as being organised and orientated in relation to objective structures. Clearly, what is being demonstrated here is a lack of competence. Operative intelligence, by contrast, displays action, that is informed cognitive manipulation of objects and the transformation of those objects by a reflecting subject. Such action exemplifies logical process and the thinking individual's freedom from the constraint of immediate experience. What operative intelligence shows, then, is competence achieved and deserved, and what it provides analytically and culturally is the established grounds for the stratification that sustains between adults and children. The control provided by adult competence justifies the supremacy of adulthood. The strictly developmental relation between the two forms of cognition further ensures that childhood must, of necessity, be viewed as an inadequate precursor to the real

---

[22] C Jenks (ed), *The Sociology of Childhood—Essential Readings* (London, Batsford, 1982); C Jenks, "Social Theorizing and the Child . . . Constraints and Possibilities" in S Doxiadis (ed), *Early Influences in Shaping the Individual*, NATO Advanced Studies Workshop (London, Plenum, 1989).

state of human being, namely being "grown-up". This prioritising of the adult, complete state is revealed in Piaget's own definition of his purpose:

> "Developmental psychology can be described as the study of the development of mental functions, in as much as this development can provide an explanation, or at least a complete description, of their mechanisms in the finished state. In other words, developmental psychology consists of making use of child psychology in order to find the solution to general psychological problems".[23]

More recently there has been a growing dissatisfaction with this well established orthodoxy in understanding human maturation. Fundamental objections have arisen concerning the view that there is a universal, standardised and inevitable programme of developmental stages.[24] As Archard has put it:

> "Piaget suggested that all children acquire cognitive competencies according to a universal sequence. Nevertheless, he has been criticised on two grounds . . . First, his ideal of adult cognitive competence is a peculiarly Western philosophical one. The goal of cognitive development is an ability to think about the world with the concepts and principles of Western logic. In particular Piaget was concerned to understand how the adult human comes to acquire the Kantian categories of space, time and causality. If adult cognitive competence is conceived in this way then there is no reason to think it conforms to the everyday abilities of even Western adults. Second, children arguably possess some crucial competencies long before Piaget says they do".[25]

But more than this criticism has arisen around the idea that biology provides an adequate model for the understanding of human cognition. This reconnects with the earlier ideas of Vygotsky who believed that human beings actively take-on or appropriate society, far from passively growing into it. Morss[26] argues that developmental psychology is irrevocably embedded in a set of pre-Darwinian ideas that have long since been abandoned in the context of their own discipline. This, for Morss, means an inevitable compulsion to reduce all human maturation to an issue of development:

> "What modern developmentalists measure, investigate, even perceive in their subject-matter is, therefore, still confined by these outdated biological concepts. What developmentalists discover in their empirical work may be determined in advance: by non-Darwinian . . . biology".[27]

Piaget's genetic epistemology has, through its measuring, grading, ranking and assessing of children instilled a deep-seated positivism and rigid empiricism into our modern understandings of the child. What the real child suffers under

---

[23] J Piaget, *Psychology and Epistemology* (trans. P Wells) (Harmondsworth, Penguin, 1972), p 26.

[24] J Morss, *The Biologising of Childhood: Developmental Psychology and the Darwinian Myth* (London, Lawrence Erlbaum, 1990); E Burman, *Deconstructing Developmental Psychology* (London, Routledge, 1994).

[25] D Archard, *supra* n 6, pp 65–6.

[26] J Morss, *supra* n 24.

[27] *Ibid*, p xiii.

the hegemony of developmental stage monitoring is not just iniquitous comparison with its peers but also constant evaluation against a "gold standard" of the normal child. Piaget's project is interested in children, not for their own sake, but in as much as they provide exemplars or typical instances in a wider endeavour to answer more deeply philosophical questions concerning the origins and growth of thought. This is much more to do with a modern concern for monitoring and controlling the person than it has to do with the realisation of unique identities and capacities. Despite the undoubtable sway of developmental psychology in our everyday thinking about the child, Burman notes its gradual erosion thus:

> "Nowadays the status of developmental psychology is not clear. Some say that it is a perspective or an approach to investigating general psychological problems, rather than a particular domain or sub-discipline. According to this view we can address all major areas of psychology, such as memory, cognition, etc., from this perspective. The unit of development under investigation is also variable. We could be concerned with the development of a process, or a mechanism, rather than an individual. This is in marked contrast with the popular representations of developmental psychology which equate it with the practicalities of child development or, more recently, human development."[28]

The unconscious child

At the turn of the twentieth century the sudden impact of the Freudian edifice and the new growth of interest in the human psyche produced something of a volte-face in our thinking about the child. After a long series of concerns with the idea of development and a continuous but unconcerted attention to futures, childhood became the province of retrospectives. Whereas children had become firmly established in both theory and everyday consciousness as pointing in the direction of tomorrow, Freud opened up a concern with the child centred on adult pasts. In one sense Freudian theory is dedicated to an account of human maturation and it has lodged a battery of incremental concepts in the modern language of becoming. The critical difference, however, is that Freud's elements of personality, stages of development and complexes are all dedicated to an understanding of the building blocks in the architecture of adult psychopathology. Freudianism and its variety of modern tributaries instigated a search from surface to depth in a manner later emulated by structuralism. The search of psychoanalysis is, however, dedicatedly diachronic, the surface being the present and the depth being the past.

Freudian development is a familiar process of the compatible bonding of the elements: id; ego; and super-ego. The id comprises an elementary and primal broth of essentially libidinal drives; it is wholly expressive and utterly inexhaustible. The

---

[28] Burman, *supra* n 24, p 9.

id can be visualised as a reservoir of the instinctive energies, it is uncontrolled and thus dominated by the pleasure principle and impulsive wishing. Here is a potential source of creativity but it is wholly incompatible with a collective life and thus needs to be curbed. Successful development is, for Freud, the proper management of this "curbing" or repression. The *id* awakens all of the images and resonances of the model of the evil child but at a later historical moment; here again is a childhood predicated on constraint, management and the fear of an evil that resides within, and this time in the form of the unconscious. The *ego* assumes the role of interaction in childhood, it enables the self to experience others through the senses and thus begins an adjustment in behaviour through which the *id* is monitored. Consciousness and rationality are finally wrought through the supremacy of the *super-ego*, the experience of the collective other which regulates the presentations of self and integrates the child into the world of adult conduct. What has become evident through the growth of psychoanalytic influence in contemporary thinking is that Freud successfully generated a new source of causality. The explanation, and in many cases the blame, for aberrant adult behaviour is the child. The resource for accounts of the deviant, the criminal and the abnormal through late-modernity has developed into equations of parental-child relationship. The child has thus become transformed into the unconscious itself and all adults, it would seem, transport their childhood like a previous incarnation, from action to action. Although this model has opened up a vast potential for adult self-exploration in line with the many journeys towards belief that modern society has spurred[29] it has done little to broaden an understanding of the child as other than a state of unfinished business or becoming. Childhood, within this model, is once again dispossessed of intentionality as this is absorbed in the vocabulary of drives and instincts. Sexuality becomes the major dimension in the development of self and amnesia emerges as the key to successful socialisation.

THE SOCIOLOGICAL CHILD

Here I introduce a series of models specifically from within the sociological tradition. As ever within any overview of sociological approaches to a particular phenomenon I need to add the caveat that the models that follow are not all part of a total mosaic nor are they necessarily compatible. Sociological perspectives on childhood, although they share certain basic premises concerning the fundamentally "social" and even "social structural" character of their object of attention, are nevertheless divided from the level of metatheory to the level of methodology. It is also the case that many theorists do not see these models as standing in splendid isolation and routinely combine elements across the boundaries. I shall attempt here to elucidate some of the commonality between these as well as expressing the sources of their differences.

---

[29] A Giddens, *Modernity and Self-Identity* (Oxford, Polity, 1991).

The socially developing child

Sociologists have always been concerned with the development of the child inasmuch as that their theories of social order, social stability and social integration depend upon a uniform and predictable standard of action from the participating members. In this sense then, they begin with a formally established concept of society and work back to the necessary inculcation of its rules into the consciousnesses of its potential participants—these are always children. The process of this inculcation is referred to as socialisation. The direction of influence is apparent; the society shapes the individual. Sociologists are not ignorant of the biological character of the human organism but are singularly committed to an explication of its development within a social context. The socially developing model of childhood does share certain chronological and incremental characteristics with the naturally developing model but it largely avoids, or indeed resists, the reduction to explanation in terms of natural propensities or dispositions. The socially developing model is not attached to what the child naturally is so much as to what the society naturally demands of the child—a major commonality between the models can be seen here in terms of the obvious essentialism that their shared positivism brings to bear.

Socialisation is a concept that has been much employed by sociologists to delineate the process through which children, though in some cases adults, learn to conform to social norms.[30] Sociology has depended upon the efficacy of socialisation to ensure that societies sustain through time. The process involves, in essence, the successful transmission of culture from one generation to another. Let us look at two definitions of the process: the first from Ritchie and Kollar (1964), writing solidly within the tradition of socialisation theory, state:

"The central concept in the sociological approach to childhood is socialisation. A synonym for this process may well be acculturation because this term implies that children acquire the culture of the human groupings in which they find themselves. Children are not to be viewed as individuals fully equipped to participate in a complex adult world, but as beings who have the potentials for being slowly brought into contact with human beings".[31]

Speier from a more critical, phenomenological stance has stated:

"Sociology considers the social life of the child as a basic area of study in so-called institutional analyses of family and school, for example. What is classically problematic

[30] See F Elkin and G Handel, *The Child and Society: The Process of Socialization* (New York, Random House, 1972); N Denzin, *Childhood Socialization* (San Francisco, Jossey-Bass, 1977); D Goslin (ed), *Handbook of Socialization Theory and Research* (Chicago, Rand McNally,1969); K Danziger (ed), *Readings in Child Socialization* (Oxford, Pergamon, 1971); A Morrison and D McIntyre, *Childhood in Contemporary Cultures* (Chicago, Chicago University Press,1971) and G White, *Socialization* (London, Longman, 1977).
[31] O Ritchie and M Kollar, *The Sociology of Childhood* (New York, Appleton County Crofts, 1964), p 117.

about studying children is the fact of cultural induction, as I might refer to it. That is, sociologists (and this probably goes for anthropologists and psychologists) commonly treat childhood as a stage of life that builds preparatory mechanisms into the child's behavior so that he is gradually equipped with the competence to participate in the everyday activities of his cultural partners, and eventually as a bona fide adult member himself. This classical sociological problem has been subsumed under the major heading of socialization".[32]

The process has been conceived of in two ways. First, what we might term the "hard" way, or what Wrong referred to as the "oversocialized conception of man in modern sociology",[33] where socialisation is seen as the internalisation of social constraints. Through this transfer from the outside to the inside the norms of society become internal to the individual but this occurs through external regulation. The individual child's personality thus becomes continuous with the goals and means of the society itself; the individual is seen as a microcosm. The "hard way" derives largely from structural sociology and systems theory and finds its most persuasive and influential exponent in Parsons who defines the process as follows:

> "The term socialization in its current usage in the literature refers primarily to the process of child development . . . However, there is another reason for singling out the socialization of the child. There is reason to believe that, among the learned elements of personality in certain respects the stablest and most enduring are the major value-orientation patterns and there is much evidence that these are 'laid down' in childhood and are not on a large scale subject to drastic alteration during adult life".[34]

What Parsons successfully achieves in his social system is a stable and uniform isomorphism, such that individual actors and their particular personalities have an homologous relation with groups, institutions, sub-systems and the society itself; they are all cut to a common pattern. What he also achieves is a universality in the practice and experience of childhood, because the content of socialisation is secondary to the form of socialisation in each and every case. The potentiality for an expression of the child's intentionality is constrained through the limited number of choices that are made available in social interaction, which Parsons refers to as pattern variables. In this way the model achieves a very generalised sense of the child at a level of abstraction and one determined by structure rather than pronounced through the exercise of agency. As this model is also based on a developmental scheme the child is necessarily considered to be incompetent or in possession of incomplete, unformed or proto-competencies. This latter understanding ensures that any research following from such a model does not attend to the everyday world of the child nor its skills in interaction and world view, except in terms of generating a diagnosis for remedial action.

[32] M Speier, "The Everyday World of the Child" in J Douglas (ed), *Understanding Everyday Life* (London, Routledge, 1970), p 208.
[33] D Wrong, "The Oversocialized Conception of Man in Modern Sociology" (1961) XXVI *American Sociological Review* 183.
[34] T Parsons, *The Social System* (Glencoe, Free Press 1951), p 101.

The second, and somewhat "softer", way in which the socialisation process has been conceived by sociologists is as an essential element in interaction, that is as a transactional negotiation that occurs when individuals strive to become group members. This is the version of socialisation that stems from the symbolic interactionism of George Herbert Mead and the Chicago School and involves a social psychology of group dynamics. This is really, however, a perspective on adult socialisation. The Meadian analysis of child development is much more of a thesis in materialism. The basic theory of the acquisition of language and interactional skills is based very much on an unexplicated behaviourism, and the final resolution of the matured relationship between the individual and the collective other (that is, the "Self" and "Other") is a thinly disguised reworking of Freud's triumph of the *super-ego* over the *id*. Symbolic interactionism has generated a wealth of sensitive ethnographic studies of small groups and communities but it begins from the baseline of adult interactional competence and thus shares, at this level, much with the socialisation theory espoused by Parsons and structural sociology. What is highly instructive of all manifestations of the model of the socially developing child (that is, socialisation theory) as they have appeared in many forms of sociology, is that they have little or no time for children. To a large extent this accounts for sociology's long neglect of the topic of childhood and also demonstrates why the child was only ever considered under the broadest of umbrellas, namely the sociology of the family.

The socially constructed child

What is now called social constructionism is a relatively new departure in the understanding of childhood which found three major landmarks in the works of Jenks,[35] Stainton Rogers et al[36] and James and Prout.[37] The perspective derives, in large part, from the 1970s backlash in British sociology to the stranglehold that varieties of positivism were exercising on the field. A wave of critical, deconstructing phenomenology had come into competition with the absolutist pronouncements of the structural sociologies and marxisms that appeared to hold sway. Such theorising also complemented the growing liberalism and relativism that were permeating the academy in the wake of the 1960s. The dominating philosophical paradigm shifted from a dogmatic materialism to an idealism inspired by the works of Husserl and Heidegger; in fact, such original phenomenology appeared rather too "wild" for the standards of British reason and was rendered acceptable through the mediation of Berger and Luckmann[38] and Schutz.[39]

[35] C Jenks (ed), *supra* n 22.

[36] W Stainton Rogers, D Harvey and E Ash (eds), *Child Abuse and Neglect* (London, Open University Press, 1989).

[37] A James and A Prout *Constructing and Reconstructing Childhood* (London, Falmer Press, 1990).

[38] P Berger and T Luckmann, *supra* n 9.

[39] A Schutz, *Collected Papers Vols I, II and III* (The Hague, Martinus Nijhoff, 1971).

To describe childhood, or indeed any phenomenon, as socially constructed is to suspend a belief in or a willing reception of its taken-for-granted meanings. Thus, quite obviously with our current topic, we all know what children are and what childhood is like but this is not a knowledge that we can reliably draw upon. Such knowledge of the child and its life-world depends upon the predispositions of a consciousness constituted in relation to our social, political, historical and moral context. Social constructionists have to suspend assumptions about the existence and causal powers of a social structure that makes things, like childhood, as they are; their purpose is to go back to the phenomenon in consciousness and show how it is built up. So within a socially constructed, idealist world, there are no absolutes. Childhood does not exist in a finite and identifiable form; Ariès[40] had already shown us this historically and Mead and Wolfenstein[41] had made early demonstrations of this cross-culturally. This moves us to a multiple conception of childhoods; what Schutz would have referred to as multiple realities. Social constructionism stresses the issue of plurality and far from this model recommending a unitary form it foregrounds diverse constructions. This model is dedicatedly hermeneutic, it therefore provides scope for exciting new development, new forms and new interpretations. It also erodes the conventional standards of judgment and truth. Therefore if, for example, as many commentators have suggested, child abuse was rife in earlier times and a fully anticipated feature of adult-child relations then how are we to say that it was bad, exploitative and harmful? Our standards of judgment are relative to our world view, therefore we cannot make universal statements of value. We can, on the other hand, attend to the socially constructed "increase" in cases of child abuse during the "Cleveland Affair" of 1987. What of infanticide in contemporary non-Western societies? Is it an immoral and criminal act or an economic necessity? Is it an extension of the Western belief in "a woman's right to choose"? Social constructionism and cultural relativism do have an intense relationship. As a model it lends itself to a cultural studies style of analysis, or the now fashionable modes of discourse analysis—children are brought into being.

Children within this model are, clearly, unspecifiable as an ideal type and childhoods are variable and intentional but, we should note, this intentionality is the responsibility of the theorist. This model demands a level of reflexivity from its exponents. It is also the case that social constructionists, through their objections to positivist methods and assumptions, are more likely to be of the view that children are not formed by natural and social forces but rather that they inhabit a world of meaning created by themselves and through their interaction with adults. The child in this model is to be located semantically rather than causally:

---

[40] P Ariès, *supra* n 4.
[41] M Mead and M Wolfenstein, *Childhood in Contemporary Cultures* (Chicago, IL, University of Chicago Press, 1955).

"There are no hard and fast principles for defining when disagreements about how things are seen become significant enough to take about them as different social realities...

When social constructionists look at childhood, it is to these different social realities that they turn. The interest is not just in learning about the constructions of childhood in history or in different cultures—it is also a technique that throws light on why we construct childhood as we do in our own time and society".[42]

Social constructionism has played an important political role in the study of childhood in that it was well situated to prise the child free of biological determinism and thus claim the phenomenon, epistemologically, within the realm of the social. While it remains important to emphasise that the model is more than a theory of the ideational, it is about the practical application of formed mental constructs and the impact that this has on the generation of reality and real consequences, it is also important not to abandon the embodied material child.

The tribal child

This model contains a quite significant alteration in thinking, and not simply in terms of the particular theoretical perspective that is to be applied to the topic. Here we witness a moral reappraisal of the stratification system and power relation that conventionally exists between adults and children, and a decision to articulate the *Weltanschauung* of what the Chicago school would have called the "underdog" in their studies of deviance and criminality. This model sets out from a commitment to childhood's social worlds as real places and provinces of meaning in their own right and not as fantasies, games, poor imitations or inadequate precursors of the adult state of being. It would be claiming too much to say that this position takes children seriously, as it would suggest that previously considered models do not, however, it can be argued that there is a seriousness here which attaches to the child's own view. We have a sense of what Mayall[43] has referred to as children's childhoods. Here we honour children's difference and celebrate their relative autonomy. In the manner of the enlightened anthropologist we desist from imposing our own constructs and transformations upon the actions of the child and attempt to treat their accounts and explanations at face value in good neo-Tylorian fashion. Within this model children are not understood as "cultural dopes", that is, we do not begin from the premise that they have only a misguided, mythological, superficial or irrational understanding of the rules of social life. Their worlds are real locations, as are our own, and they demand to be understood in those terms.

An early and well publicised excursion into the possibilities provided by this model is to be found in the copious ethnographic studies of the Opies.[44] The

---

[42] W Stainton Rogers et al, *supra* n 36, p 24.
[43] B Mayall (ed), *Children's Childhood* (London, Falmer, 1994).
[44] I Opie and P Opie, *The Lore and Language of Schoolchildren* (Oxford, OUP, 1959).

Opies, and other researchers following their lead, have argued for the long-overdue recognition of an autonomous community of children. The children's world is to be seen as not unaffected by but nevertheless artfully insulated from the world of adults; it is to be understood as an independent place with its own folklaw, rituals, rules and normative constraints. This is the world of the schoolyard, the playground, the club and the gang.

What this model encourages is an emphasis on children's social action as structured but within a system that is unfamiliar to us and therefore to be revealed. Childhood intentionality welcomes the anthropological strangeness that has been recommended by ethnomethodology. If the tribes of childhood are to be provided with the status of social worlds then it is to be anticipated that their particularity will systematically confound our taken-for-granted knowledge of how other (adult) social worlds function. There will be homologies, but the purpose of such a model as this is to ensure that the homologies do not legislate or stand in a dictatorial relationship to the child's world. We might anticipate that ethnographies of the tribes will, and should, proliferate. Work within the model has a negative potential of generating whimsical tales—quaint fables of the tribes of childhood; the kind of anecdotal accounting so favoured by the doting parent with little generalisability and less enlightenment. This, however, should not be its purpose. Much is spoken in the literature on childhood about the child's ontology but mostly as an aspiration rather than viable construct, it is within the bounds of this model that such a form of life can begin to receive annotation. The mapping of childhood practices, self-presentations, motives and assumptions provides the very basis for an attention to the intrinsic being of childhood time which in turn can enable both more effective communication and latterly more apposite policy measures. On the child's side of the equation a successful and ultimately knowing intrusion into their tribal folkways inevitably brings the threat of increased strategies of control. The ever looming panopticon vision explodes into fruition once the interior and the ontological become available.

One obvious benefit of the ethnographies that follow from within the tribal model is that it enables a sustained, and long awaited, concentration on children's language, language acquisition, language games, and thus burgeoning competence. This can help us in our relations with children and in their education, but it can also advise us about the constitution of mind as Chomsky's work on transformational grammar has done. Methodology, however, is a constant problem.

The minority group child

This model can attend to children epistemologically in any number of ways, its binding feature is its politicisation of childhood in line with previously established agendas concerning an unequal and structurally discriminatory society.

Oakley in a paper that explicitly attempts to demonstrate parallels between the politics of women's studies and childhood studies states the following:

> "This chapter considers the emerging field of childhood studies from the viewpoint of the established discipline of women's studies. Women and children are, of course, linked socially, but the development of these specialist academic studies also poses interesting methodological and political questions about the relationship between the status of women and children as social minority groups and their constitution as objects of the academic gaze".[45]

The status of a minority group is a question that seeks to challenge rather than confirm an existing set of power relations and the very title "minority" reveals a moral rather than a demographic classification that is itself intended to convey notions of relative powerlessness or victimisation. Such a model of the child begins, then, not from an intrinsic interest in childhood, though this may certainly accompany the larger purpose, but instead from an indictment of a social structure and an accompanying dominant ideology which, to quote Oakley's conclusion: ". . . deprive(s) some people of freedom in order to give it to others".[46]

It is certainly the case that sociology over the last thirty years has striven to convert the natural into the cultural. This has not simply been a completion of the Durkheimian endeavour to understand all phenomena as if they were primarily social. What has been occurring, and what has finally given rise to this model of the child, is a systematic move to re-democratise modern society and to disassemble all remaining covert forms of stratification. Whereas classical sociology attended primarily to the stratification wrought through social class, modern sociology has begun to address all of those areas that have been treated as "natural" (like our critical address of developmental psychology), or "only human nature". Thus race, sex, sexuality, age and physical and mental ability have all come under scrutiny and have all been shown to derive their meaning and routine practices from their social context. Childhood is rather late in gaining both fashion and attention but it has finally arrived. Standpoint epistemologies are being forged on behalf of the child, never more powerfully than when linked to empirical findings from within the previous model.

The strengths of this model derive from its seeming dedication to the child's interests and purposes, though it is always important with such political processes to ensure that a group is not being driven by a hidden agenda or a political sub-text. In many senses children here are regarded as essentially indistinguishable from adults, or indeed all people; it is important within such thinking not to reimport new forms of stratification. Children are therefore seen as active subjects and a sociology develops sharing characteristics with action research—a sociology for children! The weaknesses of this model derive from

---

[45] A Oakley, "Women and Children first and last: Parallels and differences between women's and children's studies" in B Mayall (ed), n 43, p 13.

[46] *Ibid*, p 32.

the necessary categorical transformation of any social group into the status of a group for-itself instead of just in-itself, that is, the imposition of a uniformity that defies the differences within. Thus the universal child becomes a minority group with demands that have to be heard, but that group is fractured and facetted in its internal diversity. This is analogous to the problems found in, for example, applying the consciousness-raising of the white middle class woman to the everyday experience of black working class women.

The social structural child

This model contains a good deal of sound sense, if not pragmatism. It begins from a recognition of the obvious—that children are a constant feature of all social worlds. As a component of all societies children are typical, tangible, persistent and normal, indeed they demonstrate all of the characteristics of social facts. Their manifestations may vary from society to society but within each particular society they are uniform. To this degree they constitute a formative component of all social structures. This model of the child begins from such an assumption, children are not pathological or incomplete, they form a group, a body of social actors and as citizens they have needs and rights. In the model of the socially developing child we saw a social structure and a society made up of rational adults with children waiting to be processed through the particular *rite de passage* that socialisation within that society demanded. Now the constancy of the child is acknowledged as is also its essentiality. From this beginning any theorising around this model can proceed to examine both the necessary and sufficient conditions that apply to childhood within a particular or indeed to children in general. Children are again very much a universal category and they are seen to properly emerge from the constraint that their particular social structure profers. Children, then, are a body of subjects but their subjectivity is not wilful nor capricious, it is determined by their society. This model concentrates not so much on the child's intentionality as on its instancing structural formation. Qvortrup's huge international survey of childhood as a social phenomenon can be more accurately understood as an analysis of the universal structural components in the recognisability and processing of childhood:

"There is . . . a more positive, and more important reason for preferring to speak about *the* childhood, namely the suggestion that children who live within a defined area— whether in terms of time, space, economics or other relevant criteria—have a number of characteristics in common. This preference in other words enables us to characterize not only childhood, but also the society in which this childhood is situated as mutually both independent and indispensable constructions; moreover it allows us to compare childhood thus characterized with other groups from the same country, perhaps most notably other age groups like youth, adulthood and old age, because they in principle are influenced by the same characterizing and formative societal parameters, although in different ways; it also permits us to ask which extent childhood within a given area has changed historically, because—typically—continuity reigns within one country more than within any other unit of that order; and finally, it becomes possible, when the concept of childhood is used, to compare childhoods internationally and interculturally, because we are availing ourselves of the same types of parameters—e.g. economic, political, social, environmental parameters".[47]

What such work demonstrates is the dual and non-contradictory view that children bear the same status as research subjects as adults, but that they may also have a different set of competencies, all of which are recognisable features of the social structure. Frones has shown that there are multiple dimensions to the "social structural" child and that it always remains possible to investigate these dimensions separately, but ultimately in relation to the integrative, inter-related and functional constraints of the institutional arrangements within the overall social structure:

"Childhood may be defined as *the life period during which a human being is regarded as a child, and the cultural, social and economic characteristics of that period* . . . most of the studies on childhood concentrate on aspects that fall into one of four main categories: relations among generations, relations among children, children as an age group, and the institutional arrangements relating to children, their upbringing, and their education. Factors from one category may, of course, be important in another, as when the institutional apparatus concerned with children is significant in an analysis of child culture or child-parent relations".[48]

The "social structural" child, then, has certain universal characteristics which are specifically related to the institutional structure of societies in general and are not simply subject to the changing nature of discourses about children nor the radical contingencies of the historical process.

[47] J Qvortrup, "Childhood Matters: An Introduction" in J Qvortrup, M Bardy, G Sgritta and H Wintersberger (eds), *Childhood Matters: Social Theory, Practice and Politics* (Aldershot, Avebury, 1994), pp 5–6.
[48] I Frones, "Dimensions of Childhood" in J Qvortrup et al (eds), *ibid*, p 148.

3

Philosophical Perspectives on Childhood

DAVID ARCHARD

I

WRITING ABOUT ARISTOTLE'S conception of the child, Gareth Matthews comments, "The common defining feature is that the child is "unfinished" relative to a human *telos*. In the biology, the child is viewed as unfinished in his or her growth as a human animal; in the ethics, unfinished in the training in virtue; in the politics, unfinished in the education for adult life as a responsible citizen".[1] This is far from untypical. Philosophy is principally if not solely interested in childhood in so far as it may be understood as that which is not adulthood but is at the same time a necessary preparation for and indicator of what will follow as adulthood. Children are viewed as "*becoming*" rather than "*being*".[2] The philosopher's child is not yet an adult but is also essentially that which will and must become the adult.

The philosopher's child is an unfinished *human*. The child is unquestionably a human being but that humanity is specified in terms of features—such as rationality, freedom and moral responsibility—which are only fully and properly possessed if at all by the developed adult. The child is unfinished relative to the accomplished nature of the fully grown human being; it is lacking that which will complete it as a human. It is not yet fully rational or autonomous or morally responsible. Thus the child's nature is defined negatively not so much in terms of what it is in and of itself but rather in terms of what it lacks. At the same time the child is that which will, and must, normally develop into an adult. A child is not, as is a higher primate, a being which essentially lacks those defining features of adult humanity and which it can never acquire. The child is an unfinished human but the work of completion is possible and normally follows in time.

This characterisation does not make childhood uninteresting. But the interest in childhood is further dependent on what view is taken as to how the particular

---

[1] Gareth B Matthews, "Socrates's Children" in Susan M Turner and Gareth B Matthews (eds), *The Philosopher's Child: Critical Essays in the Western Tradition* (Rochester, University of Rochester Press, 1998), p 21.

[2] Harry Hendrick, *Children, Childhood and English society, 1880–1990* (Cambridge, Cambridge University Press, 1997), pp 3–4.

characteristics of adulthood are acquired. On one view childhood is already an anticipation of adulthood and the adult's future features may be discerned within the present character of the child. According to Milton, "The childhood shows the man, As morning shows the day".[3] On another view the child is a blank slate on which can be written the features of adulthood. What exactly is written there will differ according to the preferred model of adult nature. Corresponding to these contrasting views childhood can also play different evidential roles in our understanding of adulthood. Philosophers might point to the behaviour of children as confirmation of what an adult's nature is. But they can do so only if the normal development of any child does not, and cannot, essentially change what has already been given as his nature. A child is, according to the theory of human development held, a possibility of becoming something else or a confirmation of what one already knows the adult in the making to be. When, thus, one describes the child as "unfinished" this can mean either that the work of completion is a work of creative construction or one merely of the realisation of a prior yet fixed potentiality.

These different accounts of development, and thus of the significance of childhood, can be combined with different theories of human nature—theories to which philosophers subscribe, even if they do not always explicitly avow them. These views can be ranged on an axis with the angelic at one end and the beastly at the other. Combining the different views of humanity's moral nature with the contrasting accounts of how far the child really does show the man gives us various possible philosophical psychologies. One might hold that humans are born good but subject to social corruption, as did Jean-Jacques Rousseau;[4] or, on the contrary, hold as did the Puritans that humans are born evil but open to moral improvement through rigorous, indeed brutal, reformative education.[5]

It should be noted that thinking about childhood by contrast with adulthood and as essentially a preface to adulthood may be considered to be both Western and modern. It is Western in so far as adulthood is viewed as an achieved state where it might, as in Eastern thinking, be considered as a continuing process.[6] It is arguably modern according to a famous thesis of Philippe Ariès who maintains that the "concept of childhood" is one lacked by pre-modern societies which had no awareness of "that particular nature which distinguishes the child

---

[3] John Milton, *Paradise Regained*, bk ii, l. 220.

[4] "Everything is good as it leaves the hands of the Author of things; everything degenerates in the hands of man". *Émile, or On Education*. Introduction, Translation and Notes by Allan Bloom (Harmondsworth, Penguin, 1979), p 37.

[5] "Is it not a fundamental error to consider children as innocent beings, whose little weaknesses may perhaps want some correction, rather than as beings who bring into the world a corrupt nature and evil disposition, which it should be the great end of education to rectify?". Hannah More, quoted in John Cleverley and D C Philips, *From Locke to Spock: Influential Models of the Child in Modern Western Thought* (Melbourne, Melbourne University Press, 1976), p 30.

[6] The contrast is discussed by William J Bouwsma, "Christian Adulthood" *Daedalus* 105, no. 2 (Spring 1976) at 77–92.

from the adult".[7] The thesis is both deeply contested and yet highly influential, being taken by some at least as uncontested historical truth. It has been associated with a further and distinct claim that the appreciation by modernity of the distinct nature of childhood has meant a humane treatment of children; pre-modernity's ignorance of childhood, by contrast, disposed to a cruel or indifferent treatment of children.[8] Whatever the merits of these views they serve to make us aware of the extent to which we are able to, and do, think of childhood as a distinct stage of human existence, yet may do so chiefly by reference to that which succeeds, and as it were justifies, childhood—namely adulthood. We may distinguish childhood from adulthood only to the extent and in order that we can negatively characterise the former in terms of the latter. In even more general terms it should make philosophical treatments of childhood sensitive to the possibility that there is no single, historically unvarying, natural kind of concept of childhood. Instead there may be socially, historically and cultural specific conceptions of childhood.

What has been outlined in schematic form is a general view of childhood which tends to inform philosophical writing about childhood. It would be contrasted, most evidently, with a view that treats childhood as a distinctive, *sui generis* and self-contained state, one whose peculiar and uniquely defining features merit consideration in their own right. It is a view most famously attributed to Rousseau who criticised those who "are always seeking the man in the child without thinking what he is before being a man".[9] Rousseau's emphasis upon the "child in the child", with its implied valuation of what is specific to childhood, has been echoed in subsequent work and has been, most notably, an inspiration for progressive, as opposed to traditional, educational thinking. It has inspired a "philosophy of childhood" which views children as, far from being immature pre-philosophical creatures, contributing a distinctive perspective upon moral, metaphysical and aesthetic issues.[10]

There is a danger here of overstatement. Let us distinguish various claims. There may be features of childhood but not of adulthood which are valuable, such as innocence, wonder, and trust. There may, correspondingly, be features of adulthood but not of childhood which are valuable, such as experience and independence. It is also evident that there may be features of childhood but not of adulthood which are *not valuable*, such as dependence and vulnerability. An emphasis only upon what childhood lacks by comparison with adulthood may lead us to ignore or neglect what childhood is in its own right. Childhood may,

---

[7] Philippe Ariès, *L'Enfant et la vie familiale sous l'ançien régime* (Paris, Libraire Plon, 1960). Translated from the French by Robert Baldick as *Centuries of Childhood* (London, Jonathan Cape, 1962), p 125.

[8] See Lloyd de Mause, "The Evolution of Childhood" in L de Mause (ed) *The History of Childhood* (London, Souvenir Press, 1976), pp 1–73.

[9] *Émile, supra* n 4, p 34.

[10] G B Matthews, *The Philosophy of Childhood* (Cambridge, MA, Harvard University Press, 1994).

as Rousseau and his philosophical successors claim, have "its own ways of feel-ing, thinking and seeing". However, it would certainly be a mistake to think that adulthood and childhood are, in this regard, strictly incommensurable. Indeed the evaluative standpoint from which these "childish ways" are appreciated can, properly, only be an adult one. One need not think childhood beyond compari-son with adulthood, nor superior to adulthood, in order to point out the narrow focus of a view that sees childhood only as the "negative other" of adulthood. Yet that does tend to be the general philosophical approach to childhood and against its background we may consider what follows for our understanding of the status of children.

II

The adult whom we seek to see the child become is, for present purposes, a responsible moral agent. The following are the principal important characteris-tics of such agency. An agent is minimally rational, that is possessed of consis-tently ordered desires, beliefs that she is aware of as consistent, and seeking when she chooses to act to act in the light of these beliefs and desires. She is appropriately held responsible for those actions of hers which are uncoerced and knowing, that is which can truly be said to proceed from her own will. This is a simplified picture but it captures the essentials for the purposes of under-standing childhood as a preparation for adult responsibility.

The adult is a reasoner; the child lacks reason and must be brought to reason. Education is variously viewed as an awakening of reason, a training of an innate faculty of reason, or as a provision to reason of materials drawn from experi-ence. But the education must be appropriate to the degree of rationality dis-played by the child and with an eye on the end of education, the mature rationality of the adult. Influential in most contemporary accounts of that edu-cation is a developmental view which represents the progress of the child towards the acquisition of full adult rationality as segmented into distinct incre-mental stages, each appropriate to a certain age band, each defined in terms of a particular set of abilities and skills, and each representing a clear advance upon the preceding stage.

The influence of a stages account of development is important for three inter-related reasons. In the first place it reinforces the teleological characterisation of childhood as a preparation for adulthood. Piaget, its most notable defender, views developmental psychology as "the study of the development of mental functions, inasmuch as this development can provide an explanation, or at least a complete description, of their mechanisms in the finished state".[11] The other two influences of a stages account pull against this simple teleology in interesting

---

[11] Jean Piaget, *Psychology and Epistemology* (1927), translated by P Wells (Harmondsworth, Penguin, 1972), p 26.

ways. First, on the stages account, it is harder to think of childhood as a single homogeneous stage in its own right. Each stage having its own identity which sets it apart from others it becomes that bit more difficult to see all the stages as bound together in a uniform identity. Indeed it is conventional now to think of childhood in at least two ways. On one understanding it is a general term for the state of pre-adulthood. On another understanding we now possess the limit stages of childhood in infancy and adolescence—the former being that stage of development immediately after birth and characterised in terms of extreme vulnerability and dependence; the latter being that stage immediately prior to adulthood and characterised in terms of impending maturity, near independence and self-sufficiency. It is possible on this understanding to see childhood proper not as that which encompasses both infancy and adolescence but as that which lies between. Whichever understanding is adopted, and wherever the precise age limits of the stages are fixed, the fact remains that childhood lacks that simple and unifying characteristic of being before adulthood.

Second, a stages account of development weakens the simplifying view of childhood as marked by the straightforward absence of adult capacities. Each stage is a progress towards adulthood, and, to that extent, the later stages display the definitive acquisition of more of those abilities, skills, and powers which are said to constitute adulthood. While it is easy to represent an infant as evidently not an adult, lacking all but the most basic, and unimportant, characteristics of the mature human being, it is correspondingly harder to do so for a late adolescent. What is true of the six-month-old baby by contrast with an adult is false of a sixteen-year-old adolescent. To the extent that this is true it is problematic to deny to the adolescent that standing which is denied to all children in virtue of their not being adults. An adolescent is much less clearly not-an-adult than an infant, but is, for the purposes of a certain ascriptive status, as much of a child.

What, then, is that status? Moral status attaches to agents, as the source of actions, and to patients, as the objects or ends of the actions of others. The status of a child as a moral patient is that of any human being. What it is forbidden to do to a human being because of its humanity it is forbidden to do to a child. This is not uncontroversial. Philosophers are divided over whether this status attaches to a human being simply in virtue of its humanity or in virtue of some independently definable set of features which are normally, and regularly, associated with humanity. Thus, most obviously, there is a moral dispute as to whether abortion is morally wrong because it is murder, and that dispute turns centrally on the question of whether a foetus has the same moral status as an adult human being. For those who think that bare humanity, being a member of the human species, is sufficient the conclusion will be that the intentional destruction of a foetus is the unwarranted murder of a full human being. Those who believe abortion to be morally permissible will normally argue for their view by denying that a foetus has this moral status. It is, of course, possible to argue further that what qualifies someone for that status, and is not possessed by a foetus, is also lacking in very young infants—an argument which would see infanticide as being as morally permissible as abortion.[12]

There are things it is wrong to do to children inasmuch as they are human beings, which would not, for instance, be wrong if done to animals. This is consistent with its being wrong to do some things to children inasmuch as they are children. That is, some wrongs are fully and properly specified as wrongful by reference to the particular status or nature of the human beings in question. By way of an example, the sexual use of another human being against their will is an evident wrong. But in the case of children, there is an additional wrong which derives from the innocence and vulnerability of the young. We may describe this in such terms as a theft of the child's innocence, as an exploitation of their particular vulnerability, and as an abuse of the trust for the child's care which is placed in any adult's hands.

A wrong is done to a human being if, other things being equal, her choices are not respected, that is if her autonomy is violated. Rape is a wrong done to a woman insofar as her sexual choice, her decision as to what happens sexually to her, is overridden. It is a particular kind of wrong inasmuch as it is a *sexual* violation of her. Children are deemed to be below the age of sexual consent. This means that they are regarded as incapable of making choices, or at least of making choices whose value should be recognised. It is a crime knowingly to have sex with someone below the age of consent. It remains a crime even if the minor is willing, that is an uncoerced and knowing party to sex. It is a crime not because it is against the will of the child, but because the child's will is not such as to license the action. There is no consent not in the sense that it is unconsented but in the sense that whatever "consent" the child gives does not count as consent.

This is not to deny the appropriateness of protecting children against the consequences of choices which they are deemed incapable of properly making. It is merely to acknowledge that what is wrongfully done to children extends beyond what is wrongfully done to adults so long as the particular nature of childhood is properly appreciated. But, at the same time, the range of wrongs done to children does not extend as far as those which can be done to adults because adults, unlike children, have a capacity for making choices which ought to be recognised and protected.

III

What of the status of children as moral agents? On a familiar Aristotelian model human beings are only responsible, and therefore blame- or praiseworthy, for those actions which they perform knowingly and willingly. Aristotle thought that ignorance of the nature or consequences of one's actions and compulsion to

[12]   Michael Tooley, "Abortion and Infanticide" (1972) 2 *Philosophy and Public Affairs* 37–65.

perform an action rendered an agent not responsible for those actions. The model is not without its critics, and there has been considerable subsequent debate as to how ignorance and compulsion should best be understood. Nevertheless, something like this account is now standard, and, on this account, children are not regarded as morally responsible agents.

This is because children lack the ability to know what it is they are doing. It is important to acknowledge that the relevant sense of knowledge should not be interpreted in too cognitivist a fashion. It also requires a degree of appreciation. Thus someone may know that firing a gun pointed at another human being will result in serious injury or worse to that person, but not appreciate what it is that he is doing in the sense of fully recognising the significance of his actions. Children may know what it is they are doing in that they are correctly apprised of the relevant facts, but, again, not see the import of these facts. In this sense a child may know that its actions will result in harm being occasioned to another child but, nevertheless, not really grasp the importance of that harm being done to another.

Children are, as a group, deemed not to be responsible for their actions inasmuch as they lack those capacities—those having chiefly to do with an appreciation of the nature and consequences of their actions—which are thought to be an essential precondition of the ascription of moral agency and responsibility. This needs to be qualified in at least three regards. First, the scope of childhood for the purposes of this particular ascription need not be co-extensive with the scope of childhood for other purposes. The child who is held not to be morally responsible need not extend in age as far, or as little, as the child who is, for instance, seen as lacking rights. Secondly, any denial of responsibility can be absolute or presumptive. One can consistently hold that children, as a group, are normally not morally responsible for their actions, that this particular child did this particular thing, and that, nevertheless, there is good reason to conclude that this particular child was morally responsible for that action. Third, it is possible in principle to see others as responsible for the child's actions. Most obviously one might see a parent or carer as, in some set of circumstances, morally responsible for the harmful deeds of the child. This will be justified through an account of the guardian's failure to rear the child in an appropriate way. But such an attribution of indirect responsibility for another's misdeeds will need to be carefully spelled out and justified.

IV

If children lack the requisite capacities to have responsibility for the actions attributed to them, they are also normally thought to lack those capacities which are a precondition for the possession and exercise of rights. This is not to deny that children are entitled to receive certain forms of protection. They are, as we have seen, moral patients to whom it is forbidden to do certain things.

However, there is a difference between protecting children and empowering them to claim, as of right, that things be or not be done to them. After all one can deny that animals have rights and yet hold that they should not be treated cruelly. The thought is that children lack the capacities, as do animals, to possess and to exercise rights in their own regard.

This claim is complicated in at least two respects. First there are a range of rights and it might be thought appropriate to possess some rights but not others. In related fashion one might view the acquisition of rights as a progressive affair, different rights being acquired at different ages. In particular there is a familiar distinction between welfare rights which allow their holder to claim protection or promotion of the constitutive elements of their well-being—such as health, personal security, education, employment—and liberty rights which accord to their holders the protection of the exercise of their freedom—of speech, religious worship, and association. One could conclude that it is proper for children to have welfare rights but not liberty rights.

The second complication arises from the fact that there are at least two major accounts of what it is to have a right—an "interest" (or "benefit") theory which sees a right as the protection of an individual's fundamental interest, and a "choice" (or "will") theory which sees a right as constituted by an individual's exercise of freedom in some important regard.[13] From each theory follows a different account of what sorts of thing can have a right—something which possesses fundamental interests which ought to be protected, or something which is capable of exercising a freedom in respect of some important matter. It is easy to see how children could be viewed as a test-case for either theory depending on whether one sees children as incapable of exercising free choice or as, nevertheless, possessed of fundamental interests meriting protection.[14]

Of course it is possible to deny that, however rights are understood, there is any good reason to deny to children all those rights which are accorded to adults. This has been argued by child liberationists, such as Richard Farson and John Holt.[15] A liberationist case can be made in at least two ways. One is by means of a straightforward denial of the claim that children lack those capacities, possessed by adults, which are seen as the qualifying properties of bona fide rights holders. This counterclaim is the more plausible the greater the reliance is upon evidence drawn from older children, and, at the same time, the lower the qualifying threshold for possession of rights is set.

The second means of making the liberationist case is by appeal to the arbitrariness of any line that might be drawn between those who do and those who do not possess rights. In the present case the line is most likely to be drawn in terms of an age. Imagine that there is a right to Ø and that the age of x is stipulated as the

[13] Peter Jones, *Rights* (London, Macmillan, 1994), ch 20.

[14] Neil MacCormick, "Children's rights: A test-case for Theories of Rights" (1976) 62 *Archiv für Rechts und Sozialphilosophie* 305–17.

[15] Richard Farson, *Birthrights* (London, Collier Macmillan, 1974) and John Holt, *Escape from Childhood, The Needs and Rights of Children* (Harmondsworth, Penguin, 1975).

threshold beyond which any person acquires the right. Now the arbitrariness critique can be informed by two different but connected kinds of thought. Both derive from the fact that age alone is insufficient to warrant the denial or ascription of a right; rather it is the regular correlation between age and the acquisition of the qualifying capacities which does the justificatory work. One thought is that the closer a child gets to x the more unjust it is that she should be denied the right to Ø. The respects in which it is true that a very young child should not have the right to Ø become less and less applicable the more that someone approaches the age of x. The second thought is that it is likely that there are some individuals who are aged x plus six months who lack the qualifying capacity just as there are some individuals aged x minus six months who possess it. Is it not then arbitrary, and unfair, to allow the achievement of x alone to qualify someone for the right to Ø?

There are a number of possible replies to the charge of arbitrariness. The first is that the fixing of *all* dividing lines or points, whose role in enforcing a distinction of prescriptive or ascriptive force relies on a correlation between the point and some further capacity or feature, is open to the same charge. Merely consider, in the context of driving, the correlation between drunkenness and a certain blood alcohol level, or between dangerousness and a certain excess of speed. It needs to be shown that the arbitrariness at work in the denial of rights to those below a certain age is noticeably worse and thus more evidently unjust. Second, any dividing point or line can be allowed to have a merely presumptive weight so that a case can be made on behalf of any particular individual that the presumed correlation of age and incapacity does not apply. Third, sufficient evidence of failed correlation (of incapacity and age) below the line would make a case for lowering the line; similarly sufficient evidence of failed correlation (of capacity and age) above the line would make a case for raising the line. Fourth, the denial of a right to Ø to those who fall below the stipulated line need not amount to a total denial of the power to command the actions of others in respect of Ø. Most contemporary legalistic documents dedicated to the defence of children's interests accord children, proportionate to their maturity and ability to form views, a fundamental right to express their views on matters affecting them.[16] If Ø-ing is central to a child's welfare, then a right to have her views listened to on whether or not she should Ø is less than a right to Ø simpliciter. But it is still a power of sorts to determine whether or not she should Ø.

There is more to the case for children to have rights than simply a denial of the claim that it is mistaken or arbitrary to distinguish between adults and children in this context. The more in question is given by what is seen as the value and significance of having and exercising rights. Even if everything which is protected by the successful exercise of one's rights is guaranteed (by, for instance, the spontaneous beneficence of others) there is an additional value in having the rights which, arguably, lies in the imputed status of being that kind of thing

---

[16] See most notably, Article 12.1 of the United Nations Convention on the Rights of the Child; but also, the Children Act 1989 s 1(3)(a).

which can claim or demand these forms of treatment, and not merely expect them.[17] By contrast lacking the imputed capacity to claim, as of right, what is due one can be viewed as amounting to a disempowerment and demotion. Certainly child liberationists see the denial to children of adult rights as associated with the modern tendency to maintain an artificial separation between the worlds of adulthood and childhood, condemning children to a false and oppressive condition of infantile dependence and vulnerability.

In stark contrast to such a view philosophical opponents of children's rights believe that the according of rights to children represents a serious mistake about the nature of both childhood and rights. Granting fundamental liberties to a child before he possesses the capacities to be the guardian of his own life is cruel, since, in the words of John Locke, it is "to thrust him out amongst Brutes, and abandon him to a state as wretched, and as much beneath that of a Man, as theirs".[18] At the least rights are inappropriate to a state which is characteristically one of weakness, vulnerability and dependence on others. The proper treatment of children, who occupy this state, can be guaranteed by the enforcement of duties or obligations on adults. One need not think that these enforceable duties correlate with rights. Moreover it devalues the currency of rights to distribute them to inappropriate subjects. Rights are too important and possess too much of a prescriptive force to be possessed by other than those suitably qualified to hold and exercise them.[19]

V

Even if one does believe that children lack at least liberty rights, it is unlikely to be denied that adults do have duties towards children. At a minimum these should guarantee to children a basic level of care which ensures that each child progresses to adulthood. This will mean the provision of certain goods and the avoidance of certain harms. Adults are the "caretakers" of those who, on the standard view, cannot take care of themselves. But what should be the guiding principle of such care when it extends beyond the provision of a bare minimum? There are three possible views. They are distinct even if they may well yield the same judgement about what, in some particular case, a child is owed.

The first view is that one's duty is to protect and promote a child's present and future interests, the latter having obviously to do with the adult which the child will become. A child may have views as to what these interests are and the adult may take into account the expression of such views, but, in the last analysis, it is for the adults who are responsible for any particular child to judge, subject to certain evident constraints consistent with the guarantee of a basic level of care,

---

[17] Joel Feinberg, "The Nature and Value of Rights" (1970) 4 *Journal of Value Inquiry* 243–57.

[18] John Locke, *Two Treatises of Government* a critical edition with an introduction and *apparatus criticus* by Peter Laslett, rev ed (Cambridge, Cambridge University Press, 1963), II, vi, §63.

[19] Onora O'Neill, "Children's Rights and Children's Lives" 98 *Ethics* 445–63.

what serves that child's best interests. There is no determinate view of what the child's interests are since this will depend on contestable opinions as to what a human's best interests are and what the nature of a particular child is. The second view is that one's duty is to do that for the child which the child, if an adult, would wish done for her. This preserves a role for autonomy inasmuch as the child chooses for herself, but it is the hypothetical autonomous choices of the child as the adult she is not yet. However, such an approach yields no determinate account of what to do for the child since everything depends on one's view of what kind of adult this child will or might become. This is not something which can be specified independently of what one does now, for how one treats a child will make a difference to the kind of adult that child develops into. The third view is that the autonomy or freedom of a child should be limited—and that is what taking care of the child amounts to—only in the name of autonomy or freedom. Thus one's aim should be to maximise the capacities of the adult the child will become to exercise free and autonomous choice for herself. This is what Joel Feinberg describes as the child's "right to an open future".[20] The view is a plausible, and influential one, but it should be noted that, on the first view, a child may have interests whose promotion constrains its future freedom. Thus, for example, it may be judged important that every person acquire an identity and sense of belonging which could be managed by being educated in the values and way of life of a particular community, that of the child's guardians. Or a child may be brought up to realise what are perceived as her innate talents and abilities, but in such a way that we thereby deny the child the possibility of choosing alternative careers and lives.

The duty to care for a child implies that its guardians have a certain power or authority which must be exercised in the caretaking, in deciding what is the most appropriate way to rear the child. On one philosophical view that duty to care is primary, and the parental authority derives its warrant, and its scope, from that prior duty.[21] On an opposed view the duty derives from a prior parental power which, according to Thomas Hobbes at least, is total: children are in "absolute subjection" to parents who may "alienate them . . . may pawn them for hostages, kill them for rebellion, or sacrifice them for peace".[22] Under Roman law a father had *patria potestas*, the absolute power of life and death over his son, who was released from this state only by the father's death or manumission.

One familiar, and very influential, source for the view that parents do have a primary power over their own children—even if it is not as absolute and unconstrained as on the Hobbesian account—is the idea that parents own their children.

[20] Joel Feinberg, "The Child's Right to an Open Future" in William Aiken and Hugh LaFollette (eds), *Whose Child? Children's Rights, Parental Authority and State Power* (Totowa, NJ, Rowman and Littlefield, 1980), pp 80–98.

[21] Jeffrey Blustein, *Parents and Children: The Ethics of the Family* (Oxford, OUP, 1982).

[22] Thomas Hobbes, *The Elements of Law, Natural and Politic* (1650), edited with an Introduction by J C A Gaskin (Oxford, OUP, 1994), 23.8.

John Locke, even though he denied parental ownership and found Hobbes's view cruel and barbarous, is the author of the labour theory of property acquisition whereby an individual justly owns that which "he hath mixed his Labour with, and joined to it something that is his own".[23] Locke's own attempt to show why parents do not own what, in procreation, they produce is unconvincing,[24] and the idea of parental proprietorship continues to cast a long shadow over thinking about parental rights.[25] At the very least parents are inclined to think that the fact that their children are their own gives them special rights—to bring them up in the ways of life, beliefs and values that are their own. In this sense a parent's right to rear her child is viewed as an extension of her right to lead her life as she chooses. It is hard too to dispense with the thought that certain natural facts—namely, in this context, the procreative relationship itself—do provide a ground for some sort of presumptive claim by a parent for her child.[26]

It is interesting to note here a problematic yet intriguing asymmetry. Both Locke and Hobbes are a source for the now widely accepted idea that the authority of the state is rooted in the freely given consent of its citizens; both rejected the idea that such authority is natural. Yet if parents have authority, at least over their children, what is *its* source? It cannot derive from the freely given consent of the children insofar as children are subject to that authority precisely because they are incapable of making free choices for themselves. The idea that the consent in question is retrospective is hard to defend, not least because it is open to a parent to strive to secure that subsequent consent and because it seems odd to allow for a denial of the legitimate, and wholly beneficent, exercise of authority after the fact. However, if parental authority is natural then it is not open to someone simply to reject the idea of any authority as natural in support of the view that all authority must rest on consent.

The exercise of any right to rear one's own child, whatever its ultimate warrant, must clearly be constrained by a duty to care for the child, whether this is construed minimally as the provision of basic goods or maximally as the promotion of the child's best interests. Certainly failure to discharge the duty of parental care, minimally construed, should be sufficient warrant for the abrogation of the parental right to rear. Whether it is sufficient for the alienation of that right to another guardian is a separate issue. Relevant here is the state which has a role in enforcing the parental duty of care and which, arguably, has itself a separate legitimate interest in the welfare of its citizens' children. It has such an interest not only because it has a duty to safeguard the weakest within its jurisdiction but also because children represent the future, and thus the

---

[23] *Two Treatises of Government*, II, v, §27.

[24] Robert Nozick, *Anarchy, State, and Utopia* (Oxford, Basil Blackwell, 1974), pp 287–9.

[25] David Archard, "Do Parents Own Their Childen?" (1993) 1 *International Journal of Children's Rights* 293–301.

[26] David Archard, "What's Blood Got to do with It? The Significance of Natural Parenthood" (1995) 1:1 *Res Publica* 91–106.

continuity of the state. The state is described as *parens patriae* ("parent of the nation") responsible in the final analysis for the welfare of the community's young.

Some have defended a greater role. Plato, infamously, urged in *The Republic* that the state, or at least its guardian ruling class, should take collective control of both the selective breeding and controlled rearing of its children. Amy Gutman neatly summarises Plato's view as that of a "family state", by contrast with a "state of families" in which parents are given an exclusive right to the rearing of their children.[27] No-one now is likely to defend either extreme, yet the interesting questions concern the precise balance of rights and duties in respect of children which are possessed by the state and the family. For just as the state's duty to act as *parens patriae* constrains the right of parents to rear their children as they choose, so that parental right constrains the right of the state to act as *parens patriae*. Moreover many think that parents not only have a right (of autonomy) to rear their children as they think best but also a right (of privacy) to do so without interference and observation by the state.[28] This raises difficult issues as to how exactly a state may best protect children if it is prevented from monitoring their progress.

VI

The claim has been made that there should be a "philosophy of childhood" in the same way that there is a "philosophy of mathematics", though it is hard to see what justifies the thought that there can be, in this sense, a second-order investigation of the nature of childhood.[29] What is true is that philosophers do have a range of things to say, as philosophers, about children and childhood. Some of these derive from and are informed by more general concerns. Epistemologists, for instance, need to have an account of how knowledge is acquired. Philosophers in their familiar mode as conceptual analysts can offer accounts of what might be meant by a term such as "child abuse".[30] Children provide a subject area in which philosophical concepts and ideas of general application can be explored, such as rights, duty, and authority. Moral philosophers should be interested in what is permitted and what is forbidden in the treatment of children, and in what grounds the claim of a parent to bring up her own child. Social and political philosophers need to address the question of the appropriate balance between the roles of the state and the family in the care of

---

[27] Amy Gutman, *Democratic Education* (Princeton, NJ, Princeton University Press, 1987), ch 1.

[28] Joseph Goldstein, Anna Freud and Albert J Solnit, *Before the Best Interests of the Child* (New York, Free Press, 1979); see also M D A Freeman, "Freedom and the Welfare State: Child-Rearing, Parental Autonomy and State Intervention" (1983) *Journal of Social Welfare Law*, 70–91.

[29] David Carr, "Review of G.B. Matthews, *The Philosophy of Child*" (1997) 47 *Philosophical Quarterly* 125–7.

[30] David Archard, "Can child abuse be defined?" in Michael King (ed), *Moral Agendas for Children's Welfare* (London, Routledge, 1999), pp 74–89.

children. To the extent that these varied matters are considered by philosophers there is a philosophy of childhood. But that there is such a philosophy is itself dependent upon an understanding of what childhood is, what its essential nature is. This more fundamental philosophical question of childhood is one that philosophers have not, as the opening of this chapter emphasised, investigated to any great degree. Rather they have assumed and exploited a particular, maybe a socially and historically specific conception, of childhood. Perhaps then there is still need for a certain kind of philosophy of childhood.

4

Psychological and Psychiatric Perspectives

QUENTIN SPENDER AND ALEXANDRA JOHN

INTRODUCTION AND DEFINITIONS

THIS CHAPTER AIMS to consider some of the legal issues thrown into relief in childhood and adolescence. We try to give some sense of the psychological and psychiatric thinking behind expert reports. These include reports on children's access to parents, complex child-care matters, after-effects of trauma, and fitness to plead.

We look first at the fundamental developmental perspective, with some examples of this, including attachment theory. We then examine risk factors contributing to delinquency. After a discussion of post-traumatic stress disorder, we turn finally to the relevance of the Mental Health Act.

The issue of the beginning and end of childhood and adolescence may on the surface appear straightforward. Birth could be considered the onset of childhood and therefore confer certain human rights, but there are theoreticians who believe the foetus has rights that should be recognised and addressed. The transition between childhood and adolescence is marked physiologically by changes and the beginning of puberty is often taken as the start of this process. In girls this is defined as the first appearance of breast buds, and for boys as the initial enlargement of testes. There is tremendous variation in the age of these milestones, but girls in general start earlier than boys. These two physiological markers herald a sequence of events that lead to the ability to procreate. Associated with this sequence are a marked spurt in growth, and a number of psychological changes that are difficult to summarise.[1] The ending of adolescence is not clear, because the psychological changes and resultant behaviours persist into adulthood. The threshold of adulthood has become steadily more diffuse through the twentieth century because of the prolongation of education for many, resulting in postponement of work choices and the need for continued financial dependence.

---

[1] P Graham, J Turk, and F Verhulst, *Child Psychiatry: a Developmental Perspective* (Oxford, OUP, 1999).

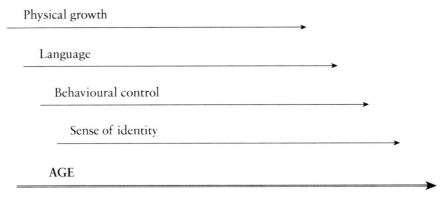

Fig.1. *Examples of developmental pathways*

The truth is that neither childhood nor adolescence has a clear endpoint. We find it more helpful to take a *developmental perspective*. By this, we mean that psychological processes—such as cognitive capacity; memory; language skills; information processing; self esteem and other emotional factors—have a time course, as illustrated in Figure 1. Physical, cognitive and emotional growth enable the child to develop representations of those around them, the means to express themselves, behavioural control, and a sense of identity. Different facets of development are clearly interrelated.

Large numbers of theorisers in psychology (including Freud, Erikson and Piaget, to name only three) have postulated a sequence of stages to psychological development. These have all been helpful in allowing our understanding to evolve, and provide a number of different ways to conceptualise developmental progress.[2] However, children are individual and come to fruition at differing rates: the ages at which psychological processes emerge and mature vary greatly. It is therefore beyond the scope of this chapter to give an outline of normal development.

An example from Erikson[3] can be used to illustrate these issues. He concluded that identity formation develops through a number of stages that logically follow one another, from diffuse uncertainty about who one is to the development of a solid, defined sense of identity. This could be seen as one of the basic tasks of adolescence. Recent research, in contrast,[4] supports a different developmental structure, with a two-dimensional concept of identity. According to this theoretical position, there are two alternative paths towards a definite identity. Some individuals foreclose on one particular choice as soon as they can. Others leave their options open for longer, allowing experimentation with a number of

---

[2] Alan Carr, *The Handbook of Child and Adolescent Clinical Psychology* (London, Routledge, 1999); Patricia H Miller. *Theories of Developmental Psychology* (New York, W H Freeman, 1993).

[3] Erik H Erikson, *Childhood and Society* (London, Vintage paperback, 1995).

[4] P Hill, "Recent advances in selected aspects of adolescent development" (1993) 34(1) *Journal of Child Psychology & Psychiatry* 69–99.

possible identities, before one of these is chosen. This could be applied to particular aspects of identity development, such as sexual identity, risk-taking or delinquent behaviour. Many currently non-offending young adults have committed a number of offences before stopping, while others have never offended. The eventual law-abiding outcome is the same.

Delayed or distorted development

The developmental perspective also helps in understanding developmental disability. Generalised learning disability affects an individual's ability to acquire an appreciation and understanding of right and wrong. Some individuals learn to understand the difference between these two positions in one area of their lives such as at school, but have difficulty transferring this concept when the context changes. This lack of understanding of the difference between right and wrong can result in criminal responsibility being attenuated. Social communication disorders such as autism or Asperger's disorder affect the individual's ability to understand the perspective of another person as well as having difficulty with the nuances of social communication. Individuals with this disorder are more concrete in their understanding and consequently may not appreciate the metaphors and analogies being used in everyday life. This may result in aggression in response to perceived social slights, which is socially unacceptable.

> *Case example: A fourteen-year-old boy with moderate learning difficulties and autism assaulted a fellow pupil at his special school. He had apparently been called "Dumbo" the previous day. He locked them both in a classroom, and hit his victim with a chair, seeming to find a degree of satisfaction in the blood that appeared, while not appearing to have any sense of the victim's experience. Staff eventually got in through the window and restrained him. Would he be deemed criminally responsible?*

The autism and learning difficulties could be held, in the absence of any mental illness, to have prevented the perpetrator from understanding the unacceptability and consequences of his actions. These combined difficulties have resulted in the individual not acquiring age appropriate understanding of how to resolve conflict and appreciate the impact of his behaviour on another.

ATTACHMENT THEORY

Another developmental theory that has achieved wide applicability is the attachment theory of John Bowlby (1907–90), child psychiatrist and psychoanalyst. He was the first to describe the importance of attachment in human development, and based his body of theory on studies of animal behaviour and children left alone in hospital, without visits from parents.

Attachment theory has since become the only part of psychoanalysis that has scientific support. The *main points* of Bowlby's theory of attachment[5] can be summarised as follows:

—human beings have a need for attachment to specific others throughout the life cycle;

—during the second half of the first year of life specific attachment behaviours develop, namely clinging to and following of the attachment figure;

—unwilling separation from an attachment figure leads to emotional distress after the age of six months;

—this distress in young children is shown in a predictable sequence of behaviours—protest, despair and detachment;

—loss of an attachment figure in adults leads to a grief reaction, with shock and anger followed by numbness and finally acceptance and reorganisation.

Two particular research techniques developing out of Bowlby's theories are worthy of mention. These are the strange situation and the adult attachment interview. Both of these techniques are useful in gaining insights into the attachment experiences of children and the recollection of these issues in adulthood. It is recognised that early attachment experiences have a profound impact on emotional development and the ability to form and sustain personal relationships.

The *strange situation* is a rigorous research technique, lasting twenty minutes, during which the child has two brief (three minute) separations from the caregiver, being left alone or with a stranger. An evaluation is made of the child's behaviour towards the caregiver upon reunion. (For the sake of simplicity, the child is referred to as "he", and the caregiver as the mother). About sixty-five per cent of children are categorised as having a *secure attachment*. This is characterised by the mother providing a secure base for exploration. After a brief separation, the child is pleased to see the mother. He does not show anger towards her. If he has been distressed, he will seek contact with her and be readily comforted, and will soon return to play.

The remainder of children have some form of *insecure attachment*, which may be due to maternal insensitivity to infant cues: this can result in a child lacking confidence in his mother's ability to be responsive to his needs. Some children (*anxious resistant*) may be clingy and become very upset during separation, with anger at the mother's return, and reluctance to be comforted. Others (*anxious avoidant*) explore readily and are relatively friendly towards the stranger, then ignore the mother's return, making little or no eye contact. Although such children do not look at all distressed, physiological tests

---

[5] A summary of the main points of Bowlby's theory can be found in his book: *A Secure Base* (London, Routledge, 1988), or in the study by Dr Jeremy Holmes: *John Bowlby and Attachment Theory* (London, Routledge, 1993). More detail can be found in Bowlby's three-volume treatise: *Attachment, Separation and Loss* (London, Pimlico paperback, 1997).

indicate that they are highly anxious, especially after mother's return. A further group of children (*disorganised*) show additional behaviours after separation in which there is a mixture of approach to the mother and avoidance of her. This is due to the internal conflict, when attempting to come to terms with the person who is both their source of safety and also a source of anxiety. This group of children with disorganised attachment includes some of the most disturbed children to come before the courts, either as the subject of care proceedings, or in the youth justice system. Many of these children have been neglected or abused, physically, emotionally or sexually, by a major attachment figure.

Children have multiple attachments, to parents, siblings, grandparents, childminders and others. It is important to emphasis that attachment is *relationship specific*. A child may therefore be secure with one parent but insecure with the other. Children are seen as having *internal working models* deriving from their major attachment relationships in the past. The overall influence on social development is generally dominated by the relationship with the primary caregiver, usually the mother.

What does security or insecurity at one year predict? Children who are secure at one year are better at making friends and better liked by teachers at the age of five years. They make fewer demands for a teacher's attention and are more likely than insecure children to get a helpful response. In other words, they seem to be good at asking for what they want and having their needs met. Their language development is slightly better than that of insecure children. Furthermore, children who are insecure at one year are less popular at school entry than those who were securely attached at one year. There is an increased risk that they will be either the victim or the perpetrator of bullying (or both). The insecurely attached children are also either unacceptably aggressive or timid. Insecure five-year-olds are less empathic than secure ones, and this difficulty may underlie their relatively poor social relationships.

Damaged attachment relationships can in principle be repaired. For instance, a child who has suffered severe neglect in the first two years of life, and is therefore adopted, is likely to have a disturbed internal working model of attachment. If the child then experiences consistent, good enough care-giving for a prolonged period, the internal model will modify, so that it becomes easier to form and maintain satisfactory relationships. This implies that the nature of the adoptive or long-term foster placement, and the age at which these begin, are crucial—and this is found in practice.

The second major research instrument to emerge from attachment theory is the *adult attachment interview*. This lengthy interview for adults can be analysed into a number of constructs that correspond to those established in the one-year-old strange situation. These are based on how the adult has processed childhood experiences. An intriguing finding is that the categories found in adult caregivers correspond closely to those found in their one-year-old children! Those parents with insecure attachment may have more difficulty showing consistent sensitivity to their children, and those with disorganised attachments seem to have particular difficulty applying parenting techniques.[6]

Attachment disorder (ICD-10)[7] is more severe than insecure attachment. It is defined as a failure to make specific attachments, associated *either* with a complete lack of interest in initiating or responding to other children and adults, *or* indiscriminate but superficial attachment to any adults encountered. (The definition excludes Autism and Asperger's syndrome, because lack of attachment is a part of these disorders, sometimes associated with an attachment to an inanimate object—such as Thomas the Tank Engine).

Attachment disorder may be due to institutional upbringing (for example a children's home), living in a succession of foster homes, or being abused. Alternatively, it can result from a parent's lack of emotional availability either due to mental health problems such as depression or through death or divorce. In particular, *neglect* may cause indiscriminate attachment, and *physical abuse* may cause "frozen watchfulness", in which the child is hypervigilant and watchful. In addition, children with attachment disorder may show a constellation of features indistinguishable from attention-deficit/hyperactivity disorder. Many children coming before the courts in child care cases have some degree of attachment disorder.

The best *treatment* for an attachment disorder is to rebuild attachments, which may be a lengthy process, and is not always successful. Rehabilitation with the child's own family must always be considered first, but is not always possible. Often the best option is a long-term foster placement with skilled, experienced parents. If appropriate, this can be supplemented by parental contact, provided this is not too disruptive to the foster placement. Adoption is often regarded as a panacea, and can be very successful for younger children, but is at more risk of breakdown with increasing age of placement. This is frequently due to the negative experiences the children have endured and their anger and resentment at a succession of failed placements, as well as the disturbance of internal attachment models, which make it too difficult to form a secure attachment to the adoptive carer.

If traumatic separations or abuse have taken place, then the child should be given an opportunity to talk about these experiences, or express his feelings in play, either with caregivers or with a therapist. This is generally of benefit only if the child's placement is settled, with his own family or with another family.

Prevention is more effective, but easier to write about than to achieve. During the first five years of life, all children benefit from as stable a family life as possible, and they should learn to cope with separation experiences from their parents. Ideally, these should be handled in such a way as to make it a positive experience, helping in the development of independence.

---

[6] C P Routh, J W Hill, H Steele, C E Elliott and M E Dewey, " Maternal attachment status, psychosocial stressors and problem behaviour: follow-up after parent training courses for conduct disorder" (1995) 36(7) *Journal of Child Psychology & Psychiatry* 1179–98.

[7] World Health Organization *The ICD-10 Classification of Mental and Behavioural Disorders: Diagnostic Criteria for Research* (Geneva, World Health Organization, 1993).

Assessment of parenting by an independent expert may be necessary to guide the courts in determining who is the most appropriate caregiver for the child, in order to maximise the child's potential and prevent further psychological difficulties. A full account of this is beyond the scope of this chapter, but it is important to emphasise that perfect parenting is not expected: *good enough* parenting is sufficient. This is a phrase attributed to Donald Winnicott (1896–1971), paediatrician and psychoanalyst. He specified and promoted the essential features of the nurturing environment that children need.[8] A framework for the assessment of parenting is described in a very useful book edited by two child psychiatrists.[9]

THE DEVELOPMENT OF COGNITIVE SKILLS

When evaluating children's evidence, it is important to have an appreciation of the development of cognitive abilities. The cognitive skills that are particularly important are processing of sensory input, language skills and memory. As a child matures, developmental progress usually occurs in all of these areas at the same rate. However, if a child has been traumatised, it is possible that the capacity to process experiences via one of these modalities will have become dissociated from the others as a means to facilitate coping. For instance, a sexually abused child may deny memories of abusive events, yet act them out with dolls, without apparently making a link.

An individual's ability to remember information is based upon six factors:

—the event itself (an event can be memorable through standing out from other events, or through frequent repetition);
—previous experiences (which can provide a template for understanding);
—contextual cues (for instance the time of an event can be remembered as being at bedtime or after a birthday);
—emotional impact;
—motivation (are the consequences of remembering positive or negative?);
—techniques to recall information (mnemonics).

In younger children, the amount of freely recalled material is significantly less than with older children, but importantly is equally as accurate. In an attempt to improve the quantity of material, children can be provided with prompts, such as open cues about possible settings, people, actions and consequences. This allows an even wider range of responses than open questions, and is very different from leading questions that can be claimed to suggest particular answers. Younger children in general remember the central events but not the

---

[8] See for instance Donald Winnicott's, *The Child, the Family and the Outside World* (Harmondsworth, Penguin Books, 1991).

[9] Peter Reder and Clare Lucey *Assessment of Parenting: Psychiatric and Psychological Contributions* (London, Routledge, 1995).

peripheral features such as, for instance in road traffic accidents, time, speed and distance. Recall can be facilitated in younger children by the use of *anchor points*, such as worst moments, the actions of adults, the sites of injuries, and hearing victims cry.[10]

When eliciting information from children following such events, the interviewer needs to be mindful of the way in which children store their memories. They will utilise verbal, visual, auditory, olfactory and behavioural information-processing capacities. The interviewer therefore has to use various means of communication, including not only words, but also drawing, play and sounds to facilitate access to all the appropriate information.

THE DEVELOPMENT OF LAW-BREAKING BEHAVIOUR

Another application of the developmental perspective is in relation to delinquency. There are two principal pathways to adolescent law-breaking.[11] A large group experiments with legal limits during adolescence only, in an exploratory way that is compatible with normal adolescence. These are known as the *adolescence-limited* group. Their offending decreases and stops after about the age of eighteen. The other, smaller, group develops antisocial behaviour in childhood, which persists in adolescence as delinquency, and continues afterwards. These are described as having *life-course persistent* antisocial behaviour. The developmental trajectory of the second group is shown in Figure 2.

The Cambridge study in delinquent development found that primary school teacher ratings at age eight years were a powerful predictor of delinquency: 45 per cent of boys rated troublesome at primary school were later convicted as juveniles (compared with 14 per cent of those not so rated).[12] Viewing it the other way, 90 per cent of recidivist delinquents had been rated as troublesome at age eight. This shows the stability of antisocial behaviour: aggressive behaviour seems to be the most stable. We will now examine the various factors in detail.

The social and cultural environment

Antisocial behaviour is more likely to develop in situations of relative poverty, and when parents are unemployed. Large family size, although often associated

---

[10] J R Spencer and R Flin, *The Evidence of Children: the Law and the Psychology* (London, Blackstone Press, 1990).

[11] T E Moffitt, "Adolescence-limited and life-course-persistent antisocial behaviour: a developmental taxonomy" (1993) 100(4) *Psychological Review* 674–701.

[12] David P Farrington, "The development of offending and antisocial behaviour from childhood: key findings from the Cambridge study in delinquent development" (1995) 36(6) *Journal of Child Psychology & Psychiatry* 929–64.

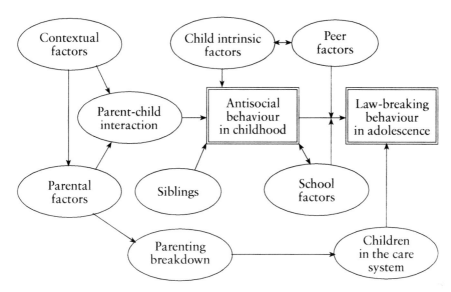

Fig.2. *The developmental pathway through childhood antisocial behaviour to delinquency*

with these two factors, is an independent predictor. A high rate of criminality in the neighbourhood encourages children to think of law-breaking behaviour as acceptable.

Parental factors

With the above contextual risk factors, parents are more likely to have their own problems. These can include:

—**Parents' own childhood.** Parents are influenced by their own experience of being a child, and are likely to parent in the way that they were parented. If they were abused as children, this may be re-enacted with their own children.
—**Current adult relationships.** Parents need support, from a partner, friends or neighbours. Not all receive this. Many mothers do not have the support of the father of their children, even if he is cohabiting. Others live alone, or with partners whose input is too short term to allow a close relationship with the children. Some parents become very socially isolated, preoccupied with chores and childcare. They may feel that people they meet in the street or in supermarkets criticise their parenting. Feelings of guilt are mixed with the need to blame the child for being so difficult. All of these factors make it difficult to manage the emotional demands of children, particularly if one or more of them have challenging behaviour.

—**Parental personality.** Even minor degrees of personality disturbance may make it difficult to sustain a long-term relationship with a partner, and may make any relationship with a child very inconsistent—in terms of both behavioural management and emotional interchange.

—**Psychiatric disorder.** *Postnatal depression* can cause a mother to be emotionally unavailable to her child during the first year of life. This encourages the child to be demanding, for instance to cry a lot to gain love or nourishment, and may contribute to difficult temperament. It is often a source of negative feelings about a child when he is older. For instance, if postnatal depression has occurred after only one pregnancy, this will be the child who is regarded in the most negative light (the naughtiest, or the most uncaring, or the family scapegoat). Subsequent *depression* may also adversely affect the parent-child relationship, leading to irritability, frequent criticisms of the child, and a tendency to respond only to negative behaviour, rather than reward positive behaviour. *Schizophrenia* may result in a parent being absent in hospital or chaotic at home. If this is the mother, then a lot depends on who else in the family is available to care for the children.

—**Drug and alcohol use.** *Drug use* may or may not interfere with parenting, depending on a number of factors including the type of drug and the social context. *Alcohol* use is more likely to lead to disinhibited behaviour, which can be very frightening for children.

—**Domestic violence.** A child is emotionally abused by witnessing violence, even if he is never the object of violence himself. It predisposes a child to express feelings in a similar way, particularly a boy who identifies with a violent father. A mother who is left looking after the son of a violent partner is prone to see in the child what she feared in the father, leading to a negative mind-set about her son.

Parent-child interactions

Work at the Oregon Social Learning Center has shown that families in which children develop antisocial behaviour are characterised by *coercive interactions*.[13] Parents attempt to make their children do what they think children should by criticising, shouting at or threatening them. If the parent gives in to the child's resistance or whines, then this behaviour is encouraged. Further work has shown that the five facets of parental behaviour necessary to engender compliant and pro-social child behaviour are: positive reinforcement, parental involvement, parental monitoring, discipline, and problem solving.[14]

---

[13] G R Patterson, *Coercive family process* (Oregon, Castalia, 1982).
[14] G R Patterson, J B Reid and T J Dishion, *Antisocial Boys* (Oregon, Castalia, 1992).

Siblings

Siblings are an important influence on development. For instance, the Cambridge study in delinquent development found that having a delinquent older sibling, or a sibling with behaviour problems, were risk factors for the development of delinquency. Siblings may also have a protective effect, for instance if older sisters take over a parenting rôle for an unavailable mother. The development of a child's siblings is subject to the same influences as the child's own development, so that the causal factors are intertwined.

Intrinsic factors in the child

It is all too easy to blame parents for everything a child does. In fact, there are aspects of the child's development that are outside parental control. Many aspects of a child's development are determined by genetic factors. So far, researchers have agreed that temperament, dyslexia, autistic disorders, attention-deficit / hyperactivity disorder, depression and aggressive behaviour have significant genetic as well as environmental causes.[15]

Temperamental differences are clearly discernible from birth, and have a genetic component. For instance, a baby who will not feed, constantly cries, and will not stay asleep is clearly *difficult*, and may present other sorts of temperamental difficulty when older. These characteristics appear to be innate, although parental factors may contribute, such as postnatal depression. A clash of personality between parent and child may also create early problems.

Various *specific learning difficulties* predispose to antisocial behaviour, and are often undetected within the educational system. Some run in families, and may therefore be exacerbated by a combination of genetic and environmental risk factors. For instance, a child with a specific reading difficulty may have parents with literacy difficulties, who may therefore be reluctant or unable to help with reading homework. Combinations of delay in reading, spelling and writing, not accounted for by overall intelligence, are commonly referred to as *dyslexia*. This is relatively common, and state education resources are insufficient to provide remedial teaching for any but the most severely affected children. The deficit has increasingly pervasive effects as the child progresses through the school system, as much of the curriculum becomes dependent on reading and writing. Low self-esteem and disaffection with school and truancy are common consequences, and depression and suicidal attempts can occur. Dyslexia is a common basis for litigation, but negligence is difficult to prove. Parental appeals against lack of statementing[16] provision are more likely to benefit the child.

[15] Peter Mcguffin and Neilson Martin, "Behaviour and genes" (1999) 319 *British Medical Journal* 37–40.

[16] We use "statement" as a shorthand for a full assessment of educational needs under the Education Act 1996.

An association between dyslexia and antisocial behaviour is well established, but the nature of the causal link is still subject to debate. It has been suggested that frustration with reading, writing or spelling leads to behaviour problems, that poor classroom behaviour leads to poor progress with literacy skills, and that both are due to common genes and environmental factors. It is possible that all three explanations could apply, in varying proportions, to different children.

Case example: A fourteen-year-old boy was referred by his family solicitor for an expert opinion. On entry to secondary school, he had immediately been found to have severe delays in reading and spelling ability. These proved a sufficiently significant handicap to justify a statement of educational needs. He received extra help in withdrawal classes, although he disliked being sin-gled out from the rest of the class. He was allowed to use a word processor, and given extra time in exams. His parents attempted to sue the education authority for the delay in detection and provision of extra help. Although he had been seen by an educational psychologist at seven years, and briefly reviewed at nine, his difficulties in class were attributed to his father's death when he was five. His headmaster ignored a letter of complaint from the boy's grandmother. The expert believed that his bad tempers at home and low self-esteem were directly attributable to his dyslexia. The opinion was that the education authority could be excused for not detecting dyslexia at age seven, but should have monitored the situation more carefully, and intervened at nine. Nevertheless, counsel advised that fault could not be proved, partly because there could be no certainty that earlier intervention would have pre-vented his problems.

Language disorder is common in pre-school children, but persists beyond the age of six years only in the most severe cases. Bad behaviour is commonly thought to be an expression of the frustration engendered by not being able to express oneself or understand what others are saying. More complex or more subtle language disorders can be associated with *autistic spectrum disorder* (which includes *Asperger's syndrome*) in which difficulties in social relating are combined with a need for sameness, often expressed in obsessions or rituals. Such disorders can lead to tremendous difficulties fitting into groups, such as a large class. Behavioural difficulties can result, although they are usually man-ageable by adapting the educational and home environments to the child. Moral sense may be impaired, as in the case example above (page 59).

Although *generalised learning difficulties* can be associated with behavioural difficulties, sometimes severe, these are often well managed in special schools. Perhaps because they occur more often in the mainstream school population, spe-cific learning difficulties seem to be associated with more behavioural disruption in the classroom. It seems that a significant *discrepancy* between abilities in one area and in another is for many children a source of distress, which for some leads to inappropriate behaviour. It is partly because professional attention is focused on the behaviour that testing for specific learning difficulties is so often omitted.

Dyspraxia is a fashionable term now that specific assessments of gross and fine motor skills (usually by a paediatric occupational therapist) are detecting it more often. It is loosely equivalent to clumsiness. Poor gross motor skills can give rise to teasing, because of the child dropping things in the classroom, or not playing adequately in team games. Poor fine motor skills can cause difficulties with writing or drawing, which can impair performance in a range of subjects. Both can significantly lower self-esteem. Dyspraxia is commonly associated with a range of other difficulties, such as for example specific learning difficulties or attention-deficit / hyperactivity disorder.

Attention-deficit/hyperactivity disorder is a combination of difficulty concentrating, motor restlessness, and impulsivity. This constellation of symptoms was found, in the Cambridge study in delinquent development, to be predictive of delinquency independently of being troublesome or aggressive.[17] Other longitudinal studies have shown it to predate the onset of behaviour problems, so that it is clearly one of the risk factors for the development of antisocial behaviour, rather than the other way round. Attention-deficit/hyperactivity disorder can be treated successfully with medication. Untreated, it can cause major difficulties for the child in academic progress, peer relationships and family relationships. All these have been shown to improve with medication. It is often associated with other problems, such as specific learning difficulties, autistic spectrum disorder, or dyspraxia. Children with attention-deficit/hyperactivity disorder, dyspraxia and other mild specific learning difficulties are sometimes grouped together with the label of "Disorders of Attention, Motor Control and Perception" (DAMP—a term which replaces the old-fashioned "Minimal Brain Dysfunction").[18] These children may have a history of minor difficulties around the time of birth.

Cognitive style contributes to the development of delinquency. One of the characteristics of antisocial children is a tendency to interpret social advances from peers as having hostile intent. This results in the potential for conflict and aggression, which is particularly likely to occur if the child is impulsive. This mis-reading of social cues can be associated with other difficulties in social interaction, which are sometimes of the sort seen in autistic spectrum disorder, even though the full diagnosis would not be appropriate.

School and peer factors

Any of these childhood intrinsic factors may combine with antisocial behaviour to lead to *failure to progress academically*. This in turn leads to low self-esteem, lack of hope for the future, disaffection with education, and the search for some alternative way to establish a sense of self. The capacity of a school to help an

[17] David P Farrington, *supra* n 12, at pp 929–64.
[18] B Kadesjo and C Gillberg, "Attention deficits and clumsiness in Swedish 7-year-old children" (1998) 40(12) *Developmental Medicine & Child Neurology* 796–804.

individual pupil with social and academic needs determines to a consider-able extent whether the child remains integrated or becomes alienated. Young people who find they have no place within the school culture are liable to drift into alternative social networks, often associated with truancy, law-breaking or drug use.

The school's intolerance of the young person's behaviour may lead to the young person being *excluded*. This can exacerbate a situation that is already dif-ficult for the child. It is common for there to follow a long gap in the young per-son's education, during which his self-esteem plummets, and he is likely to drift towards other excluded pupils, or those who have recently left school to be unemployed and have time on their hands.

CHILDREN IN THE CARE SYSTEM

Children who are abused or neglected may need to be removed from their homes. Unless it is clear that parents cannot change, there is usually a trial of rehabilitation. If this is successful, then the child or children can remain with their parents. Otherwise, they may have to stay with some other relatives. Because siblings and grandparents may have shared in the family's abusive upbringing, they may not be suitable carers. In this case, children may have to enter the care system, usually on a care order (Children Act, 1989), but some-times with no order at all (accommodated). This implies that children are looked after either in adoptive homes, foster homes or in children's homes. These *looked after children* are at higher risk than other children for a number of difficulties, including delinquency.

The trend in recent decades has been to reduce the number of children's home placements. One result of this is that the most difficult children are looked after by a group of underpaid, unsupported and under-trained residential care work-ers, for whom the task is not always possible. Nevertheless, the trend away from residential placements is in line with current thinking about the importance of attachment, and the need to ensure that children have good long-term family-based care. According to this way of thinking, children should be adopted whenever possible. This does not always work in practice: the longer a child is damaged by an unsatisfactory home environment, the more difficult he is likely to find it to settle in adoptive or foster care. This leaves a group of children that includes those whose adoption has broken down, those who are unadoptable, those in long term foster care, and those in children's homes (state and private). Many of these have experienced repeated placement breakdowns, making it even more difficult for them to form attachments than when they left their fam-ily of origin. The situation is exacerbated by a shortage of foster carers and adoptive carers. Some are asked to cope with a task that may be as impossible as for residential care workers, and therefore become disillusioned with the rôle, thus further decreasing the pool of family-based carers.

This group of damaged and vulnerable children is known to be at risk of educational failure, delinquency, and criminality in adulthood. They form a significant proportion of those before the courts for criminal offences, and may at times require secure accommodation.[19] Greater investment is required in meeting these children's needs before they enter the group of life-course persistent offenders.

> *Case example*: *James is thirteen, and was living in a children's home until the staff ceased to be able to cope with his violent behaviour, solvent abuse, and frequent criminal activity. In the past, his father sexually abused his sister and was forced to leave home. He himself was neglected and physically abused. Neither his mother nor his grandparents could manage him. He has had a succession of placements. Only one has lasted longer than a year, in a children's home with a very high staff / child ratio, and that had to close down because of being unregistered. He is currently in secure accommodation, which has involved the courts. How can he best be looked after, and what is his prognosis?*
>
> Comment: James may have a psychiatric diagnosis of conduct disorder, but this is unhelpful in planning his management. His history suggests he is capable of making attachments to adults, and that his behaviour can subside when he does. He is easily influenced by other boys who get into trouble, and gravitates towards them, which makes a placement with other children counterproductive, and also makes schooling very problematic.
>
> *One year later*: *James was placed by his local social services in a distant private children's care organisation which houses individual children with at least one professional carer. During the six months he has been there, he has established good relationships with the staff, who have learnt how to manage his violent behaviour. He has reduced his solvent abuse, almost completely stopped being in trouble with the police, and has engaged in a variety of activities. He has been having home tuition, and as yet has only attended school for two mornings per week, in spite of having a statement of educational needs. James has stated very strongly that he wishes to stay in his current placement.*
>
> Comment: James has done remarkably well, considering his care history. Many similar children get increasingly involved with the youth justice system, until eventually they are given a custodial sentence. Despite the very significant improvements James has made, he has not been able to keep up with his education. Unless he is able to get at least some qualifications, he may be very disadvantaged when he leaves the care system at eighteen, and he may be disinclined or unable to study further at college. This may lead to his being unemployable, to his joining a deviant peer group, and then becoming involved in drug use and criminal activity again.

---

[19] Using s. 25 of the Children and Young Persons Act 1969.

Two years later: James is now attending a special school full-time, and making academic progress. He relates well to adult staff in his care home, and at his school, but finds it very difficult to relate to young people of his own age (now 15). He has now been put on a care order because of repeated attempts by his relatives to remove him from his placement to unsatisfactory alternatives, and failing to keep arranged contact visits. He has been involved in minor thefts, and is seeing a probation officer weekly, on a supervision order. Comment: Fifteen is relatively late for social services to assume parental responsibility, and there will need to be careful planning to help James with leaving school, and the transition at eighteen to leaving care.

The aftermath of events of high emotional impact frequently gives rise to litigation. Like adults, children can react adversely to catastrophes such as a car crash or witnessing extreme violence. Symptoms may include nightmares or flashbacks, avoidance and increased arousal. Children may have similar symptoms after being the objects of abuse, for example sexual abuse or bullying. A useful definition of post-traumatic stress disorder in childhood,[20] which allows for the different ways in which symptoms may present at different ages, is as follows:

(a) *Exposure* to a traumatic event.
(b) *Re-experiencing*, in play, which may be uni-themed, nightmares, flashbacks, memories or response to reminders.
(c) *Non-specific effects*, such as social withdrawal or regression (in language skills, toilet training or a return of earlier behaviours).
(d) *Increased arousal*, such as night terrors, decreased concentration, hypervigilance or an exaggerated startle response.
(e) *New fears*, for instance of the dark, of separation or of toilets, or new aggression.
(f) Symptoms must last for *at least a month*.

Children should have one example of behaviours in each category (b) to (e). For older children, the adult definition can be used, but this definition is probably satisfactory up to the age of sixteen years. When children with this disorder are interviewed, they may not articulate their traumatic experiences coherently, due to the way they have processed their original experience, and may therefore come across as unreliable witnesses.

Processing of the memories seems to be necessary for the symptoms to subside. For some children, this can occur with family or friends: this may not be possible if family members are also suffering from the after-effects of the

[20] M S Scheeringa, C H Zeanah, M J Drell and J A Larrieu, "Two approaches to the diagnosis of post-traumatic stress disorder in infancy and early childhood" 34 (2) *Journal of the American Academy of Child and Adolescent Psychiatry* 191–200.

trauma, or if the events are too terrible or socially unacceptable to recount. Psychological treatments have been shown to reduce symptoms, particularly behavioural therapy and eye-movement desensitisation and reprocessing.[21] Children should have the opportunity to make sense of the memories, preferably with family members, and preferably as soon as possible after the trauma. Professional involvement may be necessary when family members are unable to do this, but may also prejudice any court proceedings.

Compensation is often sought for the effects of an accident or other trauma on the home and school life of a child. Clinical practice suggests that the prolongation of symptoms until compensation is obtained (*compensation neurosis*) does not occur in quite the same form in children as in adults. A parent may be eager for the child to be badly enough affected to gain financial recompense, and may consciously or unconsciously find ways to maintain the symptoms, but the child herself seems usually unaffected by this motivation (and may indeed be far less affected by the trauma than the parent claims). An alternative to lengthy litigation to obtain damages is application to the Criminal Injuries Compensation Board. This is particularly useful in cases of sexual abuse where a successful prosecution has not occurred.

IS THE MENTAL HEALTH ACT RELEVANT TO CHILD PSYCHIATRY AND PSYCHOLOGY?

There is no minimum age for application of the Mental Health Act, 1983. In practice, it is seldom used in young people under sixteen. This is because parents' wishes are usually regarded as over-riding the young person's if she is mentally ill. For instance, a girl with anorexia nervosa who requires hospital treatment can be taken to hospital by her parents and admitted according to their wishes. According to the Children Act 1989, she may have a right to withhold her consent to this, but this may not apply if she is deemed too ill to exercise sound judgment. Thus an admission against the young person's wishes can be sustained without the application of any holding orders.

Difficulties with this approach can occur in two circumstances. First, the young person may not submit to her parents' wishes. Secondly, the parents may not agree to the recommended treatment.

If the young person resists admission, or runs away frequently, then the Mental Health Act can be applied with the agreement of the next of kin, to enforce admission to a psychiatric hospital. In the case of a clinic for eating disorders that is not a psychiatric hospital, the Mental Health Act cannot be used, and the court may be asked to give specific directions.

---

[21] Michelle L Van Etten and Steven Taylor, "Comparative efficacy of treatments for post-traumatic stress disorder: a meta-analysis" 5 *Clinical Psychology and Psychotherapy* 126–44.

If the parents oppose the use of the Mental Health Act, then they can be displaced as next of kin (probably in favour of social services) by a specific court order. Alternatively, care proceedings can be used to give parental responsibility to social services. This would be appropriate if the parental refusal were seen as part of a general pattern of failing to meet the child's needs.

> *Case example: A fourteen-year-old girl with anorexia nervosa was failing to respond to treatment on a paediatric ward. Her mother (a single parent) was undermining the treatment, for instance by supplying the girl with very low fat yoghurts, and saying that the problem was all because she had been bullied at school. The girl was gaining no weight on the ward, and lost weight every time she went home. Admission to a specialist unit was indicated. The mother refused to comply with this recommendation. Social services were involved, and their assessment was that the girl's life would be in danger if she did not receive more appropriate treatment. A case conference agreed that the girl's name should be on the child protection register. The mother was told that care proceedings would be instituted if she did not agree to the transfer to a specialist unit. She backed down, and the girl received the specialist treatment, which helped her to reach a normal weight.*

As we go to press, new legislation is expected. Current guidance is that in cases of doubt, for instance when a Gillick-competent young person refuses treatment but a parent consents, the courts should be asked to decide.

CONCLUSIONS

We have highlighted some of the conceptual issues behind expert psychological or psychiatric reports. These may use one or more of the theoretical perspectives described above, which are not necessarily stated explicitly. The nature of the evidence collected during the expert's assessment should indicate some of the underlying models. For instance, an assessment of fitness to plead is likely to rely heavily on psychiatric diagnosis and an appraisal of cognitive ability. In contrast, an assessment of parenting is likely to use the ideas of attachment theory and parents' ability to understand their child's developmental needs. Appraisal of the damage resulting from trauma needs to evaluate the quality of the evidence, as well as the extent of emotional symptoms. Assessments of young offenders need to be viewed in the context of the longitudinal development of delinquency.

PART II
The Child in Law

5

Youth and Justice

JULIA FIONDA

INTRODUCTION

THE CHILDREN ACT 1908 effectively gave birth to the modern youth justice system since this was the legislation which established the juvenile court. Prior to that there was a gestation period of around sixty years during which there was a distinct move towards a child-centred and welfare-based treatment of young offenders within the adult criminal justice system. The creation of the juvenile court symbolised the recognition of the incapacity and sensitivity of child defendants, since its *raison d'être* was to take them out of the adult courts and to create a discrete system of punishment.

In just less than a century since then, the youth[1] justice system has neared completion of a lifecycle and the child-centred approach to the punishment of youth crime is much less clear cut. In the latter part of the twentieth century and the beginning of the twenty-first, children who commit crimes have been increasingly viewed, and therefore treated, as though they are fully competent, aware of the significance and repercussions of their actions and mature enough to accept responsibility for them in the form of a proportionate punishment. The notion of children as objects of concern, as lacking competence to think their actions through and as capable of outgrowing their troublesome and immature behaviour has, to some extent, been sidelined in the quest for a politically expedient and therefore highly retributive response to youth crime. Childhood is often perceived politically as synonymous with leniency and care, the state acting as *parens patriae* or the stern but caring parent. Political parties compete to express greater intolerance and machismo in their policy on crime and thus perceive their role in relation to young offenders as less parental and more combative.

However, there is a contradiction within the criminal justice system and two dichotomous notions of childhood have emerged. Children who are victims of crime are regarded much more as an object of concern lacking in moral

---

[1] Even the change of terminology is significant. The Youth Justice system and references to and youth offenders marked a new trend started by the re-naming of the Juvenile Court as Youth Court in the Criminal Justice Act 1991 (s 70). This reflects a perception of the "clientele" of the court as youths rather than children or juveniles.

consciousness, especially where the relevant authorities are trying to elicit a statement or other evidence from them.[2] This dichotomous view of childhood is also reflected in media reporting of crime involving children.[3] Paradoxically, the children perceived in such different ways are often the same people. A much publicised example was Aliyah Ismail, a thirteen-year-old who died of methadone poisoning, having drifted into a life of drug and alcohol abuse and prostitution. She had also, though, complained of abuse and exploitation by others and an enquiry into her death suggested that she had been sorely failed by the two hundred and thirty social services professionals who had worked with her and her family.[4] Recent research has further shown that most children who offend are also likely to have been victimised, possibly more frequently than they have victimised others.[5]

This chapter will briefly discuss this lifecycle of the youth justice system and contemporary constructions of childhood implicit within it. It will also explore how both policy and practice in recent years have contributed to a more confused, and perhaps weaker, construction of childhood for young offenders and the consequent "adulteration" of parts of the system.

THE LIFECYCLE OF THE YOUTH JUSTICE SYSTEM: FROM BIRTH TO OLD AGE

Pre natal developments

In the early part of the nineteenth century the criminal justice system made little, if any, distinction between children and adults. There was no separate punishment system for children. They were tried through the same procedures and were subject to the same sanctions as adults, including imprisonment and corporal punishments.[6] Punishments were aimed at preventing crime through deterrence rather than reform of the offender. The science of criminology had only recently been founded and the criminal justice system functioned under the influence of classicist free-will theories.[7] Theorists of the classical school had argued that crime was the result of a rational choice on the part of the offender who had weighed up the benefits or otherwise of both crime and obedience to the law and had concluded that crime was more advantageous. Therefore the most appropriate form of crime prevention was deterrence which could

---

[2] This is incisively discussed by Allan Levy in ch 6 in this volume.

[3] See A Young, *Imagining Crime: Textual Outlaws and Criminal Conversations* (London, Sage, 1996), ch 11.

[4] D Brindle, "Drug death girl shuttled among carers" *The Guardian*, 5 October 1999.

[5] J Hartless, J Ditton, G Nair and S Phillips, "More sinned against than sinning" (1995) 35 *British Journal of Criminology* 114.

[6] See L Radzinwicz and R Hood, *The Emergence of Penal Policy* (Oxford, OUP, 1990), chs 6 and 7.

[7] See for example, Beccaria's *Of Crimes and Punishments* (Indianapolis, Bobbs-Merrill, 1764). The classical school is eruditely discussed in G Vold, T Bernard and J Snipes, *Theoretical Criminology* (Oxford, OUP, 4th ed, 1998).

influence this decision on the part of the offender and others considering the same options. Holding the offender accountable for their actions was also important and so retribution was a key feature of punishment. On this argument the age of the offender is largely irrelevant—where a rational decision to offend has taken place the offender has to be held accountable.

Later in the nineteenth century a more welfare-based approach to punishment emerged, partly as a result of the development of positivist criminology which revealed other explanations for criminal behaviour, typically those attributable to the inadequacies of the individual and his environment. Criminal statistics also showed that those in the fifteen to twenty age band were a highly criminogenic group.[8] This heralded the start of a more individualised approach to young offenders, evidenced by developments such as the opening of Parkhurst prison in 1842 as a separate custodial institution for children only and the establishment of a number of reformatory schools, founded by Mary Carpenter, as a form of residential after care for those leaving custody.[9] Welfare reformers began to recognise the vulnerability of children and the fact "that proper training can counteract the imposition of poor family life, a corrupt environment and poverty, while at the same time toughening and preparing delinquents for the struggle ahead".[10] Hence children were viewed as less than wholly accountable for their criminal actions and incomplete in their development. Noticeably this coincided with broader trends in social policy which reflected a similar view of childhood. The Factory Acts recognised young children's need for legal protection in the workplace and restricted the number of hours that children could work in factories and the age at which they could be sent to such work, partly in order to ensure that they were able to attend school.[11]

Birth

The new concept of childhood found expression in the criminal justice system in a number of pieces of legislation at the turn of the century. For example, the Prevention of Crime Act 1908 established borstals, a series of educational establishments for young boys aged sixteen to twenty. Courts could send young offenders to a borstal for an indeterminate period of between one and three years to learn new skills and receive moral education and discipline. The 1907 Probation of Offenders Act created the national Probation Service and the first form of supervision in the community—a key element in the drive for the decarceration of young offenders.

---

[8] Morris and Giller, *Understanding Juvenile Justice* (London, Croom Helm, 1987), p 7.

[9] See A Rutherford, *Growing out of Crime: The New Era* (Winchester, Waterside Press, 1992), pp 39–43.

[10] A Platt, *The Child Savers* (Chicago, Chicago University Press, 1969), p 53.

[11] See H Cunningham, *Children & Childhood in Western Society since 1500* (London, Longman, 1995), pp 138–45.

Most notably, however, the Children Act 1908, known as the "Children's Charter", marked the real birth of the youth justice system. Part V of the Act created the juvenile court which Morris and Giller describe as partly "the logical outcome of increased awareness of the differing needs of juveniles and adults".[12] David Garland has similarly acknowledged the importance of this new court which endorsed "the conception of the child or juvenile as a special category and prompted a separate institutional basis for the future development of social work and criminological initiatives".[13] Many magistrates' courts had begun holding separate hearings for young offenders prior to this enactment, but after 1908 formal separate courts were established with specially trained magistrates and restricted but more flexible sentencing powers.

The Children and Young Persons Act 1933 went further in codifying the new welfare approach. Section 44 of that Act states that:

> "Every court in dealing with a child or young person who is brought before it, either as [. . .] an offender or otherwise, shall have regard to the welfare of the child or young person and shall in a proper case take steps for removing him from undesirable surroundings, and for securing that proper provision is made for his education and training".

The Act also widened the jurisdiction of the juvenile court to incorporate seventeen-year-olds. At the other end of the age group the Children and Young Persons Act 1932 raised the minimum age of criminal responsibility from seven to eight, whilst also abolishing corporal punishment as a sentence of the court. These had been just some of the sixty-five recommendations of the Malony Committee[14].

Middle age

The modern history of the youth justice system is well-documented as a continual pendulum swing between broadly punitive and welfare approaches to youth justice.[15] It is therefore not possible to trace a seamless path through this lifecycle from birth in 1908 to a pinnacle of child-centred welfarism in middle age. In between there have been many returns to the punitive, hardline approach of

---

[12] *Supra* n 8, p 30. They also see this provision as reflecting "concern for the future; juveniles' health and well-being was one of the nation's greatest assets" in a time of radical political and economic change.

[13] *Punishment and Welfare: A History of Penal Strategies* (Aldershot, Gower, 1985), pp 22–3.

[14] A Home Office committee set up in 1925 to investigate the "treatment" and "protection" of young offenders which reported in 1927—*Report of Departmental Committee on the Treatment of Young Offenders* Cmnd 2831 (London, Home Office, 1927).

[15] See for example, A Rutherford *supra* n 9, chs 2 and 3; T Newburn, "Youth, Crime and Justice" in R Morgan et al, *Oxford Handbook of Criminology* (Oxford, OUP, 2nd ed, 1997); Morris and Giller, *supra* n 8, chs 1 and 3 and M Cavadino and J Dignan, *The Penal System: An Introduction* (London, Sage, 2nd ed, 1997).

the early nineteenth century.[16] However, the Children and Young Persons Act 1969 is highlighted here as the centrepoint of middle age because of its particular significance in shaping the latter part of this lifecycle.

If the 1969 Act had been properly implemented in full, many of the changes now taking place in the youth justice system would simply not have been possible. The Act was the product of two benevolent White Papers in the 1960s[17] as well as at least some absorption of the radically liberal developments in Scotland at that time.[18] The Act proposed to raise the age of criminal responsibility from ten[19] to fourteen, to replace criminal proceedings gradually with care proceedings, to phase out both forms of custody for young offenders (borstals and detention centres), to place cautioning on a legislative footing and to expand the use of intermediate treatment (community based, therapeutic methods for preventing offending and re-offending).

These radical provisions reflect not only a particular conception of childhood, involving lesser accountability and the need for a more sensitive and reforming approach to offending behaviour, but they also identify youth crime less as a crime problem and more as troublesome childhood or adolescent behaviour which requires guidance and support. Notions of blame, guilt and punishment would have faded away with the gradual disappearance of criminal procedures. Very young children under fourteen would have been excluded from any criminal responsibility at all and later debates (to be discussed below) on the application of the doctrine of *doli incapax* would have been avoided.

Nevertheless, large parts of the 1969 Act were never implemented[20] and the 1970s saw a return to a punitive, heavily incarcerative approach to youth crime. By the mid 1980s, however, there had been a further change in the pendulum swing. Rutherford describes the approach adopted briefly between the mid 1980s and early 1990s as the "developmental approach".[21] This essentially consisted of minimal intervention by criminal justice authorities in order to allow young people to grow out of offending behaviour naturally where possible. Heavy intervention, in particular custodial provisions or care orders which took

[16] For example, the phrase "short sharp shock" was first used in 1942 to describe the regime of the new detention centres introduced by the Labour Government in the 1950s. Stanley Cohen has also famously discussed the hardline reaction of the media and criminal justice authorities to some minor public disorder by mods and rockers in Clacton in the early 1960s: *Folk Devils and Moral Panics* (Oxford, Martin Robertson, 1972).

[17] *The Child, The Family and the Young Offender* Cmnd 2742 (London, Home Office, 1965) and *Children in Trouble* Cmnd 3601 (London, Home Office, 1968).

[18] The Kilbrandon Committtee had reported in 1964 and recommended that the juvenile justice process be viewed more as an educational process with less emphasis on punishment and blame. As a consequence the non-criminal Children's Hearings system was established in the Social Work (Scotland) Act 1968 and replaced the juvenile court.

[19] It had been raised from 8 to 10 in the Criminal Justice Act 1963.

[20] Andrew Rutherford explores some of the reasons for the failure of the Act in "A Statute Backfires: The Escalation of Youth Incarceration in England during the 1970s" in J Doig (ed), *Criminal Corrections: Ideals and Realities* (Massachusetts, Lexington Books, 1983).

[21] See *supra* n 9, particularly ch 1 where Rutherford describes this "new era" in youth justice in some depth.

the young person away from their natural environment, were thought to be harmful and a hindrance to the growing up process. Youth crime was seen in most cases as no more than a symptom of the rebellious adolescent phase of child development, which would, with adequate guidance, naturally cease as the young person matured into adulthood. If the criminal justice system hindered this developmental process then crime had less chance of burning itself out. Therefore it was thought by many at that time that a heavily retributive approach could actually increase the crime problem rather than prevent or reduce it.

In practice, many practitioners, including probation officers, social workers, police officers and even magistrates, favoured an approach where the criminal justice system acknowledged juvenile responsibility with a caution wherever possible, so that more natural discipline networks such as the parents, school and wider community could take over to address more constructively the problems of the offending behaviour. The heavier forms of intervention could thereby be reserved for the more serious cases where it eventually became clear that the offending behaviour had deeper underlying causes and required a more intrusive approach.

Hence in the late 1980s the Home Office criminal statistics show a sharp increase in the use of formal cautions by the police for young offenders, a spectacular reduction in the use of custody, particularly for males aged fourteen to seventeen and a steady fall in the numbers of juveniles being tried in the youth court. As Rutherford points out, "This transformation is all the more striking for having occurred during the 'Thatcher Years' and it must be regarded as one of the most remarkable developments of post-war criminal justice".[22] A key part[23] of this "remarkable development" was the strong belief by practitioners and others in the developmental process and the capacity of children, even those who offend, to grow up, mature and change their behaviour. This was the real antithesis of the retributive nineteenth-century approach based on a theory of personal responsibility.

Old age?

The 1990s was a decade of retreat from this liberal position and marked the beginning of the end of a child specific youth justice system. The decade began with the enactment of the Criminal Justice Act 1991 which, while supposedly liberal and decarcerative in tone,[24] set out a new universal sentencing frame-

---

[22] See *supra* n 9.

[23] Others, including Cavadino and Dignan, *supra* n 15, argue that these developments were as much due to a new systems management approach emanating from the influential work of a number of academics at Lancaster University, see pp 254–61.

[24] The official rationale for the new sentencing structure was to reduce pressure on the prison system by encouraging sentencers to use strengthened and more credible community alternatives, see the Green Paper *Punishment Custody and the Community* Cm 424 (London, Home Office, 1988).

work for judges and magistrates to be used in the sentencing of both adults and juveniles. With the exception of provisions relating to parental responsibility[25] few of the significant changes made by the Act were child specific.[26] More importantly the sentencing framework was heavily offence based; the gravity of the offence should determine a proportionate "deserts" based sentence.[27] This left little room for the youth panel to take into account maturity or any incapacity of a young offender to understand the implications of his behaviour.

By 1993 the decarcerative intent behind this Act had become a political embarrassment to the weak Major government which at the same time had embarked upon the "Back to Basics" political campaign for electoral support. "Back to basics" as far as young offenders were concerned meant a return to the nineteenth century law and order approach. This is what prompted John Major in his now (in)famous response to the Bulger murder later that year: "We should condemn a little more and understand a little less". Michael Howard also echoed the sentiments of Beccaria when he told the Conservative Party Annual Conference in October 1993 that "crime is caused by criminals".

In 1994 this sentiment was embodied in the Criminal Justice and Public Order Act. This hotch-potch of provisions criminalised the behaviour of a number of groups of "outsiders"[28] whom the media had hysterically vilified in some way, including young offenders after the Bulger murder and joy riding panic of 1992–3. The relevant provisions of this Act will be discussed in more detail below. However, what is of particular significance in the wider historical context is the fact that the Act targeted ten to fourteen-year-olds for the most punitive changes to the law. Indeed, this very young age group were brought within the provisions which allow for young offenders to be tried and sentenced in the Crown Court (and thereby effectively lose their right to childhood in this context). The Act also created a new custodial sentence for children as young as twelve for the first time in many decades.

Youth justice was a key area of interest to the Labour Party throughout their period in opposition between 1979 and 1997. In 1996 they had pledged to "end the confusion over punishment and welfare at national and local levels".[29] They were pledging to end the pendulum swing of the previous one hundred and fifty years in youth justice policy, although they were coy about where the pendulum's final resting place was to be. In reality the legislation that they went on to propose after the election in 1997 did no such thing and the Crime and Disorder

[25] Ss. 56–58 inclusive—the requirement for parents to attend court proceedings, duties on parents to pay financial penalties incurred by their children and the new parental bindover respectively.
[26] There were provisions in Part III relating to children's evidence in court which were inevitably child specific—ss. 52–55.
[27] Ss. 1(1)(a) and 2(2)(a).
[28] H Becker, *Outsiders* (New York, Free Press, 1963). The "outsiders" in this case included taxi touts, football hooligans, terrorists, travellers, ravers and young offenders.
[29] Labour Party, *Tackling Youth Crime, Reforming Youth Justice* (London, Labour Party, 1996).

Act 1997 has been heavily criticised for its lack of a clear focus and political ideology.[30]

One of the many and varied themes in the Act is that of "Taking Responsibility". The Government were insistent that:

> "[y]oung people who commit crime must face up to the consequences of their actions for themselves and for others and must take responsibility for their actions . . . the response of the youth justice system should be rapid, consistent and effective. No young person should be allowed to feel that he or she can offend with impunity . . . Punishment is important as a means of expressing society's condemnation of unlawful behaviour and as a deterrent. Punishment should be proportionate to the offence but progressively tougher if young people continue to offend".[31]

This was to be achieved in practice through such measures as the abolition of the *doli incapax* presumption,[32] the Detention and Training Order,[33] the Child Safety Order[34] and Reparation Order.[35]

In other parts of the Act the Government claimed that they were trying to be "tough on crime and its causes"[36] and trying to " prevent youth crime" among the under tens.[37] These aims involve increasing intervention through measures such as the action plan order,[38] the reprimand and warning[39] and the child safety order.[40] Whilst there are elements of a 1960s style welfare based approach here and some genuine attempts to tackle the underlying problems of childhood and youth which are producing youth crime,[41] the Act and its underlying policy is heavily reminiscent of the classical approach of the nineteenth century. The language of the Consultation and White Papers is dogmatic, intolerant and punitive (even when discussing constructive intervention):

> "Within our youth justice system, punishment is important to signal society's disapproval of criminal acts and to deter offending. It is the appropriate response to children and young people who wilfully break the law".[42]

> "An excuse culture has developed within the youth justice system. It excuses itself for its inefficiency, and too often excuses the young offenders before it, implying that they

---

[30] See J Fionda, "New Labour Old Hat: Youth Justice and the Crime and Disorder Act 1997" [1999] *Criminal Law Review* 36; L Gelsthorpe and A Morris, "Much ado about nothing—a critical comment on key provisions relating to children in the Crime and Disorder Act 1998" (1999) 11 *CFLQ* 209.

[31] Home Office White Paper, *No More Excuses—A New Approach to Tackling Youth Crime in England and Wales* Cm 3809 (London, TSO, 1997) pp 1–2.

[32] Crime and Disorder Act 1997 s. 34.

[33] *Ibid* s. 73.

[34] *Ibid* s. 11.

[35] *Ibid* s. 67.

[36] Home Office, *supra* n 31, pp 12–17.

[37] *Ibid*, pp 18–20.

[38] Crime and Disorder Act 1997 s. 69.

[39] *Ibid* s. 65.

[40] *Ibid* s. 11.

[41] Further examples include the Drug Treatment and Testing Order which is clearly designed to alleviate an addiction problem which may be causing criminal behaviour.

[42] Home Office, *supra* n 31, p 12. This quote appears under the heading "Tough on crime and its causes".

cannot help their behaviour because of their social circumstances . . . we must stop making excuses for youth crime. Children above the age of criminal responsibility are generally mature enough to be accountable for their actions and the law should recognise this . . . Public protection is best served if punishment is combined with rehabilitation so that young offenders are equipped to lead law-abiding and useful lives once they are released from custody".[43]

These are typical of many statements in recent policy documents on youth crime which make it clear that the youth justice system expects children both above and below the age of ten to take responsibility for their criminal (or pseudo-criminal) behaviour and accept the proportionate punishment they deserve (although retribution may be served with a side dish of rehabilitation).

The Youth Justice and Criminal Evidence Act 1999 goes a step further and expects young offenders to negotiate their own penalty with a youth offending panel (this will be discussed further below). The dichotomy emerging between the way in which young offenders and young victims are perceived as children (or not) is illustrated with both lucidity and irony in Parts I and II of that Act.

CONTEMPORARY CONSTRUCTIONS OF CHILDHOOD

This section will examine the boundaries of the youth justice system in its current form in order to analyse what, if any, coherent analysis of childhood can be made. These boundaries include the statutory parameters of age groups considered in legal terms to be children, young persons or adults, and the extent to which the adult criminal justice system overlaps with the youth justice system in the trial and sentencing of children in the Crown Court.

Age ranges

The minimum age of criminal responsibility in England and Wales rose gradually throughout the twentieth century and is now set at ten. This has been the minimum age since 1963 with only a brief, and ultimately abortive, extension to fourteen in 1969.[44] Children below this age are considered *doli incapax*, and incapable of forming criminal intent. However, the minimum age is much more than a test of incapacity; it is more significantly a symbolic threshold for the criminal justice system. It is the age at which the state has decided that children can or should be subject to the punishment processes of the law. To some extent the historical and international debates on an appropriate minimum age are more about the age at which we choose to punish children (the policy view) and only partly about their mental capacities in relation to criminal intent (the legal

---

[43] Home Office, *supra* n 31, pp 1–2.
[44] Children and Young Persons Act 1969, s. 4 and s. 70(1).

view). It is inconceivable, for example that the authorities in Belgium or Spain consider that young persons under the age of eighteen and sixteen respectively are incapable of forming criminal intent, but rather they prefer to deal with unlawful behaviour by young offenders in a non-criminal way. Similarly in Scotland the comparatively low minimum age of criminal responsibility has remained at eight in part because the consequences for children at that age are less serious due to the youth justice system having been effectively de-criminalised since 1968. The debate continues to rage in England and Wales as to whether the lower end of the youth justice age range is appropriate. Two developments here have indicated a desire on the part of the youth justice system and the Government to lower it further: the fate of the presumption of *doli incapax* and the introduction of the Child Safety Order.

The presumption of *doli incapax* for ten to fourteen-year-olds came under attack in the early 1990s when the High Court[45] purported to abolish it on the grounds that it was "perverse", "contrary to common sense" and that it did a "serious disservice to the law".[46] Laws J in this case took into account both the legal and policy views of the purpose of the presumption. On the one hand he argued that it was a test of competence which should prevent the prosecution bringing a case where a child was incapable of knowing that their actions were seriously wrong.[47] This accounted for the perversity of the presumption where children who had received a conventional moral education would be more likely to be prosecuted successfully than one who had not. Not only did he find it abhorrent to assume that all children under fourteen had lesser mental competence than adults (although this could be rebutted) but he argued that, where such lesser mental capacity existed, that was exactly what the criminal justice system should be punishing:

> The prosecution are in effect required to prove, as a condition of his guilt, that he is morally responsible: But it is because he is morally *irresponsible* that he has committed the crime in the first place (original emphasis).[48]

On the policy view the presumption was seen as an ancient means of protecting the child from the horrors of the punishment system which have existed from time to time, such as the death penalty, transportation, and the infliction of physical pain or humiliation. Laws J argued that, since the youth justice system now contains no horrors of this nature, children need no such protection.

Despite a brief resurrection by the House of Lords on the grounds that the High Court had acted unconstitutionally in abolishing it, the presumption was

---

[45] *C v. DPP* [1994] 3 WLR 888.

[46] *Ibid* at 894, *per* Laws J.

[47] Sue Bandalli argues, however, that it afforded no such protection as it was so easily rebutted by a prosecutor who was well prepared and a good advocate—"Abolition of the Presumption of *Doli Incapax* and the Criminalisation of Children" (1998) 37 *Howard Journal* 114.

[48] *C v. DPP* [1994] 3 WLR 888 at 896.

abolished in the Crime and Disorder Act 1998.[49] Having toyed with the idea of reversing the presumption so that some protection might still be afforded to a very immature child who pleaded it as a defence, the Home Office decided that complete abolition was the "simplest course and would provide the least hindrance and delay to court proceedings".[50] The outcome is that symbolically the youth justice system no longer makes any distinction between a ten-year-old and a fifteen-year-old both in terms of their maturity and their ability to withstand the stigma and stress of the punishment system.

The Child Safety Order was introduced by section 11 of the Crime and Disorder Act 1998. Under this provision children may be placed under such an order where they have either contravened a local curfew, have committed an act which would constitute an offence if the child was aged over ten or has acted in a manner which has or is likely to cause harassment, alarm or distress. The terms of any order are entirely a matter for the discretion of the court, except that the length of the order must not exceed twelve months. The child will report to a responsible officer during the currency of the order and this officer may be a youth offending team member or a social worker.

The rationale behind this measure was to protect children from a life of crime: "children under ten need help to change their bad behaviour just as much as older children".[51] It was also designed to protect the community from: ". . . the criminal and anti-social activities of unsupervised young children [which] can make life a misery for those who have to endure their disorder".[52]

Under the Children Act 1989[53] children under ten whose naughty or "anti-social" behaviour became a problem too great for parents alone to deal with could be assisted by social workers to change their behaviour. It has never before required the intervention of the youth justice system or the youth offending team. The claim that prosecution (or, in this case, quasi-prosecution) is necessary in order to instigate ameliorative action to change a young person's behaviour is anachronistic and wrong. This provision is clearly a surreptitious abandonment of the minimum age of criminal responsibility and a statement that children under ten are now ready for exposure to formal legal (if only quasi-criminal) procedures in taking responsibility for their actions.

The youth court jurisdiction was extended to include seventeen-year-olds in 1991.[54] Hence eighteen, the legal coming of age for so many other purposes[55] effectively marks the end of childhood for young offenders. That said those aged

---

[49] Section 34. For critiques of this decision see Fionda, *supra* n 31, pp 38–9 and P Cavadino, "Goodbye doli, must we leave you?" (1997) 9 *CFLQ* 165.

[50] Home Office, *supra* n 31, para 15.

[51] *Ibid*, para 99.

[52] *Ibid*, paras 99–100.

[53] Particularly Parts III and IV.

[54] Criminal Justice Act, s. 70.

[55] Such as voting in an election, buying alcohol, having a homosexual relationship and marrying without parental consent. These age limits are discussed by John Muncie in *Youth and Crime* (London, Sage, 1999), ch 1.

eighteen to twenty inclusive are not quite regarded as full adults and are referred to as young adults. This group are tried and sentenced in the adult courts but serve any custodial sentence in a Young offenders' institution[56] and may be sentenced to an Attendance Centre Order until the age of twenty-one. Further, the Criminal Justice Act 1991 created a grey area in terms of childhood between sixteen and eighteen. The parental responsibility provisions[57] are all compulsory in respect of parents of offenders under sixteen but discretionary between sixteen and eighteen. This is perhaps an attempt to mirror the sentiment of *Gillick*[58] in civil law and acknowledge diminishing parental responsibility, albeit in a more stilted way.

Grave Offences

Childhood therefore technically runs from the age of ten to seventeen in the youth justice system, with just a few concessions made between the ages of eighteen and twenty to acknowledge that full maturity may only be reached at twenty-one. However, to some extent childhood in criminal justice terms is dependent on the gravity of the offence. The commission of a (very) serious offence can mean that a child essentially transcends their own childhood—they have committed an adult act and therefore are treated as an adult on that basis. This might alternatively be seen in more emotive terms as the withdrawal of the privilege of childhood for the most serious offenders.

When the juvenile court was established in 1908 special measures were put in place for young offenders who committed murder. Detention during Her Majesty's pleasure[59] replaced the death penalty for those under eighteen. In 1933 the Children and Young Persons Act (CYPA) amended these provisions and sections 53(1) and 53(2) set out a procedure whereby young offenders may be tried and sentenced in the Crown Court.[60] Section 53(1) relates to young persons aged ten to seventeen inclusive charged with murder; in these cases trial in the Crown Court is mandatory. On conviction, the mandatory penalty remains detention during Her Majesty's pleasure, an indefinite period of detention. Recent litigation by Venables and Thompson, appealing against the tariff element of their

---

[56] At least for the time being—a Home Office Consultation Paper has suggested a "more flexible" approach to their custody in which they could be sent to an adult prison at the age of 18: *Detention in a Young Offender Institution for 18–20 year olds: A Consultation Paper* (London, Home Office, 1999).

[57] Ss. 56, 57 and 58.

[58] *Gillick* v. *West Norfolk and Wisbech AHA* [1986] AC 112. Michael Freeman and Penney Lewis discuss this case further in chs 11 and 9 in this volume respectively. See also the Family Law Reform Act 1969, s. 8.

[59] Children Act 1908 ss. 103 and 104.

[60] S. 53 has now been re-worded and replaced by s. 91 of the Powers of the Criminal Courts (Sentencing) Act 2000. The effect of the provisions is identical and the wording is not significantly changed. The new enactment simply brings these provisions into line with other, more recent, sentencing provisions for young offenders.

penalty under this section, resulted in the House of Lords making important statements about the long term imprisonment of very young children.

Venables and Thompson had claimed that the mandatory penalty is child-specific and that the Home Secretary was wrong to equate it with a life sentence for adults for the purposes of determining the length of a tariff.[61] The majority in the House of Lords agreed with them and while the setting of a tariff was in itself lawful, the House of Lords reminded the Home Secretary that when acting in a quasi-judicial capacity he should have regard to the welfare principle set out in section 44 CYPA 1933. This principle was, according to Lord Browne-Wilkinson, just as important in assessing the appropriate date for release as any consideration of the retributive and deterrent aspects of the penalty and any risk to the public.[62] Furthermore, it was held that the cases of these young offenders had to be reviewed regularly and a tariff must reflect that. This was in order that a young person is able to see the light at the end of a long sentence and, most importantly, that their capacity to change and rehabilitate greatly in a short period of time is taken into account in any decision on release. The penalty of detention during Her Majesty's pleasure derived from an earlier use of the term for the indefinite detention of "lunatics", whose detention was also designed to end after a suitable period of psychological change and rehabilitation. Hence very young children sentenced under this procedure must be treated with due consideration of their capacity to mature.

Section 53(2) of the CYPA 1933 relates to young persons charged with serious offences for whom trial and sentencing in the Crown Court is a matter for the discretion of the youth court. The Crown Court can order a custodial sentence up to the maximum for the offence.[63] This provision is far more controversial and has undergone more profound changes since 1933. Originally it only applied to offenders aged fourteen to seventeen who were charged with attempted murder, manslaughter or wounding with intent, that is, the most serious of offences against the person. The Criminal Justice Act 1961 amended the provision so that young persons over fourteen who were charged with any offence carrying a maximum penalty of fourteen years or more (in the case of an adult) could be sent to the Crown Court. This significantly widened the range of offences to which the procedure applied and subsequent changes in the substantive criminal law have meant that a number of property offences are included.[64] In 1991 seventeen-year-olds were brought into the procedure by

---

[61] R v. *Secretary of State for the Home Department, ex parte Venables and Thompson* [1997] 2 WLR 67 (CA) and [1997] 3 All ER 97 (HL). For a critique see J Fionda, "The Age of Innocence?—the concept of childhood in the punishment of young offenders" (1998) 10 *CFLQ* 77; C McDiarmid, "Children Who Murder: What is Her Majesty's Pleasure?" [2000] *Crim LR* 547.

[62] *Ibid* (HL) at p 126.

[63] The juvenile court at that time could only impose short periods of custody. Even today the youth court cannot make a custodial order for more than 2 years, only half of which is actually served in an institution—Crime and Disorder Act 1998 s. 73.

[64] Offences falling within the s. 53 procedure include: rape, wounding with intent, unlawful sexual intercourse with a girl under 13, arson, burglary of a dwelling, aggravated burglary and s. 1(2)criminal damage (Criminal Damage Act 1971).

default since they were included for the first time in the jurisdiction of the youth court.[65]

In 1994 section 53(2) was widened to include those aged under fourteen.[66] Their exclusion from this procedure was seen as an unacceptable loophole in the law rendering the youth court virtually powerless to sentence serious offenders adequately at this age.[67] It is therefore now the case that children as young as ten may be tried in the Crown Court.[68] The Court of Appeal has sounded a note of restraint in their guidance on the use of section 53(2), which is especially pertinent in the light of these changes. The essence of the guidance accords with that given by the House of Lords in *Venables and Thompson*[69] and focuses on the length of the sentence being appropriate not just to the gravity of the offence and retributive requirements but also to the age of the offender. In *Storey* the Court of Appeal suggested that a sentence under s 53(2) should not be so long:

> ". . . that it would seem to the young [offender] involved, particularly if they are not outstanding intellectually, that the far end of it is out of sight . . . The sentencer should take care to select a duration on which the offender can fix his eye with a view to emerging in the foreseeable future".[70]

However, the fact remains that trial in the Crown Court, under full public gaze and in auspicious surroundings is a distressing experience for any defendant and particularly one as young as ten.[71] It was not surprising therefore that Venables and Thompson (who were only eleven at their trial in 1993) were successful in their claim to the European Court of Human Rights that such a distressing experience denied them their right to a fair trial.[72]

It should be noted that the outcome of the Venables and Thompson case has not challenged the legality of trying young children in the Crown Court *per se* but the conditions under which they are tried have to be appropriate to their age

---

[65] Criminal Justice Act 1991 s. 70. This may account in part for the extraordinary rise in use of s. 53(2) between 1992–3—from 93 to 315 cases respectively. In 1997 this had risen to 722 (Home Office *Criminal Statistics* (London, TSO, 1999)).

[66] Criminal Justice and Public Order Act 1994, s. 16.

[67] Home Office criminal statistics at this time suggest there were few of these; in fact there was a fall generally in the numbers of 10–13-year-olds being tried up to 1995. Home Office commissioned research also indicated that few of their offences are extremely serious, see J Graham and B Bowling, *Young People and Crime*, Home Office Research Study no. 145 (London, Home Office, 1995). In any event the Children Act 1989 contains provisions enabling children who are dangerously violent or out of control to be remanded into care—s. 31.

[68] Indeed in 1997 the media reported, with some disapproval, on the youngest ever child to be tried in the Crown Court—a boy aged 10 years and 6 days charged with arson. See "The boy is ten. He is in an adult court, accused of being an arsonist", *Daily Mail*, 5 February 1997. A further example involving a 12-year-old drug dealer was reported in "Please, I want Mummy: How the youngest crack dealer in Britain aged only 12 reduced a judge to tears", *Daily Express*, 24 June 2000.

[69] *Op cit*, n 61.

[70] *R v. Storey* (1984) 6 Cr App R (S) 104 at 106. See also *R v. Cummins* [1986] Crim LR 483; *R v. Kearsley* [1992] Crim LR 130; *R v. Wainfur* [1996] Crim LR 674 and *R v. Mills* [1998] Crim LR 220.

[71] Their names were also released into the public domain—this would never have happened had they been involved in civil litigation in the family courts.

[72] *V v. UK; T v. UK* (2000) 30 EHHR 121.

and understanding. As a result of this decision the Home Secretary requested the Lord Chief Justice to issue some guidance on the treatment of children in the Crown Court and this was set out in a Practice Direction.[73] The Lord Chief Justice made an important statement of principle before giving more practical guidance:

> "Some young defendants accused of committing serious crimes may be very young and very immature when standing trial in the Crown Court. The purpose of such trial is to determine guilt (if that is in issue) and decide the appropriate sentence if the young defendant pleads guilty or is convicted. *The trial process should not expose the young defendant to avoidable intimidation, humiliation or distress. All possible steps should be taken to assist the young defendant to understand and participate in the proceedings. The ordinary trial process should so far as necessary be adapted to meet those ends. Regard should be had to the welfare of the young defendant as required by section 44 of the Children and Young Persons Act 1933*". (Emphasis added)

In practical terms the Lord Chief Justice went on to suggest some of the ways in which the trial process could be made less intimidating and distressing. These include a pre-trial visit for the young person to the courtroom where the trial is to take place, holding the trial in a room without a raised bench if possible, allowing the young person to sit with members of his family if he wishes, the removal of wigs and gowns and taking frequent and regular breaks in the proceedings where the young person is unable to concentrate for long periods. These provisions coincide to some extent with the protections afforded to child witnesses under the Youth Justice and Criminal Evidence Act 1999 Part II and recognition of the need to protect child defendants in the courtroom in a similar way is to be welcomed.

YOUTH CRIME: THE RHETORIC

Arguments about what I call the "adulteration" of youth justice are less tenable in relation to older teenagers who fall within the jurisdiction of the youth court. Family lawyers, for example, have recognised the need to retreat gradually from a paternalistic view of childhood as the young person develops maturity.[74] The family law approach, however, is more focused on the maturity of the individual litigant whereas the youth justice system tends to have abrupt cut off points and rather less concern for individual levels of development, which is an important factor in many of the problems discussed throughout this chapter. In many cases young offenders aged fifteen, sixteen or seventeen may (or may) not merit a less child-centred approach and be rightly expected to take full responsibility for their actions, although this can only be judged on an individual's circumstances

---

[73] Practice Direction—Trial of Children and Young Persons in the Crown Court [2000] 1 Cr App R 483.

[74] See further ch 11 in this volume.

and competence and never through the gravity of the criminal law label attached to their behaviour.

Of greater concern is the "adulteration" of youth justice policy in the 1990s in particular relation to children aged ten to fourteen. At this age group a child-centred approach is more justified, a fact borne out by a long history of special protections against the more rigorous aspects of punishment for this age group.[75] Given the socio-political context of the 1990s, changes to the law at that time may have been an angry rejoinder to the murder of James Bulger. It is difficult to justify them with conviction on any other level. Nevertheless the changes outlined below collectively render this age group more likely to be prosecuted in the youth court and more likely to be sentenced with greater severity and, for the first time since the beginning of the twentieth century, to find themselves in custody.

Pre trial initiatives

During the 1980s the cautioning rate for ten to seventeen-year-olds reached its highest ever level. In 1980 44 per cent of male offenders in this group were cautioned, by 1990 this had risen to 75 per cent.[76] For ten to fourteen-year-olds the number of prosecutions in the juvenile court fell from 18,900 in 1980 to 2,700 in 1990. Cautioning was a useful response to offending at this age at a time when dealing with youth crime was heavily influenced by the developmental ideal.[77] Indeed it was not uncommon for young offenders to receive multiple cautions during this growing up period.[78] In 1994, however, the Home Office decided it could no longer tolerate this practice and in issuing guidance on cautioning Michael Howard, the then Home Secretary, claimed that multiple cautioning brought the youth justice system "into disrepute".[79] Thereafter the use of multiple cautioning fell.[80]

The Crime and Disorder Act 1998 gave a legislative footing to the cautioning system for young offenders in the form of reprimands and warnings.[81] A young offender can only ever receive one of each of these penalties before prosecution becomes the standard response to further offending behaviour. Where criminal activity has started early a child in the ten to fourteen age bracket is likely to find themselves more swiftly propelled towards the youth court. This propulsion will be assisted by the fact that with a new statutory framework the future use

---

[75] Including the presumption of *doli incapax* discussed above and the ban on imprisoning children under 14 since the 1908 Children Act.

[76] Home Office, *Criminal Statistics* (London, TSO, 1991).

[77] See above.

[78] R Evans, "Cautioning: Counting the Cost of Retrenchment" [1994] *Criminal LR* 566–75.

[79] Home Office Circular 18/1994.

[80] R Evans and D Ellis, *Police Cautioning in the 1990s*, Home Office Research Findings No. 52 (London, Home Office, 1997).

[81] Crime and Disorder Act 1998, ss. 65 and 66.

of informal, unrecorded (or "unofficial") cautions is uncertain. Furthermore, the changes made to the CPS Code at the same time as the publication of Circular 18/1994 suggested that the previously inhibited policy towards prosecution of children was likely to change.[82]

Sentencing options

Once convicted in the youth court sentencing options are now more varied but to some extent more punitive and expectant of a greater degree of mature accountability. For those who have received a warning under the new framework outlined above, they will not be eligible for a conditional discharge on a subsequent prosecution within two years.[83] In this way their first prosecuted offence is automatically up-tariffed (as it is unlikely that the courts will resort to using absolute discharges instead). The courts will have no choice but to consider a fine or even a community penalty where they might previously have used the conditional discharge. Offenders aged over ten who are convicted for the first time and who have pleaded guilty will be automatically sentenced to a referral order and be referred to a youth offending panel.[84] In a series of meetings with the panel the child will be expected to negotiate a "contract" containing the precise terms of his punishment. These meetings will require the attendance of a primary carer where the offender is under sixteen and another adult may attend with the offender if the panel agrees, but no lawyer will be present. The contractual symbolism used in the language and provisions of this legislation has been criticised as inappropriate, given that any contract drawn up under these conditions is likely to be void for duress and lack of any consideration on the part of the panel.[85] Moreover, it is quite remarkable that the Government considers children under eighteen able to negotiate such a contract without any professional assistance whatsoever, particularly given the reluctance to allow children under eighteen to make binding contracts in civil law.[86] The younger the offender the more potentially difficult and unfair this exercise in personal autonomy will be.

For those not subject to a referral order, the youth court has two important new options in relation to ten to fourteen-year-olds. The curfew order has been extended to include twelve to sixteen-year-olds.[87] This legislative action

---

[82] See A Ashworth and J Fionda, "Prosecution, Accountability and the Public Interest" [1994] *Crim LR* 894.

[83] Crime and Disorder Act 1998 s. 66(4).

[84] Youth Justice and Criminal Evidence Act 1999, Part I.

[85] See C Wonnacott, "The Counterfeit Contract: reform, pretence and muddled principles in the new referral order" (1999) 11 *CFLQ* 271; C Ball, "Youth Justice and Criminal Evidence Act 1999 Part I—A significant move towards restorative justice or a recipe for unintended consequences?" [2000] *Crim LR* 211.

[86] See for example, Cowan and Dearden in ch 10 in this volume.

[87] Crime (Sentences) Act 1997, s. 43.

was taken by Michael Howard prior to the general election in 1997 but Jack Straw has intimated repeatedly that he is intending to implement this section in the near future. More significantly the 1994 Criminal Justice and Public Order Act extended the use of custodial sanctions to twelve to fifteen-year-olds through the introduction of the Secure Training Order.[88] This was the brain-child of Kenneth Clarke during his time in the Home Office in the early 1990s and was supposed to plug a gap in the sentencing powers of the youth court. Children under fifteen had not been eligible for custodial sentences since the turn of the twentieth century but by the end of the century this was clearly seen as an inadequacy of the system. Persistent offenders (those committing three or more imprisonable offences) could, after 1994, receive a secure training order of up to two years, exactly half of which would be served in a new custodial institution, the secure training unit built (and run privately) especially for this age group. When New Labour tidied up the various custodial provisions for young offenders and created the new, single detention and training order they surreptitiously[89] added that ten to twelve-year-olds would now be eligible for this penalty. At the same time as this provision was passing through the leg-islative process, Her Majesty's Chief Inspector of Prisons stated that: "The Prison Service should relinquish responsibility for all children under the age of 18".[90] While acknowledging that some young people might need to be held in some form of custody, he argued that the prison estate was not the appropri-ate place for them to be held and in any case it should be a last resort. Indeed, in all his strongly worded rightist rhetoric on youth justice and his radical transformation of policy in this area, Michael Howard never once suggested that the age of eligibility for custody be lowered to ten. At this early age the offender must be both persistent and dangerous[91] so the provision should be sparsely used.[92] Children at this age should also be a priority for occupation of any local authority secure accommodation rather than serving their sentence in a Prison Service institution. It is, however, a meaningful reform which is redo-lent of the early Victorian model of youth justice. It is interesting to note that although the Detention and Training Order was implemented for nationwide use on April 1 2000, this did not include the provisions relating to ten and eleven-year-olds. This suggests that the enactment of these provisions was partly a symbolic gesture, but that they remain on standby on the legislative shelf awaiting the next media panic or high profile case involving a defendant at this age.

[88] Criminal Justice and Public Order Act 1994, Part I.

[89] There was no discussion at all of custody in the three Consultation papers and the White Paper preceding the Act—the provision was directly drafted into the Bill.

[90] HM Chief Inspector of Prisons, *Young Prisoners: A Thematic Review* (London, HMIP, October 1997), p 75.

[91] Section 73(2)(a) and (b).

[92] Ann Hagell and Tim Newburn found very few persistent offenders aged 10–12 in their survey based on the statutory definition of persistence (three or more arrests)—*Persistent Young Offenders* (London, Policy Studies Institute, 1994).

Ironically, at the same time as these provisions extend the personal responsibility of young children for offending behaviour, Parliament has also ensured that parents are mindful of their responsibilities in this area. The Criminal Justice Act 1991 had re-affirmed the legal duty of parents to attend youth court proceedings concerning their child[93] and to pay any financial penalty given.[94] That Act also introduced the parental bindover, where a parent can be ordered to take care and control of their child or to ensure that the requirements of a community penalty are not breached by their child.[95] The Crime and Disorder Act 1998 went a step further and introduced Parenting Orders[96] the terms of which are highly discretionary and flexible but which will include attendance at a weekly parenting class for up to two months.

It is questionable how far these provisions are really about parents sharing the responsibility for their child's miscreant behaviour or how far they are again symbolic acts of retribution. The Home Secretaries responsible for each enactment justified the provisions in relation to empirical research which showed clear links between parenting styles and offending behaviour.[97] However it is ironic that the parenting order was announced by the Home Office in the consultation paper on youth crime[98] instead of that which discussed reforms to family law and welfare benefits[99] and subsequently enacted in criminal justice legislation. The contrast in approach with the Children Act 1989 could not be greater. Where offending behaviour is viewed as symptomatic of "need"[100] that Act also seeks to ensure that parents adequately deal with it, preferably within the home and not in the courts. To this end the Children Act seeks to work in partnership with the parent, social services being required to provide assistance to the parents in alleviating the child's needs without an apportioning of blame or any allegation of failure on the part of the parent.[101] Allocation of responsibilities and duties under this civil legislation is designed to be more facilitative and less accusatorial.

---

[93] Criminal Justice Act 1991 s. 56.

[94] *Ibid* s. 57.

[95] *Ibid* s. 58 (as amended by the Criminal Justice and Public Order Act 1994, Sched 9, para 50).

[96] Criminal Justice Act 1991 s. 8.

[97] For example, the Black Report *Report of the Children and Young Persons Review Group* (Belfast, HMSO, 1979); Graham and Bowling, *Young People and Crime* (1995) discussed further below; and D Utting, J Bright and C Henricson, *Crime and the Family: Improving child-rearing and preventing delinquency* (London, Family Policy Studies Centre, 1993). These are the most influential research reports quoted in both Home Office *Crime Justice and Protecting the Public* White Paper Cm 965 (London, HMSO, 1990) and Home Office, *supra* n 31.

[98] Home Office, *supra* n 31.

[99] *Supporting Families: A Consultation Document* (London, TSO, 1998).

[100] Defined by the Children Act 1989, s. 17(10).

[101] See further M D A Freeman, *Children, Their Families and the Law: Working with the Children Act* (London, Macmillan, 1992).

YOUTH CRIME: THE REALITY

Empirical research on the offending behaviour of young people does not indicate that children aged ten to fourteen are a growing criminogenic group. It also reveals much about the extent of childhood and the age at which desistance (often linked to reaching maturity)[102] begins. Research commissioned by the Home Office and published in 1995[103] revealed important data on the offending behaviour of young people. Although the self-report study did not include data gathered from children under fourteen,[104] those surveyed most commonly started offending at fifteen,[105] one year later than the onset of truancy for both sexes. From that age onwards a majority of the sample admitted to committing no more than one or two offences within the previous year[106] although half of the males and one third of the females[107] admitted to at least some offending behaviour. Property offending was more common than violence.[108] Offending behaviour was linked to poor parental supervision, poor attachment to parents, poverty, low attachment to school, truancy and having delinquent peers.

Females most commonly stopped offending after their mid-teens and by their early twenties their crime rate was five times lower than among teenage females. Males continued to offend at a relatively high level until the age of eighteen and beyond into their early twenties. Serious offending for males had also significantly decreased by their mid-twenties although their participation in property crime increased with age. Desistance was linked to making a successful transition from adolescence into adulthood. In females this was measured through life changes such as leaving school, leaving home, forming stable relationships and having children. In males important factors were living at home, avoiding delinquent peers, not using drugs or drinking heavily.

Although the methodological difficulties of such studies are well known[109] many other surveys have produced similar results. Farrington's longitudinal studies have suggested that criminals careers tend to begin at fourteen or fifteen.[110] A research review by Rutter and others found that international studies reveal relatively little criminal offending or antisocial activity in pre-adolescent years.[111] The second Youth Lifestyles Survey conducted in 1998/99 also found a

---

[102] See M Rutter, H Giller and A Hagell, *Antisocial Behaviour by Young People* (Cambridge, Cambridge University Press, 1998) ch 10.
[103] J Graham and B Bowling, *supra* n 67.
[104] The sample consisted of 1,721 young people aged 14–25 plus a booster sample from ethnic minority groups.
[105] Graham and Bowling, *supra* n 67, pp 23–4.
[106] *Ibid*, p 18.
[107] *Ibid*, pp 11–18.
[108] Twice as common in males and three times as common in females.
[109] See for example T May, *Social Research* (Milton Keynes, Open University Press, 1997), ch 5.
[110] D Farrington, "Criminal Career Research in the United Kingdom" (1992) 32 *British Journal of Criminology* 521.
[111] M Rutter and others, *supra* n 102, pp 98–105.

peak age of offending onset at thirteen-and-a-half for males and fourteen for females.[112] Those aged twelve to thirteen were less likely to have offended and the peak ages of offending were fourteen for females and eighteen for males. Even Home Office criminal statistics indicate a peak age of offending for males at eighteen and females at fifteen.

CONCLUSION

This research would tend to show that where offending occurs under the age of fourteen it is relatively infrequent and usually non-serious. Until the mid 1990s this was reflected in the youth justice system procedures which only applied to offenders of this age in exceptional cases where the *doli incapax* presumption was rebutted. Where they were prosecuted, offenders at this age were shielded from the most rigorous of punishments and excluded from Prison Service custody altogether. This chapter has shown how in less than ten years the child-centred approach of the legal system in respect of offenders at this age has been eroded and how recent changes in the law have marked a return to the early Victorian approach to punishing youth crime for all age groups.

The conception of childhood at the heart of the youth justice system has fundamentally changed over the last decade. Concomitant with the erosion in the recognition of children's incapacity and lack of awareness is a trend towards punitive treatment and many of these policy changes are politically motivated rather than based on any real change in the nature of childhood or the competence of children. The changes make little legal sense when the criminal justice measures are assessed alongside perfectly adequate civil measures also aimed at tackling troublesome behaviour (albeit with a very different philosophy and technique). However, policy makers during this bleak period in youth justice have failed to connect, or to use New Labour's own phrase to "join up", the criminal and the civil in the way that "old Labour" had done in the Children and Young Persons Act 1969. The consequence of this criminal justice tunnel vision is that policy makers (and others) are blinded by the label of "crime". The behaviour in question is abnormalised, the child in question is de-personalised and becomes an "offender". Offenders become the focus of hatred and a hysterical reaction results. In jurisdictions where the criminal label is avoided until the age of fifteen, sixteen or even eighteen, the legal system avoids such hysteria and is in a position to more constructively identify the abnormal troublesome behaviour of teenagers and deal with it as a health or social work problem. In England and Wales this is seen as being "soft" in a culture where we are no longer prepared to tolerate children being children.

---

[112] C Flood-Page, S Campbell, V Harrington and J Miller, *Youth Crime: Findings from the 1998/99 Youth Lifestyles Survey*, Home Office Research Study 209 (London, Home Office, 2000).

6

Children in Court

ALLAN LEVY QC

THE CONSEQUENCES OF children appearing in court, whether as witnesses or defendants, have not received much attention until comparatively recent times. The landmark event was probably the Pigot Report[1] in 1989 which focused the spotlight on the plight of the child witness in the criminal court. A series of criminal appeal decisions going back some eighty years had concentrated in the main on the question of the child alleging sexual abuse being physically confronted by the accused in court. Judge Pigot and his committee were asked to consider the video recorded evidence of children and the report attracted a wide audience and the attention of government. Subsequent statutes,[2] containing, in the main, compromise provisions, attempted to ameliorate the child's experience prior to and in court. More recently the high profile Bulger case,[3] the subject of post-trial litigation here and in Strasbourg, has resulted in a re-assessment of the criminal trial procedures for children and the application in particular of international human rights standards. This chapter attempts to assess the progress, if any, in the criminal justice system in making the lot of the child witness less traumatic and the trial of the child accused fairer, and also considers the attitudes to children that are revealed.

THE CHILD WITNESS

Confrontation

The ordeal of a child giving evidence in a criminal trial was highlighted as long ago as 1919. George Smellie[4] was convicted at Middlesex Sessions on the 24 November 1919 of assaulting, illtreating and neglecting his daughter Frances, aged eleven, in a manner likely to cause her unnecessary suffering or injury to her health. He was sentenced to twelve months imprisonment. He appealed to

---

[1] Report of the Advisory Group on Video-Recorded Evidence (Home Office, London, 1989).

[2] The Criminal Justice Act 1988 (as amended) and Criminal Justice Act 1991.

[3] R v. *Thompson and Venables*, Preston Crown Court, 1–24 November 1993; R v. *Secretary of State for the Home Department, ex parte Venables and Thompson* [1998] AC 407, HL; *V v. UK; T v. UK* (2000) 30 EHHR 121.

[4] R v. *George Smellie* (1919) 14 Cr App R 128.

the then Court of Criminal Appeal raising one argument. When his daughter was called to give evidence at the trial her father was compelled by the warder, by order of the court, to sit on the stairs leading out of the dock, out of sight of Frances, while she gave her evidence. The father's counsel gave three reasons why what happened in his view invalidated the trial. First, a prisoner at common law is entitled to be within sight and hearing of all the witnesses throughout the trial. Secondly, on the particular charge George Smellie faced, the effect on the minds of the jury of the removal of the prisoner from the dock by order of the judge at the moment when his daughter was entering the witness box was incalculable; and thirdly, that in this specific case, because it was admitted that he had beaten her for stealing, she might be inclined to say untrue things in his absence which she would not have said under the restraining influence of his presence.

The Court of Criminal Appeal gave short shrift to the ground of appeal. Mr Justice Coleridge stated that "if the judge considers that the presence of the prisoner will intimidate a witness, there is nothing to prevent him from securing the ends of justice by removing the former from the presence of the latter". In more recent times the renamed Court of Appeal (Criminal Division) in 1990 in the case of *R* v. *X, Y* and *Z*[5] considered the use of screens to protect child witnesses. The applicants were seeking leave to appeal against conviction and sentence and the child victims were all related to each other. The children had been abused in almost every permutation of sexual perversion imaginable. Each applicant had pleaded guilty to some charges and not guilty to others. The not guilty pleas were heard before a judge and jury at the Old Bailey in November 1987. The five child victims' ages ranged from eight to twelve years. The judge was Judge Pigot QC who subsequently in June 1988 was asked by the Government to look in greater depth than had so far been possible into the idea that video recordings of interviews with child victims (and possibly other victims of crime) should be readily admissible as evidence in criminal trials. He was to report in December 1989,[6] a month after the appeal concerning *X, Y* and *Z* was heard in the Court of Appeal (Criminal Division).

Screens

Before the jury were empanelled in the trial of *X, Y* and *Z* the Crown Prosecution Service received information from social services that some of the children were likely to be affected adversely if they gave evidence in court. This was brought to the attention of the judge who assembled counsel and asked for their views as to the propriety or otherwise of having a screen erected in court so as to stop the children seeing or being seen from the dock. Defence counsel

---

[5] *R* v. *X; R* v. *Y; R* v. *Z* (1990) 91 Cr App R 36.
[6] *Supra*, n 1.

objected to the use of the screen but the judge permitted the screen to be used. At the outset of the trial the judge told the jury not to allow the mere presence of the screen in any way to prejudice them against any of the defendants. Four of the children gave evidence. The applicants were convicted and appealed. One of the grounds was that it was an unfair and prejudicial act to erect the screen and as a result the jury might have been unduly influenced and unfairly prejudiced against X, Y and Z. The inference being that the people in the dock had already in some way intimidated the child who was going to give evidence. The Court of Appeal said that the judge in the trial has to see that the system operates fairly—that is fairly not only to the defendants but also to the prosecution and to the witnesses. The judge rightly came to the conclusion that in the circumstances the necessity of trying to ensure that the children would be able to give evidence in court outweighed any possible prejudice to the defendants by the erection of the screen. The defendants' applications were refused.

Subsequently the use of screens was challenged under the European Convention on Human Rights[7]. In *X* v. *UK*[8] the European Commission of Human Rights decided that, as the accused's advocate was able to see and cross-examine the witness on his behalf, there was no breach of the accused's right to a fair trial under Article 6.

Tainting evidence

A few years later in December 1993 the Court of Appeal (Criminal Division) again had to grapple with a case concerning a child witness: *R* v. *Smith*.[9] The appellant was charged with rape and gross indecency with a twelve-year-old girl. During the girl's evidence a social worker sat beside her. When the girl broke down in tears the social worker consoled her and talked quietly to her. After lunch, before the judge came into court, but while the jury were present, the girl left the court through the judge's door in the company of a number of people including the judge's clerk and the social worker. She returned a few minutes later. Letters and statements obtained later, including a communication from the judge, showed that the girl had asked to go to the toilet. She was taken to a toilet in the judge's corridor because there were relatives of the defendant outside the court.

Smith was convicted and appealed arguing that two irregularities had occurred. First, the fact that the social worker had been talking quietly to the girl after she had broken down in tears, and secondly, the circumstances in which the complainant left the court to go to the toilet could have suggested to the jury that she had spoken to the judge. At the appeal hearing the first ground was not

[7] Convention for the Protection of Human Rights and Fundamental Freedoms (4 Nov 1950, Rome; TS 71 [1953]; Cmd 8969).
[8] (1993) 15 EHRR CD 113.
[9] (1994) Crim LR 458.

pursued. However, the Court of Appeal observed that it was the task of the judge to reduce the strain on child witnesses without prejudicing the interests of the accused. It was important that anyone providing comfort and support to a child witness should not talk to him or her while the evidence is being given and this should be made clear publicly. If a social worker talks or whispers more than a consoling word or two, the suspicion may be aroused that something is being said about the evidence. Anyone fulfilling that role should say as little as possible, preferably nothing to the witness.

In respect of the second ground of appeal, the Court of Appeal stated that there had in fact been no contact between the witness and the judge when she went through his door. The test was: was there or may there have been a real danger that the jury may have been prejudiced or affected against a defendant by what they may have seen?

In this case there was no risk that justice was not done, although it may have been better to have avoided the actual route used. The Court of Appeal also pointed out that similar problems may arise where the witness is segregated from the defendant, for instance by screens or a video link. Court buildings are such that it is not uncommon for a child to be brought to the live-link room by a tortuous route in the course of which it might be theoretically possible for improper communication to take place. However the judge should not be expected to say anything to the jury on the matter unless there is some real reason to suppose an impropriety has occurred.

USA and Canada

The difficulties facing child witnesses in a criminal trial have, of course, arisen in other jurisdictions. In the USA, for example, the Supreme Court in the landmark case of *Maryland* v. *Craig*[10] dealt with the Confrontation Clause of the Sixth Amendment to the Constitution. In a trial in a Maryland court the testimony of a six-year-old boy, an alleged child abuse victim, was received by one way closed circuit television. The procedure involved the child, the prosecutor and defence counsel withdrawing to another room where the child was examined and cross-examined. The judge, the jury and the defendant remained in the courtroom, where the testimony was displayed. Although the child could not see the defendant, the defendant remained in electronic communication with his counsel and objections could be made and ruled on as if the witness were in the courtroom.

It was argued in the Supreme Court that the procedures used violated the Sixth Amendment ("In all criminal prosecutions, the accused shall enjoy the right . . . to be confronted with the witnesses against him"). The Supreme Court held (by five to four) that the Confrontation Clause does not guarantee criminal

---

[10]   (1990) 497 US 836.

defendants an absolute right to a face-to-face meeting with the witnesses against them at the trial. The clause's central purpose, to ensure the reliability of the evidence against a defendant by subjecting it to rigorous testing in an adversarial proceeding, is served by the combined effects of the elements of confrontation: physical presence, oath, cross-examination, and observation of demeanour. Face-to-face confrontation is not an indispensable element of the confrontation right. If it were, the clause would abrogate virtually every hearsay exception, a result long rejected as unintended and too extreme. Maryland's interest in protecting child witnesses from the trauma of testifying in a child abuse case is sufficiently important to justify the use of its special procedure. In Canada, in the case of *R v. L (D O)*[11] a videotaped statement of a young complainant in a sexual abuse case was admitted in evidence. Objection was taken to it on the basis that it infringed the Canadian Charter of Rights and Freedoms because it offended against the admission of hearsay evidence and prior consistent statements. It also violated the right to direct cross-examination. On appeal, the Canadian Supreme Court held that the evidence was admissible as it did not offend against the Charter. The videotaping not only made the participation in the criminal justice system less stressful and traumatic for the child but also aided the preservation of evidence and the discovery of truth.

The Pigot Report

The Pigot Report published in December 1989 eloquently described[12] the stresses and strains facing the child witness:

> ". . . all the submissions which we received that addressed the matter indicated that most children are disturbed to a greater or lesser extent by giving evidence in court. The confrontation with the accused, the stress and embarrassment of speaking in public especially about sexual matters, the urgent demands of cross-examination, the overweening nature of courtroom facilities and the sense of insecurity and uncertainty induced by delays make this a harmful, oppressive and often traumatic experience. Moreover, because children are less clearly able to understand the reason for the demands which are placed upon them and have fewer developed intellectual and emotional resources than adults to help them cope with these, the effects are generally agreed to be peculiarly injurious and very often long-lasting".

The Report added[13] that:

> ". . . we are satisfied that a majority of children are adversely affected by giving evidence at trials for serious offences under existing circumstances. We attach particular importance to the psychiatric opinion we received which suggests that not only do abused children who testify in court exhibit more signs of disturbed behaviour than

[11] [1993] 4 SCR 419.
[12] See para 2.10 of the Report, *supra* n 1.
[13] See para 2.12 of the Report, *supra* n 1.

those who do not, but that the effects of a court appearance are most severe and pro-longed in those who have suffered the worst abuse and those without family support. We received evidence on this point from paediatricians, psychiatrists, social workers and a range of individuals with professional and voluntary responsibility for child care and the care of victims. This led us not only to endorse the case already explained for relieving the stress upon child witnesses, but also to wonder whether the nature and extent of the problem is fully comprehended by the legal profession and the wider pub-lic. We cannot emphasise strongly enough that those children who are clearly upset or who break down in the witness box simply manifest openly the effects of a much more generally harmful experience".

In view of their findings the Pigot Committee made radical recommendations. The most controversial was that the complete evidence of the child should be videotaped prior to the trial, so taking him or her out of the formal trial alto-gether. This so-called "full Pigot" met with, and continues to meet with strong opposition.[14] Section 32 of the Criminal Justice Act 1988 had allowed child wit-nesses to give oral evidence at the trial through a live video link. Following Pigot the Government produced the Criminal Justice Act 1991[15] which, subject to the judge's discretion and rules of court, permitted a videotaped interview of the child's evidence in chief to be shown at the trial in cases involving sexual offences or offences of violence or cruelty. However, crucially, it required the child to attend court for cross-examination many months later, thereby driving a coach and horses through the letter and spirit of the Pigot Report. In addition the leg-islation did not entitle the child witness as of right to use the video link or screen and did not provide for an "interlocutor" to relay questions from the advocates and the court as recommended in the report. A report from the Royal College of Psychiatrists in 1996[16] highlighted some medical and legal concerns: for instance, the adverse effect on the children who are interviewed when the video recordings are not subsequently used, the way in which children are interviewed, the delay in the hearing of the trial, whether the video link was an adequate protection for the child at trial, and the methods of cross-examination used at trial.

Almost a decade after the Pigot Report, following demands for further reforms, the Government produced the Youth Justice and Criminal Evidence Act 1999[17] which in Part II provides "Special Measures Directions" for "Vulnerable and Intimidated Witnesses",[18] including children. Some measures are new, others were already available. In specific circumstances (sections 16

[14] For discussions of the recommendations and the subsequent history, see for example, J R Spencer and R H Flin, *The Evidence of Children, The Law and the Psychology* (London, Blackstone, 2nd ed, 1993), ch 15; J Fortin, *Children's Rights and the Developing Law* (London, Butterworths, 1998), ch 18; and L Hoyano, "Variations on a Theme by Pigot: Special Measures Directions for Child Witnesses" [2000] *Crim LR* 250.

[15] S. 54 inserted a new s. 32A into the Criminal Justice Act 1988.

[16] *The Evidence of Children*, Council Report CR 44, Jan 1996, para 3.7.

[17] This was preceded by *Speaking up for Justice: Report of the Interdepartmental Working Group on the Treatment of Vulnerable or Intimidated Witnesses in the Criminal Justice System* (London, Home Office, 1998).

[18] For an analysis of the provisions, see L Hoyano, *supra* n 14.

and 17) a criminal court may direct that the following measures are taken: screening the witness from the accused (section 23); evidence by live link (section 24); evidence in private (section 25); removal of wigs and gowns (section 26); evidence in chief by pre-recorded videotape (section 27); pre-trial cross examination or re-examination by videotape (section 28); evidence of a witness through "an intermediary" (section 29); and "aids to communication" are used (section 30). Where a child witness under seventeen has to give evidence against a person accused of a sexual offence (but not other offences) the court will be obliged to make a "special measures direction" under section 28 unless the witness chooses to give live evidence (section 21). The 1999 Act has not in fact provided the full model envisaged by the Pigot Report except in child sexual abuse cases. It has, however, significantly moved matters on and it gives further recognition to the special needs of child witnesses.

The child witness and the criminal justice system: a view

Recent wide-ranging reforms, aimed at trying to reduce the trauma suffered by children giving evidence in the criminal courts, underline how little was done for so long. The welfare of the child has never been of primary importance in the criminal justice system. Suggested measures in the past which would have ameliorated the child's position were often firmly rejected because of a fear that they would undermine the rights of the accused. Increasing recognition of the child as a person in his or her own right, with rights, has in more recent times produced improvements. It is probably no coincidence that the late 1980's which brought the UN Convention on the Rights of the Child[19] and the Children Act 1989, also saw the setting up of the Pigot Committee. Although much ground needs to be covered before the special needs of the child are fully recognised in the criminal justice system, the plight of the child witness has received serious attention and further necessary reforms may ensue.

THE CHILD AND THE CRIMINAL TRIAL

The sensational trial at Preston Crown Court before a judge and jury in November 1993[20] of the then eleven-year-olds Jon Venables and Robert Thompson, for the abduction and murder of two-year-old Jamie Bulger, received national and international attention. Despite much lurid media coverage and extravagant comment, some serious attention eventually focused on the nature of their trial and its appropriateness for children. The debate about how the criminal justice system tries young children for serious crimes was stimulated

[19] 20 Nov 1989, New York; TS 44 [1992]; Cm 1976.
[20] *Supra*, n 3. See also D J Smith, *The Sleep of Reason* (London, Century, 1994); and B Morrison, *As If* (London, Granta Books, 1997).

by the boys' application under the European Convention on Human Rights[21] to Strasbourg, complaining that there had been in particular a breach of Article 6, in that they had not had a fair trial at Preston Crown Court before a judge and jury. Subsequently the European Court of Human Rights found in their favour on this aspect,[22] holding that they had been denied the opportunity to participate effectively in their trial, in particular to consult and instruct counsel and to understand the proceedings. This decision has had a significant effect on our domestic procedure and provides a useful yardstick to measure contemporary attitudes to children on trial in the criminal courts. Complaints about the sentencing process are met with mixed results.

The Bulger case

On 12 February 1993, when each defendant was aged ten, they played truant from school and abducted two-year-old Jamie Bulger from a shopping precinct. They took him on a journey of over two miles and then battered him to death and left him on a railway line to be run over. The defendants were subsequently arrested and stood trial before a judge and twelve jurors in an adult Crown Court. Prior to the trial the boys were taken by social workers to visit the courtroom and introduced to trial procedures and the people involved by the use of a "child witness pack" containing books and games. There was enormous national and international media coverage. Throughout the trial the arrival of the defendants was marked by a hostile crowd who on occasion tried to attack the vehicles bringing them to court. The courtroom was packed.

The full panoply of an adult criminal trial was modified to some extent in view of the defendants' age. They sat next to social workers in a specially raised dock and their parents and lawyers were seated nearby. The hearing was shortened and a ten minute interval was taken every hour. The defendants spent time during adjournments with their parents and social workers in a play area. On 24 November 1993 each defendant was convicted of murder and abduction and sentenced to detention during Her Majesty's pleasure. The judge recommended a minimum period of eight years to be served by the boys to satisfy the required "tariff" for retribution and deterrence.[23] No appeal was made to the Court of Appeal (Criminal Division) against conviction. Following conviction the judge modified an earlier order[24] and allowed the defendants' names, but no other details to be published.

---

[21] *Supra*, n 7.

[22] *V v. UK; T v. UK* (2000) 30 EHRR 121, para 89.

[23] This was later raised to 10 years by the then Lord Chief Justice, Lord Taylor, and further raised to 15 years by the then Home Secretary, Michael Howard. However, the latter decision was quashed by the House of Lords on judicial review, *supra* n 3. As a result of the decision of the European Court of Human Rights a new tariff has to be set, not by the Home Secretary, a politician, but by the present LCJ, Lord Woolf.

[24] Made under s 39(1) Children and Young Persons Act 1933.

The decisions of the European Court of Human Rights

The seventeen judges of the European Court of Human Court Rights rejected some of the complaints about the sentences passed. They decided that detention at Her Majesty's pleasure did not amount to inhuman or degrading treatment in breach of Article 3; nor did it violate the right to liberty and security under Article 5, paragraph 1 of the Convention. However, they were persuaded that there was a breach of Article 5, paragraph 4, the right to have the continuing lawfulness of detention decided by a court, and a breach of Article 6 in that the initial tariff had been decided upon by a politician, the Home Secretary, who could not be considered as independent of the executive; and there had been no opportunity subsequently for a judicial body to assess the lawfulness of the detention. The Court further found that the trial itself did not amount to degrading treatment under Article 3, but did amount to an unfair trial which breached Article 6, the right to a fair trial.[25]

THE UNFAIR TRIAL

The European Court of Human Rights noted that Article 6, read as a whole, guarantees the right of an accused to participate effectively in his criminal trial. It also observed that it was the first time it had been called upon to consider how this guarantee applies to criminal proceedings against children, and in particular whether procedures which are generally considered to safeguard the rights of adults on trial, such as publicity, should be abrogated in respect of children in order to promote their understanding and participation. The judges recognised that there was no clear common standard among the member States of the Council of Europe as to the minimum age of criminal responsibility. However they considered it essential that a child charged with an offence is dealt with in a manner which takes full account of his age, level of maturity and intellectual and emotional capacities, and that steps are taken to promote his ability to understand and participate in the proceedings. The Court considered it noteworthy that in England and Wales children charged with less serious crimes are dealt with in special youth courts, from which the general public is excluded and in relation to which there are imposed automatic reporting restrictions on the media. Moreover there was an international tendency towards the protection of the privacy of child defendants.[26]

---

[25] See paras 52 to 121 of the decision, *supra* n 22.

[26] See Art 40(2)(b) of the UN Convention on the Rights of the Child, *supra* n 19; and Rule 8 of the Beijing Rules (UN Standard Minimum Rules for the Administration of Juvenile Justice, 29 Nov 1985, General Assembly); Recommendation no. R(87)20 of the Committee of Ministers of the Council of Europe, adopted 17 September 1987, paras 5 and 8; and Art 8 of the European Convention on Human Rights, *supra* n 7.

Despite the special measures taken in the Crown Court, such as the pre-trial visit to the court and the shortened hearing times, the European Court took the view that "the formality and ritual of the Crown Court must at times have seemed incomprehensible and intimidating for children of eleven". It noted that certain modifications of the courtroom, in particular the raised dock which was designed to enable the defendants to see what was going on, had the effect of increasing the boys' sense of discomfort during the trial, since they felt exposed to the scrutiny of the press and the public. There was a high level of press and public interest both inside and outside the courtroom which caused problems. On occasions hostile crowds tried to attack the vehicles bringing the defendants to court. Both boys were suffering from post-traumatic stress disorder throughout the trial and had not had any therapeutic work since the offence. This limited their ability to follow the proceedings or participate.

The Court took the view that in all the circumstances it was not sufficient for the purposes of Article 6, paragraph 1, that the defendants were represented by skilled and experienced lawyers. In the tense courtroom and under public scrutiny it was highly unlikely that the boys would have felt able to consult with their lawyers during the trial or, because of their immaturity and their disturbed emotional state, to co-operate with them and give them instructions. Accordingly they were unable to participate effectively in the criminal proceedings and, in consequence there was a breach of Article 6. They did not seek damages but were awarded legal costs and expenses.

THE PRACTICE DIRECTION

Following the Strasbourg decision the Lord Chief Justice issued a Practice Direction[27] which took on board the observations of the European Court of Human Rights. In particular it provided for improving arrangements in the courtroom, explanations to the young defendant, frequent breaks where necessary, restricting public and media attendance at court, and the avoidance of exposure to abuse and intimidation when attending the trial. Subsequently in *McKerry v. Teesdale and Wear Valley Justices*,[28] the Lord Chief Justice said that the privacy of juveniles in legal proceedings, reflected in international instruments, had to be carefully protected, great weight being given to their welfare.

The continuing effect of the Strasbourg ruling has been seen in three particular cases. In the first a judge at Southwark Crown Court[29] refused to permit two twelve-year-old boys to face a jury trial in respect of allegations of indecently assaulting a thirteen-year-old girl. He cited the Strasbourg decision as applied to the individual circumstances of the case before him. In a second case five boys

[27] Trial of Children and Young Persons in the Crown Court, 16 Feb 2000.
[28] Queen's Bench Divisional Court, *The Times*, 29 Feb 2000.
[29] *The Guardian*, 14 Jan 2000.

accused of indecently assaulting two young girls had their case stayed because it would be too intimidating for them to face trial at the Old Bailey.[30] The judge said that in the light of the European Court decision, it would be an abuse of the boys' rights to put them on trial in an adult court. However, in a third case,[31] the Court of Appeal upheld a judge who had ruled that a child could be tried in an adult court despite defence submissions based on Articles 3 and 6 of the European Convention on Human Rights.[32] He had correctly exercised his discretion.

CONCLUSIONS

The Bulger case has clearly had a profound effect on the trial process for children. The unprecedented comments of the judges of the European Court of Human Rights, one of whom was British, have to some extent brought forward a more child-orientated procedure. It has rightly been said that the judgment is "significant for the treatment of all children in criminal trials because it recognises the difficulty children can have in understanding and participating in adult-focused adversarial court proceedings".[33] There is, however, no sign of the juvenile facing a serious charge being taken out of the Crown Court altogether, except on an individual basis and as an exercise of discretion. In not having specialised youth courts to deal with serious allegations we are out of line with many other countries such as Canada, Germany and Spain. The age of criminal responsibility, at ten years, is also significantly below most other countries.[34] A provision in the Children and Young Persons Act 1969 would have raised the age to fourteen, although not for homicide, but was never implemented and was repealed by the Criminal Justice Act 1991.

It is somewhat chastening that it was only events at the very end of the twentieth century that have precipitated some measure of reform of children's trials in the criminal courts. At least there has been some recognition of the special position of the child. Against this movement, however, has been the abolition[35] of the protection provided to ten to thirteen-year-olds by the presumption of *doli incapax*[36] for any offence committed on or after 30 September 1998, so putting the child in the same position as an adult, and the sentencing measures which put children as young as twelve at potential risk of incarceration in

---

[30] *The Times*, 1 Jun 2000.

[31] R v. C *(a Minor) The Times*, 5 Jul 2000.

[32] *Supra*, n 7.

[33] E Henderson, "The European Convention and Child Defendants" (2000) 59 *Cambridge Law Journal* 235 at 238.

[34] For example, in France it is 13, in Germany, Austria and Italy 14, in Scandinavia 15 and Spain 16 (in Scotland it is 8).

[35] By s. 34 Crime and Disorder Act 1998.

[36] Formerly at trial the prosecution had to prove, not only the facts of the allegation, but that the child knew that what had occurred was seriously wrong and not merely naughty or mischievous.

children's prisons. Indeed an apparent inclination on occasion to treat the child as if he or she was an adult is a disturbing feature of the last few years.

The Bulger case and a general public alarm about juvenile offending has produced mixed consequences. It is instructive that the main reforming initiative affecting the trial process has come from an external source in Strasbourg. It was long overdue, although seemingly not welcomed in some quarters. It highlights the strong disinclination here to grant children all the protection their young age and stage of development merits. Now that the European Convention on Human Rights is part of our domestic law[37] and some more attention is being paid to the UN Convention on the Rights of the Child,[38] there may be some hope that there will be more respect for the fact and disabilities of childhood and a more tolerant and understanding attitude. A recent Justice Report *Children and Homicide*,[39] for example, recommended that the age of criminal responsibility should be re-examined, and that children under fourteen should not be liable for public trial in adult criminal courts, but should be tried in private so that their identities are protected, and only the facts of the case and the sentence are made public.[40] In the case of children accused of homicide or other crimes which might now fall to be tried in a Crown Court, it was suggested that the proceedings be heard before "a specially convened panel of a judge and two magistrates with relevant experience and training".[41] Children are entitled to look for a fundamental re-assessment of the criminal justice system which is more attuned to their rights and responsibilities. It is long overdue.

[37] Human Rights Act 1998.
[38] *Supra*, n 19.
[39] February 1996.
[40] See paras 7.2 and 7.3.
[41] Para 7.3.

7

Law, Literature and the Child

IAN WARD

CHILDREN AND LITERATURE

THE INTERDISCIPLINARY STUDY of law and literature has emerged as one of the most dynamic and challenging of contemporary approaches to legal study. In this chapter, we will take a particular look at the situation of children and law within literature, and within one particular and canonical source, William Shakespeare. In doing so, we will necessarily enjoin an ongoing debate with regard to the ability of literature to both describe, and constitute, imagined conceptions of ideality. Such images, it is suggested, play a crucial role in the process of constructing individual identities within political communities; a process of especial pertinence to the education of children. In his *Sources of the Self*, Charles Taylor sought to establish a sense of civic identity, and responsibility, on the premise that "we grasp our lives in a narrative". The liberating potential of self-identity is released by our participation in the dialogues which describe our situations within established political communities.[1] Accordingly, individuals, and communities, can only refashion themselves if they enjoy a proper appreciation of the historical and literary formation of central social conceptions, such as the "law" or the "child".

In similar vein, Martha Nussbaum has emphasised the critical relation between identity formation and education. The ambition of a liberal education, she suggests, must be one which seeks to liberate the "mind from the bondage of habit and custom" and which can then produce "citizens who can function with sensitivity and alertness". A "community is formed by author and readers", and the morality of such a community is fashioned by the dialogic interaction between citizens. Education, she notes, has always been dedicated to the translation of "ideal" images into "real" political conceptions, through the medium of literary texts. Accordingly, literature has always played the "vital" role of "cultivating powers of imagination that are essential to citizenship".[2] It is an observation which again has a particular pertinence for any study of

---

[1] C Taylor, *Sources of the Self: The Making of Modern Identity* (Cambridge, Cambridge University Press, 1989), p 47.

[2] M Nussbaum, *Cultivating Humanity: A Classical Defense of Reform in Liberal Education* (Massachusetts, Harvard University Press, 1997), pp ix, 8–11, 85–6.

children's literature; for there is no genre of literature which enjoys a comparable capacity to define the imagination of the putative citizen.

In general terms, "law and literature" is commonly defined by two particular approaches. First, there is law *as* literature, which seeks to suggest that law is a literary entity, meaning something which is subject to the various rules of dialogue and interpretation. In other words, the study of law, its theory and its application, must be undertaken within the terms of literary theory and criticism. Secondly, there is law *in* literature, which looks at the portrayal of law in literary texts. While this demarcation enjoys the benefits of convenience, it must be remembered that the study of any literary text necessarily enjoins both law *as* and law *in* literature. Both the "child" and the "law" are imagined conceptions described *as* literature and *in* literature. Accordingly, in this chapter, there are two issues of immediate concern; first, how do children read literature, particularly that which includes legal or political commentary, and secondly, within these texts, how are children portrayed in relation to law? In other words, in texts that are to be read by children, what is the ideology of the text and how is the imagination of the child to be fashioned?[3]

The particular study of children's literature, like law and literature, is very much an emerging discipline. Indeed, much of the debate surrounds the issue of whether children's literature can be determined as a discrete discipline. The perceived simplicity of language has tended to lead to its diminution as a distinct genre. Of course, the determination of children's literature is not easy, primarily because of the inherent instability of defining what "children" are.[4] The demise of authorial intent, in literary theory in general, has militated against a determination on the grounds of what the writer may think, while the inadequacy of determining children's literature from the text itself has also been repeatedly alleged.[5] Style is a more viable possibility, and Nicholas Tucker has suggested that if "a writer is aiming at a young audience" he or she must concentrate on "certain" necessarily limited "areas of experience and vocabulary".[6] The most obvious such area, of course, is that of the struggle for self-determination over and against patriarchal authority; a theme which, as we shall shortly see, provides the essential frame for Shakespeare's treatment of children and the law.

Concentration on the experience of the child reader has consolidated a belief that children's literature, like any literary genre, is defined by its audience. According to Peter Hunt, children's literature "uniquely" defines itself in terms of its audience. Thus "classic" children's texts are defined less as classic because

---

[3] For a discussion of the various approaches to "law and literature", see I Ward, *Law and Literature: Possibilities and Perspectives* (Cambridge, Cambridge University Press, 1995), ch 1.

[4] For a general discussion of these definitional problems, see A Hunt, *Criticism, Theory and Children's Literature* (Oxford, Blackwell, 1991), pp 5–6, 21, 60.

[5] See Felicity Hughes's observations, in A Hunt (ed), *Children's Literature* (London, Routledge, 1990), p 60.

[6] N Tucker, *Suitable for Children: Controversies in Children's Literature* (Falmer, Sussex University Press, 1976), pp 18–19.

of their being "better" than other texts, but because they are more ideologically "useful".[7] While it may be different in terms of audience and utility, children's literature is subject to the same critical and intellectual fashions which vie for control of the literary academy. Unsurprisingly, given its tendency to determine itself in relation to audience, theories of the "reader-response" type have proved popular in children's literature criticism. Lissa Paul has tried to advance a semiotics of children's literature, while Peter Hunt has referred to "oral discourse markers" which can be used as "signifiers" in children's literature. According to such a thesis, developed from orthodox "sign-system" theories, the child reader is led through a text, from one signpost to "correct" meaning to another.[8]

Of course, there is the ever-present danger of over-intellectualism in all areas of literary theory. A century ago, the likes of Dickens, Ruskin and Chesterton were warning of the particular dangers of the moralising intellectual. More recently, Peter Hollindale advised that the attempt to intellectualise a genre of children's literature is often merely an attempt to replace one ideology with another.[9] Yet, even here, in the advice against a ready identification of a genre of children's literature, critics are unavoidably joining a critical position which suggests that words are power. Peter Hunt has suggested that the linguistic style of C S Lewis presents a particularly good "example of the covert control of the audience so common in children's books". For Hunt, children's literature presents a "very obvious power relationship between writer and reader".[10] Relatedly, the peculiar relation between children and women has been commonly noted. Both have consistently suffered silencing and exclusion through subjection to "closed" texts; texts which do not invite the constructive participation of the female or child reader, but which seek to pre-establish certain conceptual and thematic "rules".[11]

Words present power, and a child audience is a particularly receptive and impressionable one. According to Hollindale, there is an implicit "passive" ideology in all children's literature. At the same time, there are also "constraints" upon this ideology, represented by the need to write within specific contexts which the child can understand. It is not, then, a matter of recapturing children's literature for the cause of modern democracy, but more a matter of recognising the ever-presence of ideology rather than seeking either to constrain or to promote it.[12] Once it is recognised that meaning can be "fragmented" between readers, then children's texts can both subjugate and liberate; any text can.[13] The inevitability of this "fragmentation" has been strongly argued by

[7] Hunt, *supra* n 4, pp 44–64.

[8] Deconstructionism has also attracted its supporters among students of children's literature. See L Paul, "Intimations of Imitations", in A Hunt (ed), *Literature for Children: Contemporary Criticism*, (London, Routledge, 1992), pp.66–77, and Hunt, *supra* n 4, pp 9, 66, 105–17.

[9] P Hollindale, "Ideology and the Children's Book" in Hunt (ed), *supra* n 5, pp 24–5.

[10] Hunt, *supra* n 4, p 109, and Hunt (ed), *supra* n 5, p 18.

[11] For a commentary, see L Paul, "Enigma Variations: What Feminist Theory Knows About Children's Literature", (1987) 54 *Signal* 1987 at 186–201.

[12] Hollindale, 'Ideology and the Children's Book' in Hunt (ed), *supra* n 5, pp 19–40.

[13] Hunt, *supra* n 4, pp 151–4.

New Historicists, who have concentrated on the hermeneutic model of interpretive understanding. Here, rather than resting with any ultimate authority, the meaning of any text is dependent upon the interplay of author, text and audience. Such a thesis stresses the historicity of language, the characterisation of society as the expression of power struggles, the socio-cultural nature of the subjective, the nature of reading as a communicative discourse, and above all the centrality of ideology in all children's texts.

According to Tony Watkins, the child's identity is determined by a narrative and communicative experience. "Stories", he suggests, "contribute to the formation and re-formation in our children of the cultural imagination". Such an imagination represents a "network" of "patterns and templates through which we articulate our experience". Accordingly, "the stories we tell our children, the narratives we give them to make sense of cultural experience, constitute a kind of mapping, maps of meaning that enable our children to make sense of the world". Above all, they "contribute to children's sense of identity, an identity that is simultaneously personal and social: narratives, we might say, shape the way children find a 'home' in the world".[14] It is, perhaps, the most compelling of all theses in contemporary children's literature scholarship, and it is one which is particularly pertinent for this chapter, and its necessarily historical engagement with Shakespeare; the Shakespeare of the sixteenth and seventeenth centuries, and the Shakespeare of today's child audience.

THE POLITICS OF PATRIARCHY

Before embarking upon a discussion of certain Shakespearean texts, and their treatment of the relation between children and the law, it is necessary to establish an immediate context. The family was the central unit of government in early modern England. Accordingly, the running of a good household, founded upon the harmony of marriage and family, was not just desirable for the greater good of the commonwealth. It was a matter of honour. Any man who misruled an unruly household and permitted a woman or a child to destabilise it was without honour. According to Richard Brathwaite: "As every man's house is his castle, so is his family a private commonwealth, wherein if due government be not observed nothing but confusion is to be expected".[15]

The family was commonly perceived to be a micro-constitutional model. Sir Robert Filmer described his constitutional polity in terms of a family. His *Patriarcha* was established on an image of ideal government which, at both macro and micro levels, was founded upon a common familial model: "as the

---

[14] T Watkins, "Cultural Studies, New Historicism and Children's Literature" in Hunt (ed), *supra* n 8, p 183.

[15] See A Fletcher, *Sex, Gender and Subordination in England 1500–1800* (Yale University Press, 1995), pp 139, 205, 380–1.

father over one family so the king, as father over many families, extends his care to preserve, feed, clothe, instruct and defend the whole commonwealth". Filmer's theory of absolute sovereignty was founded upon the Biblical idea of Adamic succession; authority had passed, since the Genesis, from one supreme patriarch to another. It is the "secret will of God".[16] Sir Thomas Smith similarly believed that the beginnings of a godly commonwealth lay in the family, the "first and most natural beginning and source of cities, towns, nations, kingdoms, and of all civil societies".[17] Thus, the matter of regulating families is a matter of government. According to Jean Bodin, "all will be well with the commonwealth where families are properly regulated", while Thomas Cromwell informed the clergy in his *Injunctions* of 1536, that the well governed family was the "great commodity and ornament of the commonweal".[18]

The root of the cultural model of the ideal family was, of course, theological. The Nowell catechism, dedicated to explicating a social and political interpretation of the "godly word", was clear: "For by the name of parents, we are charged not only to yield and obey to magistrates, but also to honour and love them. And likewise, on the other part, superiors are taught so to govern their inferiors, as a just parent useth to rule over good children".[19] The propagation of children was the only justification for copulation, and while for some the child served to remind adults of their fallen sinful status, for others, the perfection of the child could serve to purge the adult of this sinfulness. As Sir Simonds D'Ewes observed: "Parents are especially bound to instruct the children, pray for them and train them up in fear of God because they drew original corruption from their loins".[20]

The education of children was, thus, central to the Protestant image of the ideal family. John Downame referred to the family as a "seminary of the church and commonwealth, and as a private school, wherein children and servants are fitted for public assemblies". The great prescriber of puritan family values, William Gouge, described that godly family as "a little commonwealth", a "school wherein the first principles and grounds of government and subjection are learned".[21] According to the Puritan commentator, William Perkins, the only purpose of marriage, "ordained of God in paradise", was to procreate children for the service of God. Government of the family, thus, becomes more than merely a matter of civic responsibility. It was also the mark of godly status. The "elect" ran ordered families, with subjugated wives and perfected children. In

---

[16] R Filmer, *Patriarcha and Other Writings* (Cambridge, Cambridge University Press, 1991), pp 1–2, 7–11.

[17] In S Amussen, *An Ordered Society:Gender and Class in Early Modern England* (Oxford, OUP, 1988), p 199.

[18] In P Collinson, *The Birthpangs of Protestant England* (London, Macmillan, 1988), p 60.

[19] In E Talbert, *The Problem of Order: Elizabethan Political Commonplaces and an Example of Shakespeare's Art* (University of North Carolina Press, 1962), p 15.

[20] In Fletcher, *supra* n 15, p 207.

[21] *Ibid*, pp 204–5.

the 1650s, the Calvinist divine, Richard Baxter, urged that a new commonwealth of the godly should be founded on the reformed family.[22]

In the context of such cultural and political capital which attached to the ideal of patriarchal government, the perceived crisis in family government took on almost hysterical proportions. "Was there ever seen less obedience in youth of all sorts", Philip Stubbes inquired, "both menkind and womenkind, towards their superiors, parents, masters and governors?".[23] The evidence seemed to be compelling. During the 1590s, it was repeatedly reported that children played in the yard of St Pauls, broke windows and disturbed services. At Wimborne in 1629, churchwardens lamented that "our church and the seats thereof have often been beastly abused and profaned by uncivil children". At Exeter Cathedral, in 1658, a cage was erected in which unruly children could be placed during services. Anxieties were not reserved to ecclesiastical authorities. In 1651, the London Grocer's Company complained of the "resort and confluence of boyes and children to play, wherefore the windowes are broken, and other prejudice and damage about the Hall and Garden". Roaming children, like roaming vagabonds in general, provided immediate and public evidence of a perceived social crisis. In 1663, one observer commented: "It must needs pity any Christian heart, to see the little dirty Infantry, which swarms up and down in Alleys and Lanes, with curses and ribaldry in their mouths, and other ill rude behaviour".[24]

The unruly child was one of two overriding hazards to good patriarchal government. The other was the unruly woman. King James I blamed nagging women for the destabilisation of provincial government.[25] Popular contemporary literature was obsessed by shrews. The unquiet woman, according to Nicholas Breton, was "the misery of man", for "she looks at no law and thinks of no lord, admits no command and keeps no good order". Of course, the law was employed precisely to restore social order and the image of patriarchal authority. Thus, in 1620, for example, Ann Weekes of Langridge was presented as a "common scold, a raiser of idle reports and fames, and a common sewer and breeder of discord between her neighbours".[26] The marginalisation of women was always most acute in the institutions of state, and most acute of all, in the doctrines of the Church. Tydale's *Obedience of a Christian Man*, affirmed that women, being "that weak vessel", were put by God, "under the obedience" of husbands. The Puritan commentator, William Gouge, confirmed that the

[22] R Baxter, *The Holy Commonwealth* (Cambridge, Cambridge University Press, 1994), pp 115–6, 205–7. For a commentary, see K Wrightson, *English Society 1580–1680* (London, Routledge, 1982), p 67.
[23] In D Underdown, *Revel, Riot and Rebellion: Popular Politics and Culture in England 1603–1660* (Oxford, OUP, 1987), p 116.
[24] For a commentary on these examples, and others, see K Thomas, "Children in Early Modern England" in G Avery and J Briggs (eds), *Children and Their Books: A Celebration of the Work of Iona and Peter Opie* (Oxford, OUP, 1989), pp 53–5.
[25] See C Hill, *Society and Puritanism in Pre-Revolutionary England* (Harmondsworth, Penguin, 1991), p 444.
[26] Both in Underdown, *supra* n 23, p 119.

husband and father, is a "Priest unto his wife and children", the "highest in the family, and hath both authority over all and the charge of all is committed to his charge; he is as a king in his own house".[27]

The contemporary perception that both women and children were becoming ever more disruptive caused widespread consternation in early modern England. As Antony Fletcher has observed, it was commonly felt that society "as a whole" was "tottering towards dissolution".[28] Given the identified problems of unruly women and unruly children, it is unsurprising that the figure of the unruly female child was one of particular horror and repugnance. The root cause of a shrewish woman, it was commonly agreed, lay in weak parenting, and the inability to control their necessarily "lustful imaginations"; imaginations which, as Helkiah Crooke affirmed, "have no repugnance or contradiction of reason to restrain them".[29] Only the reason of men could constrain the potentially destructive irrationality of young women.

The example of this irrationality most commonly visited in contemporary literature, was the propensity of young women to fall in love. Young men, of course, also fell in love, but their fate was more generally described in terms of their susceptibility to female wiles. The idea that women should choose their partners, for reasons of love or anything else, threatened social dislocation at many levels, not least the economic one, which saw women as marketable commodities to be traded, for the benefit of the entire family unit, on the marriage market.[30] Marriages perceived to be outwith established class and interest demarcations caused widespread criticism. Queen Elizabeth famously monitored marriages involving her courtiers in order to ensure that matches were socially and economically suitable. It was commonly felt that only matches between partners from families which enjoyed social consonance could themselves be settled and harmonious. Of course, it was quite acceptable to fall in love with all sorts of unsuitable matches, even to indulge in affairs and liaisons. Those given to reading Spenser or Sidney, or, of course, Shakespeare, could scarcely think otherwise. But it was entirely unacceptable for any child, male or female, to disobey patriarchal injunctions as to marriage.

SHAKESPEARE'S CHILDREN

This figure of the unruly young woman is of particular interest in the context of this chapter, because, as has been commonly noted, Shakespeare seems to have been particularly obsessed with the relation between incompetent or insensitive

[27] See Fletcher, *supra* n 15, p 74, Wrightson, *English Society*, *supra* n 22, p 90, and Hill, *supra* n 25, pp 443–6.

[28] Fletcher, *supra* n 15 p 109.

[29] *Ibid*, pp 71–2.

[30] As Lawrence Stone has emphasised, a series of ill-conceived matches could ultimately destroy an aristocratic or even middle-class family. See his *The Crisis of the Aristocracy* (Oxford, OUP, 1967), pp 285–91.

fathers and rebellious, self-assertive, daughters. Kate Chedgzoy has recently re-
iterated the Freudian interpretation of Shakespeare; one which sees the author
constantly attempting to mediate the necessarily destructive urge of the child to
self-determine. For Freud the epitome of such a destructive urge was the Oedipal
relationship between Hamlet and his mother. But the thesis, according to
Chedgzoy, is equally applicable for father-daughter relationships; the most obvious example being the destruction which is visited upon Lear and Cordelia.[31]

In many ways, *Lear* is indeed the most pertinent example of the disaster which
can befall a dysfunctional family; a fate which is writ still larger by the fact that
this is a royal family. When asked to define the extent of her love for her father,
Cordelia talks in strictly legal terms, of "bonds" and "duties" (1.1.90–106). Law
does not admit the emotions of love and family. Cordelia is trapped by her
unwillingness to indulge in hypocrisy. Shakespearean England, as we have
already noted, was one which defined familial relations in precisely such terms;
as matters of bond and duties. Of course, in terms of private relations, it was
quite permissible to talk in terms of love and affection. Indeed, it was expected.
But Cordelia refuses to subscribe to such a deceit; one which presents a public
face of duties in order to mask a private face of love. Lear, as king, is the representative of a political culture dedicated to this deception, and he cannot then
expect his daughters to make public gestures which do not subscribe to precisely
this culture. Cordelia plays by the rhetorical rules of family engagement which
Lear, as king, has sought to enforce.[32]

Of course, *Lear* does not seem, at least at first glance, to be a piece of children's literature. Indeed, in an immediate sense, Shakespeare would not appear
to be a children's writer at all, while his plays, the complexity of which have baf-
fled generations of adults, would not be readily defined as children's literature.
Yet, if the determinant of a literary genre does indeed lie with the audience of
readers, then Shakespeare is one of the most influential of all authors encountered by children. Given the demands of the national curriculum, there are few
children in the UK who do not encounter Shakespeare at some point in their
education. Indeed, most will read more Shakespeare at school than any other
writer. Moreover, as we shall note in the final part of this chapter, before they
arrive at the "real" Shakespeare, they will already have encountered a number
of pre-school Shakespeares; in pop-up books, cartoon and fairy-tale form, and so
on. In these terms, Shakespeare is very definitely a writer of children's literature.

[31] K Chedgzoy, *Shakespeare's Queer Children: Sexual Politics and Contemporary Culture*
(Manchester, Manchester University Press, 1995), pp 7–9, 33–6, 55–7.

[32] A continuing debate surrounds the question of whether the deceit can be overcome. In his sem-
inal *Shakesperean Tragedy*, Bradley suggested that the destruction of the family, and particularly
the fates of Lear and Cordelia, do not lead to any suggested redemptive. They are indeed quite point-
less. Wilson Knight, on the other hand, in his *The Wheel of Fire*, preferred to think that they are
both redeemed ultimately by love, and the appreciation that it cannot be suppressed by political for-
malism. See A Bradley, *Shakespearean Tragedy* (London, Macmillan, 1992), lectures 7 and 8, and
G Wilson Knight, *The Wheel of Fire: Interpretations of Shakespearian Tragedy* (London,
Routledge, 1995), pp 193–202.

Less immediately dour than tragedies such as *Lear*, the romantic comedies can be more readily situated within a genre of children's literature, of fairy-tales and fantastic stories, love affairs and, in general at least, happy endings. Certainly, in their *Tales from Shakespeare*, Charles and Mary Lamb saw fit to concentrate on these plays as more readily translatable to a young audience, and this tendency has persisted into the twentieth century. Yet, as in *Lear*, in a number of these comedies the catalyst for the various adventures which befall the primary characters lies in a singular act of disobedience to patriarchal injunction. One of the most immediate examples is *A Midsummer Night's Dream*. Written for a courtly audience, and riven with allusions to Queen Elizabeth, the *Dream* is one of Shakespeare's most fantastic romances. It is, as Duke Theseus admits, a world of ideals and dreams, a "rite of May" (4.1.132). As Barber recognised, in his pioneering study of the romantic comedies, it is the epitome of the sequential structure of disobedience, followed by disorder, followed by a restoration of harmony.[33]

The initial act of disobedience is immediately jurisprudential. The play opens with Egeus demanding that Theseus enforce the civil law against his daughter, Hermia, and her suitor, Lysander. Lysander has "bewitch'd" Hermia with "rhymes" and "love-tokens", such that she now refuses to obey her father's order that she marry Demetrius. The "ancient privilege" of Athens, by definition a common law of the realm, allows the father to demand the "death" of a child who disobeys a specific injunction to marry (1.1.22–45). In appealing to Theseus, Hermia seeks recourse to justice. But Theseus is unmoved, merely willing to commute the sentence of death to internal exile in a nunnery (1.1.58–66). Hermia is subject to an unjust law, but a law all the same; just as she appears to be subject to an unjust father, but one who still enjoys the patriarchal authority which attached to sixteenth century theories of family government. As Theseus observes, there is no public-private distinction in Athens. The law is pervasive, and so the resolution of Egeus's family dispute becomes a matter of concern for the stability of the wider commonwealth itself (1.1.116–21).

Faced with such a fate, Hermia and Lysander flee beyond the jurisdiction of Athens, to the woods and into the political imagination. As Freud noted, children seeking to rationalise disobedience do so by projecting alternative ideal images of legitimate authority. But the fairy world into which they venture is one which, despite its initial attractions, quickly appears to be itself dislocated. The queen of the fairies, Titania, is in open defiance of her husband, Oberon, and the realm has descended into chaos. Ultimately, the run-aways return to Athens and submit themselves to Theseus's will. Somewhat belatedly, Theseus exercises his sovereign prerogative to "overbear" Egeus's "will", and secures harmony through the marriage of the two couples (4.1.178). In doing so, it has been suggested that Theseus represents something of an ideal Shakespearean

---

[33] C Barber, *Shakespeare's Festive Comedy: A Study of Dramatic Form and its Relation to Social Custom* (Princeton University Press, 1959), pp 119–62.

magistrate, able to mitigate the harshness of the common law by judicious exercise of his prerogative. The balance of law and prerogative founds the law of the constitution, just as the assertion of patriarchal authority, which Theseus is also able to resecure, founds the well-ordered commonwealth.[34]

Most important of all, perhaps, Theseus appreciates that good government is about governing the imagination, at least insofar as it can be governed. The "gentle concord of the world" will be "triumphantly" restored by reasserting authority within the "strong imaginations" of the audience, and the institutions which are immediately dedicated to facilitating precisely this are the family and marriage (4.1.86–9, 142). Patriarchy will be reasserted, the balance between the public and private reasserted through its complementarity, and then sealed by Theseus's own marriage. As he noted in the very first scene, marriage is the "everlasting bond of friendship" which must be sealed by the threatre of "pomp, with triumph, and with revelling" (1.1.19, 85). The celebration of marriage, the ceremonial assertion of patriarchy, is not something which is merely enjoyed by a private family. Rather it is a public event dedicated to preserving the stability of the commonwealth. The play closes with Oberon dedicating his fairy-land to preserving the harmony of the commonwealth of Athens and its constituent family units, and sealing this harmony through the regenerative potential of the marriage bed (5.1.389–408).

While the *Dream* is commonly acknowledged to be one of Shakespeare's lightest romances, others suggest a rather darker side to juvenile disobedience. Helena in *All's Well That Ends Well* is probably the most self-assertive of all Shakespeare's disobedient children. She ridicules the court, which she comes to as an outsider, refuses to accept any proposed matches, and rejects any received notions of natural or civil order. "Our remedies in ourselves do lie", she advises, "Which we ascribe to heaven" (1.1.212–50). Yet, Helena is a conspicuously poor judge of marital material, and so attracted to an idiot courtier that she is willing to disobey all parental and sovereign injunctions. In one sense, as Helena declares at the close, all that "ends well" is well. But it is clear that all is far from well at the end of the play, and the future security of the French court remains decidedly uncertain. Happy endings are only ever superficial, and never removed from the vicissitudes of real life, or the potentially destructive urges of self-willed children.

There is certainly no happy ending in *Romeo and Juliet*, a play in which the idea of the family unit as the key constituent of public politics is placed in direct contradiction with dynamics of private affection. The natural force of love challenges the apparently unnatural force of patriarchal authority, and the resultant dynamic threatens to destabilise an entire commonwealth. Patriarchy appears to provide a thin veneer of civility masking a primitive and brutal society in which the redemptive qualities of youth and of love struggle to survive, and are

---

[34] L Montrose, "Shaping Fantasies: Figurations of Gender and Power in Elizabethan Culture" (1983) 1 *Representations* 1983, 85.

ultimately exterminated. The play closes with the Duke and the other ageing representatives of patriarchy noting the destruction of their progeny, and with it the potential for regeneration. Not least distressing is the Duke's admission that the responsibility for failing to recognise the need to nurture youth in order to channel its energies away from private dispute and towards public harmony, lies with him in his capacity as the supreme civil magistrate. The whole commonwealth is "punish'd" by a patriarchy unable to appreciate that the government of any family must be dedicated to the well-being of the entire community (5.3.294).

While not as immediately tragic as *Romeo and Juliet*, another distinctly ambiguous story of a child's disobedience seemingly crushed by patriarchal forces, is *The Taming of the Shrew*. The brutality with which Kate is "tamed" led George Bernard Shaw to exclaim that "no man of any decency of feeling" could be anything but "extremely ashamed".[35] Kate, like Juliet, and Hermia in the *Dream*, represents the particular threat of a disobedient female child. Although it is emphasised that she has advanced beyond the recognised age of marriage, she remains bound to the authority of her father. Indeed, the essential theme of the play is that she will only escape his authority when she transfers to that of another patriarch. The entire play is set within a play, performed for the education of Sly, an aspiring patriarch (Ind.1.134–6). With the seeming exception of Petruchio, the play is beset with inept patriarchs who consistently fail to appreciate that marriage is a public institution, and, accordingly, that it is the duty of the father to secure a match that will prove to be harmonious and thus secure. Coppelia Kahn has convincingly argued that Kate's disobedience is not against patriarchy, but against incompetent patriarchs. Kate understands the responsibilities of parenting far better than her father, who is readily tempted by "desperate" matches (2.1.320). It is this realisation which forces Kate to attempt to determine her own marital fortunes in order to secure her own future family.[36]

The submission that Kate ultimately makes, and which so shocked Shaw, must be seen within this context. In submitting to Petruchio, she submits to an ideal patriarch; ideal in that he appreciates the theatrical responsibilities of patriarchalism. She does not submit directly to her father, who remains studiously incompetent. Her submission is then conditional, upon the good performance of Petruchio's duties. As Peter affirms, harmony will follow from their mutual appreciation of each other's theatrical competence (4.1.167). Moreover, it is a very public submission, because, once again, the restoration of harmony in familial matters is a matter of public recognition and celebration. The placing of Kate's hand under Petruchio's foot, which echoes a tradition which was

---

[35] In L Boose, "Scolding Brides and Bridling Scolds: Taming the Woman's Unruly Member" (1991) 42 *Shakespeare Quarterly* 1991, 179.

[36] See C Kahn, "*The Taming of the Shrew*: Shakespeare's Mirror of Marriage" (1975) 5 *Modern Language Studies* 1975, 89.

all but dead by Shakespeare's time, is employed to further emphasise the theatricality of the submission. Kate is submitting to an entire culture; one which places demands upon both patriarch and putative matriarch.[37]

The idea of ultimate conformity in a previously unruly child reaches its epitome in the much-debated "fashioning" of Prince Hal. It has been suggested that the maturing of the young Hal, into the future "image of all Christian Princes", *Henry V*, represents the classic evolution of the young, potentially unruly child, into the adult representation of political and social conformity. Against this, it has also been suggested that Hal's conformity is in fact an illusion. Appreciating that any conformity is merely a matter of appearances, Hal merely seems to conform in order to secure the throne. Indeed, his greatest strength, as becomes apparent in *Henry V*, is an appreciation that all the various structures of magistracy are ultimately illusory, dependent upon a necessarily tenuous hold on the political imagination.[38]

At the outset of the first part of *Henry IV*, Hal is engaged in the festive world of "misrule", dedicated to drinking and various forms of minor criminality with the "good lads" of Eastcheap. His patriarchal figure here is not his father, the king, but Falstaff, the "lord of misrule". It is Falstaff who urges the young prince to turn the world upside down once he is king, making it a commonwealth in which thieves are no longer hanged (1.2.59–60).[39] From the very beginning of the sequence of plays, in act 1 scene 2 of the first part of *Henry IV*, Hal reminds his audience that he is playing a role, and so the critical ambiguity is set. Later, Warwick confirms that the young man is being educated in the art of government. He "but studies his companions/ Like a strange tongue, wherein, to gain in language/ 'Tis needful that the most immodest word/ Be look'd upon and learnt" (4.4.74–8). The implication is clear; as Hal learns the arts of government, and self-determination, he will shake off his patriarchal models and fashion his own. "Presume not", Hal advises the audience at the close of part one, "that I am the thing that I was" (5.5.56).

The second part of *Henry IV* sees Hal submit to the authority figures of his father and the Lord Chief Justice, to patriarchy and to the law (5.1.73–101). Yet, the submission, as we have already noted, is fatally wounded by the haunting knowledge that Hal knows how to deceive. If he can flirt with anarchy, as in Eastcheap, and then turn against, as he did against Falstaff, the same might be the case with regard to formal justice. No child, it seems, can ever be depended

---

[37] For a commentary, see Boose, *supra* n 35 at 182–4.

[38] For the classically sceptical interpretation of Hal's "fashioning", see S Greenblatt, "Invisible Bullets: Renaissance Authority and Subversion in *Henry IV* and *Henry V*", in J Dollimore and A Sinfield (eds), *Political Shakespeare: New Essays in Cultural Materialism* (Manchester, Manchester University Press, 1985), pp 18–47, and N Rabkin, "Rabbits, Ducks and *Henry V*" (1997) 28 *Shakespeare Quarterly*, 279–96. I have discussed these alternative theories in I Ward, "A Kingdom for a Stage, Princes to Act: Shakespeare and the Art of Government" (1997) 8 *Law and Critique*, 189–213.

[39] According to Barber, Hal's engagement with the world of misrule is necessary if he is to gain experience of all the constituents of the commonwealth over which he will later rule. See Barber, *supra* n 33, pp 192–219.

upon not to strike against patriarchal authority, no matter how theatrical and public their submission. Hal's anxiety to seize the crown, and the corresponding lack of emotional affinity with his dying father, serves to enhance the feeling that relations within the royal family are far from ideal or harmonious. Moreover, what is most striking about *Henry V* is the absence of family, or even familial remembrance. Indeed, not only does Henry abandon his family, as he had his surrogate family in Eastcheap, but he abandons his commonwealth in order to seek glory as the ideal imaginary Christian prince. The public persona of the patriarch entirely obliterates the private.

What is most striking about the wooing of Princess Katherine, aside from the extent to which it is couched in terms of the ridiculous, is the absence of any expression of affection which is not cast in terms of duty. Henry is proud of his inability to express his affections. It is quintessentially English. More worryingly, he seems to view patriarchal responsibility in pretty much the same terms as Lear; a matter of "duty", "bond" and "articles". It is not him that Henry urges Katherine to marry, but England. Katherine, in turn, only agrees to the match if her father approves it. She too conforms. At no time does she ever protest the slightest affection for Henry. Moreover, once she has conceded that she is willing to obey her father's injunction, Katherine is completely silenced. She plays no further part in proceedings, merely listening to her father and future husband discuss the political implications of the match. Of course, this is entirely as it should be, at least in the orthodox early modern conception. The French king closes by affirming that the match, dedicated as it must be, to procreation, will ultimately produce a child who will unite the two hitherto warring countries (5.2.366–73). There is, however, a final and crushing ambiguity, for, as the Chorus immediately suggests, the product of their marital alliance will be the weak, sickly, ultimately insane, Henry VI; a king during whose rule England will "bleed" much and lose all of his father's conquests (Ch.5.2.9–12). The image of ideal patriarchy guarantees nothing.

READING SHAKESPEARE

For centuries children have been educated into conformity, at school and at home. The forms of education can be various. Exposure to literature is just one of these forms. Another is exposure to the law. A Tudor textbook informed its schoolboy readers that on London Bridge could be seen the heads of disobedient adults, adding that it "is a straunge sight to se the heere [hair]" fall or moulder away "and the gristell of the nose consumed". It is a "spectacle for ever to all yonge people to beware". A Jacobean divine commented that "When theeves are hanged, or whoores carted, we shew them to our children".[40] On a more positive note, children were consistently encouraged to play games which

---

[40] In Thomas, *supra* n 24, p 68.

encouraged conformable habits. Thus boys were encouraged to play at fighting, while girls cooked. Even playing at marriage ceremonies, while for some potentially blasphemous, was more generally approved, as an essential part in the education of the young godly.[41] Gillian Avery has suggested that the origins of an identifiable children's literature lay with the Protestant desire to educate the future "elect", most particularly against the potentially evil influences of the imagination. James Janeway's *A Token for Children* concentrated on accounts of children dying pure and virtuously. Any child who read Janeway's *Token* could not fail to note that anyone who disobeyed their parents would necessarily go straight to hell when they died, and all children, it was emphasised, died eventually.[42]

Ultimately, then, education is about the inculcation of habits, even if, at a radical level, this might be a habit of questioning received wisdom.[43] The ability of a child to make critical or moral judgments has long been seen as a pivotal aspect of successful education. Similarly, the ability to make rational moral judgments defines the political responsibility of the "good citizen". It is an ability nurtured, as Iris Murdoch has suggested, by an appreciation of art and literature. Indeed, in a world devoid of any deeper philosophical foundations, it is the only means by which a modern community can legitimate itself.[44] An educated child is, then, someone who can apply reason to moral judgment. Nicholas Tucker has applied Jean Piaget's theories of child psychology to the interpretation of children's texts. In his *The Moral Judgment of the Child*, based on empirical surveys, Piaget constructed a picture of children of various ages attempting to make sense of life experiences, and in such a way, learn to make moral judgments. He identified three stages, a first from birth to the age of seven, when children are entirely governed by parental opinion, a second from around seven to ten, when children develop the need for a common understanding of social rules, and a final from eleven to fourteen, when they learn to evaluate and apply these behavioural rules.[45]

Literature plays a critical role in equipping the child to develop their own sense of moral obligation; in terms of an obligation to the community, rather than merely to parents. According to Tucker, therefore, the kinds of literature encountered by children varies in line with their stage of development. Following Piaget's demarcation, the very youngest children encounter literature which makes no demands on individual evaluative capacity. Between the ages of seven and eleven, children encounter a rather different literature, one which portrays children in situations of some independence, required to reach their

---

[41] In Thomas, *supra* n 24, pp 59–60.

[42] G Avery, "The Puritans and the Heirs" in Avery and Briggs, *Children and Their Books*, pp 96–8, 109–12.

[43] See Thomas, *supra* n 24, pp 63–5.

[44] I Murdoch, *Existentialists and Mystics: Writings in Philosophy and Literature*, (London, Chatto & Windus, 1997), pp 3–30, 66–70. In her opinion, Shakespeare's drama reveals a world slowly coming to grips with the reality that there are no certainties in life. See p 222.

[45] J Piaget, *The Moral Judgment of the Child* (London, Routledge and Kegan Paul, 1932).

own judgments about good and bad behaviour. An ability to make certain moral judgments is assumed. From eleven to around fourteen, and then beyond, children are increasingly beset with a literature which refuses to provide simple solutions and interpretations. Such texts are riven with ambiguity and seemingly irresolvable moral dilemmas.[46] Shakespeare, of course, riven with ambiguities, in matters of familial relations, the law, and much else, most closely fits the latter category.

However, children certainly encounter alternative Shakespeare's at a much younger age. These alternatives seek to erase the most intransigent dilemmas, and instead present a Shakespeare entirely more susceptible to simple rationalisations. Perhaps the most famous of these alternative Shakespeares is Charles and Mary Lamb's *Tales from Shakespeare*. Written at the turn of the nineteenth century, the *Tales* enjoy their own immediate context, commissioned by the radical dissenter William Godwin, as part of a conscious strategy to educate younger readers in the joys of radical liberalism. Reading, Godwin held, was itself an expression of intellectual liberty. The Lambs agreed. But the *Tales*, addressed to an audience markedly less sophisticated than that which could decipher the actual texts, presents moral stories strikingly devoid of ambiguity.[47] The Lambs do make sense of Shakespeare, but it is a very particular sense; one which accords with the principles of Godwin's *Political Justice* in seeing justice as a necessary constituent of law. Thus, each of the patriarchs in the *Dream*, *Lear* and *Romeo and Juliet*, are roundly condemned for their inability to appreciate the immanent relation of law and justice. By implication, in these cases disobedience is justified. But it is only justified insofar as can be excused in the name of justice. Where disobedience is not so legitimated, as in *The Taming of the Shrew*, disobedience is equally roundly condemned. Lamb's Shakespeare is, ultimately, no more liberal than the politics of radical liberalism would permit, and children who encounter Shakespeare through this particular refraction are as constrained by the context of early nineteenth century England, as they are by that of the late sixteenth and early seventeenth.[48]

The Lambs' Shakespeare is a very particular Shakespeare; theirs. The idea that there are various different Shakespeares, each particular to its interpretive audience or mediator, enjoys considerable contemporary academic support. Jan Kott famously suggested that each Shakespeare is "our" Shakespeare; particular to each age and to each audience. Accordingly, just as we can construct our

---

[46] N Tucker, *The Child and the Book: A psychological and literary exploration* (Cambridge, Cambridge University Press, 1981), pp 5–17, 46–132, 144–87.

[47] For commentaries on the relation between the Lambs and William Godwin, and the ideology which is reflected in the *Tales*, see W St Clair, "William Godwin as Children's Bookseller', in Avery and Briggs, *Children and Their Books*, pp 165–79, and M Butler, *Romantics, Rebels and Reactionaries: English Literature and its Background 1760–1830* (Oxford, OUP, 1981), pp 163–4, 174–7, noting the extent to which Lamb, despite Godwin's injunctions, presented a distinctly conservative and conformist Shakesperean ideology.

[48] C and M Lamb, *Tales from Shakespeare* (Harmondsworth, Puffin, 1994), pp 16–30, 133–51, 182–95, 266–88.

interpretation of Shakespeare, so too we can construct our interpretation of Shakespeare's children and Shakespeare's law. All are images pertinent to us, the empowered reader. But, ultimately, as Kott recognises, our ability to interpret is constrained by the context within which we operate, and that context is already saturated by received interpretations and images of Shakespeare.[49] Such an historicist understanding is commonly shared, as we have already noted, by a number of scholars of children's literature. Thus, although children who today encounter Shakespeare, at whatever level, enjoy an empowering creative potential, it is one which is immediately limited by the context of "Shakespeare" itself. The most canonical of sources are those which are defined by the rigidity of their meaning within the interpretive community. As Terry Hawkes has emphasised, the very fact that Shakespeare is used so widely in the educative process testifies to the perceived importance of providing an established "meaning".[50] Although radical Shakespearean scholarship may seek to deconstruct Shakespeare, to locate inconsistencies and contradictions which militate against meaning, these strategies generally require a degree of literary sophistication which is rarely approached by a young audience.

Rebellious children in Shakespeare either conform, such as Hermia and Lysander, or Hal, or die, such as Romeo and Juliet or Cordelia. Happy endings require conformity, and although an audience may admire the inner virtue and wisdom of a character such as Cordelia, the fates of Hermia and Hal are wholly more ideal. Romeo and Juliet's Verona, like Cordelia's England, are communities entirely destroyed by filial disobedience, no matter how morally justified it might have been. Certainly, Shakespeare writes to warn against the hazards of ineffective parenting, and there are occasions where individual instances of disobedience against individual patriarchs are at least morally justifiable. But at no point does he justify general disobedience, and when force of necessity legitimates a degree of disobedience it is either temporary or entirely destructive. Various generations of children may interpret and reinterpret "their" Shakespeare's. They may approve or disapprove of Cordelia, of Romeo and Juliet, of Kate and Helena, of Hermia and Lysander, to greater or lesser degrees. They may even appreciate that conformity to patriarchal authority requires a loss of freedom, barely legitimated by the need to submit to an essentially illusory and imagined notion of ideal public and private government. But ultimately, it cannot be said that Shakespeare's presentation of families, of children and their relation to the laws of patriarchy, does anything other than seek to impress the importance of conformity. The good child is someone who obeys the law and obeys their parents, because such obedience is the mark of an individual equipped to enter society and to act as a good citizen in the common cause of the common good.

---

[49] J Kott, *Shakespeare: Our Contemporary* (London, Routledge, 1967).
[50] See T Hawkes, *Meaning By Shakespeare* (London, Routledge, 1992), particularly ch 1.

8

Children Through Tort

RODERICK BAGSHAW

THE LAW OF torts imposes duties on, to and about children. This chapter seeks to provide an overview of these duties. But the law of torts does not purport to provide an exhaustive catalogue of the entitlements or obligations of children. For instance, it is orthodox doctrine that duties which are imposed by statute, including duties backed by criminal sanctions, will not support a tort-style claim for damages unless there is evidence that Parliament intended the duty concerned to support such claims. And it is equally orthodox that obligations which are categorised only as moral or social duties will not support such claims. The law of torts does not deny the existence of such duties or their utility; it merely leaves their enforcement to other mechanisms. The apparent gaps in tort law's protection of the interests of children may be a product of tort law's perception of the purpose of tort law rather than tort law's perception of children.

OBLIGATIONS RELATING TO INJURIES CAUSED BY CHILDREN

Responsibility of children for injuries to others

The primary position is that children of all ages are subject to the same tort obligations as adults.[1] Thus children must not, for instance, utter slanders or commit assaults.[2] While many children will lack such resources as would make a tort action against them worthwhile, in some contexts they will be insured.[3]

This equation of children with adults is subject to three qualifications. First, the courts have refused to hold minors liable for torts where the effect would be to circumvent the rules which make many contracts unenforceable against minors.[4] In this context a distinction has been drawn between attempts to

---

[1] J Salmond, *The Law of Torts*, 6th ed (London, Sweet and Maxwell, 1924), p 69, "A minor is in general liable for his torts in the same manner and to the same extent as an adult". This can be contrasted with the law in Germany where a child cannot be liable until the age of 7 (§ 828 I BGB) and the Netherlands where a child cannot be liable until the age of 14 (Art 6:164 BW).

[2] *Jennings* v. *Rundall* (1799) 8 TR 335, 337 *per* Lord Kenyon CJ, "If an infant commit an assault, or utter slander, God forbid that he should not be answerable for it in a Court of Justice".

[3] Seventeen-year-old motorists are an obvious example.

[4] For the rules in contract see, G H Treitel, *The Law of Contract*, 10th ed (London, Sweet & Maxwell, 1999), ch 13.1.

present an action for breach of contract as a tort and tort claims arising out of behaviour "outside the purview of the contract".[5]

Secondly, in some circumstances children may be effectively immune from certain forms of tort liability because they are judged to be incapable of forming the state of mind necessary for commission of the particular tort. A child judged incapable of anticipating that his or her actions may have deleterious effects for people in the claimant's position cannot be found to have been negligent.[6] This has made it important to clarify what state of mind a claimant must demonstrate in a defendant in order to prove a trespass to the person.[7]

Thirdly, even when children are subject to ordinary tort duties they are not expected to meet adult standards.[8] Instead the standard of care demanded of a child will be moderated to reflect the child's age. This proposition is supported by *McHale* v. *Watson*,[9] a case arising from Barry Watson, aged twelve, throwing a metal spike at a wooden post. He intended the spike to spear into the post, but instead it was deflected into the claimant's eye. Windeyer J held that Barry's age was not a personal characteristic which could be disregarded when evaluating his behaviour: "Childhood is not an idiosyncrasy".[10] Upholding this conclusion on appeal,[11] Kitto J argued that:

> "In regard to the things which pertain to foresight and prudence—experience, understanding of causes and effects, balance of judgment, thoughtfulness—it is absurd, indeed it is a misuse of language, to speak of normality in relation to persons of all ages taken together. In those things normality is, for children, something different from what normality is for adults".[12]

---

[5] *Ballett* v. *Mingay* [1943] KB 281, 283 *per* Lord Greene MR, distinguishing between *Jennings* v. *Rundall* (1799) 8 TR 335 and *Burnard* v. *Haggis* (1863) 14 CBNS 45. Tort claims arising from a child's participation in the making of a contract (e.g. deceit) have also been forbidden: *R Leslie Ltd* v. *Sheill* [1914] 3 KB 607.

[6] Such children are often referred to as "of tender years". There is no fixed age below which a child qualifies as "of tender years" but cases on contributory negligence suggest that children of 6 or 7 may qualify: *Lynch* v. *Nurdin* (1841) 1 QB 29 (seven); *Gough* v. *NCB* [1954] 1 QB 191 (six-and-a-half); but Bramwell B suggested that a 4-year-old could be liable in *Mangan* v. *Atterton* (1866) LR 1 Ex 239, 240.

[7] In *Fowler* v. *Lanning* [1959] 1 QB 426, Diplock J held that the plaintiff must prove either that injury was intended by the defendant or that the defendant was negligent. See also *Walmesley* v. *Humenick* [1954] 2 DLR 232. In *Morriss* v. *Marsden* [1952] 1 All ER 925, Stable J held that only the act which amounted to trespass had to be intended and that it was sufficient if the defendant was shown to have understood the nature and quality of the act. Professor John Fleming has pointed out that these decisions entail "the incongruity that an infant, too young for negligence because incapable of appreciating the risk, may well be old enough for a more heinous 'intentional' wrong although equally innocent of moral culpability" (J G Fleming, *The Law of Torts*, 9th ed (Sydney, LBC Information Services, 1998), p 29). But is it really peculiar to suppose that most children understand the wrongness of hitting others with roller-skates before they understand the wrongness of leaving roller-skates on the stairs?

[8] By contrast in France, "a civil *faute* is determined solely by the act committed: the age of the tortfeasor, his character, intelligence and ethical capacity are of no relevance" C v. *Bar, The Common European Law of Torts, Volume I* (Oxford, Clarendon Press, 1998), para 68.

[9] (1964) 111 CLR 384 (High Court of Australia: first instance); (1966) 115 CLR 199 (High Court of Australia: appeal).

[10] (1964) 111 CLR 384, para 23.

[11] (1966) 115 CLR 199.

[12] *Ibid*, p 214.

Applying this to the facts of the case he stated:

> "It is, I think, a matter for judicial notice that the ordinary boy of twelve suffers from a feeling that a piece of wood and a sharp instrument have a special affinity. To expect a boy of that age to consider before throwing the spike whether the timber was hard or soft, to weight the chances of being able to make the spike stick in the post, and to foresee that it might glance off and hit the girl, would be, I think, to expect a degree of sense and circumspection which nature ordinarily withholds till life has become less rosy".[13]

This approach was accepted in England by the Court of Appeal in *Mullin* v. *Richards*.[14] Although the facts were never finally settled, one view is that a plastic ruler broke while two fifteen-year-old girls were battling, and a shard from it pierced one girl's eye. The injured girl sought damages for the other's negligence. The Court of Appeal held that in asking the two relevant questions about foreseeability—whether the defendant girl ought to have realised that her actions gave rise to a risk of injury,[15] and whether the injury actually sustained was of a different kind from that which the defendant ought to have foreseen as the likely outcome of her lack of care[16]—the trial judge should have considered what ought to have been foreseen by an ordinarily prudent and reasonable fifteen-year-old schoolgirl. The test was objective to the extent that the defendant could not rely on being abnormally dim-witted, quick-tempered, absent-minded or inexperienced[17] compared with ordinary children in her own age group, but the test was subjective to the extent that it took account of what could ordinarily be expected as to knowledge, understanding and experience from a child in that age group. A child's age will cease to be relevant in setting an appropriate standard of care when the child reaches the "years of discretion", but this status does not depend on reaching any fixed age.

Responsibility of children for their own injuries

Injured children may have their damages reduced for contributory negligence. Since 1945 such reductions are calculated on the basis of the child's responsibility for his or her own injuries[18] and in assessing the child's degree of responsibility the child's age is taken into account. Very young children are treated as "unable, in consequence of their tender age, to take care of themselves"[19] and hence cannot be found to have been contributorily negligent. Even if the child

---

[13] *Ibid*, p 216.

[14] [1998] 1 WLR 1304.

[15] A question relevant to whether a duty of care was owed.

[16] A question relevant to whether the damage caused was too remote a consequence of the carelessness.

[17] Language used by Kitto J in *McHale*, *supra* n 11, at 214.

[18] Law Reform (Contributory Negligence) Act 1945.

[19] *Cooke* v. *Midland Great Western Railway of Ireland* [1909] AC 229, 236 *per* Lord Macnaghten (a case involving a 4-year-old).

does not fall within this category the standard expected is still only that of an ordinary child of the particular age. Salmon LJ explained the idea of the "ordinary child" in *Gough* v. *Thorne*:[20] "I do not mean a paragon of prudence; nor do I mean a scatterbrained child; but the ordinary girl of [the particular age]". Importantly, the test asks whether the child has shown more disregard for its own safety than is reasonable at its age, not whether it has been more disobedient than it ought to have been.[21]

At one time a child incapable of protecting itself was "identified" with its custodian so that carelessness by the custodian was attributed to the child as contributory negligence.[22] This doctrine has now been "exploded" on the basis that a careless custodian should be treated as a joint tortfeasor.[23] It seems, however, that in some circumstances a defendant will be able to argue that he was not careless at all because it was reasonable in all the circumstances to expect the custodian to protect the child.[24]

A defendant may also avoid liability if the child accepted the risk of injury.[25] In *Buckpitt* v. *Oates*[26] John Stephenson J held that a child could be found to have appreciated a risk sufficiently for the defence of *volenti* to apply even when that child was not capable of making an enforceable contract.[27] An important distinction has been drawn, however, between children knowing that it is disobedient or wrong to do something and appreciating the risk that the action posed.[28]

Responsibility of parents and others for injuries caused by children

Children who break their tort obligations are personally responsible for paying any required compensation. Importantly English law does not make the parents of a child vicariously liable for the child's torts *qua* parents.[29] Parents will be vicariously liable, however, if the child committed the tort in the course of employment

[20] [1966] 1 WLR 1387, 1391.
[21] *French* v. *Sunshine Holiday Camp (Hayling Island) Ltd.* (1963) 107 SJ 595 (6-year-old disobedient in climbing onto low wall but not contributorily negligent because not expected to anticipate risk of falling onto glass covering concealed lights).
[22] *Waite* v. *North Eastern Ry Co* (1858) E B & E 719 (5-year-old injured while crossing railway with grandmother).
[23] *Oliver* v. *Birmingham & Midland Motor Omnibus Co* [1933] 1 KB 35.
[24] See below p 136 and p 143.
[25] The defence known as *volenti non fit injuria*.
[26] [1968] 1 All ER 1145.
[27] Although it seems odd that the law of contract should save a child from wasting its money while the law of tort is happy for a child to bear the consequences of choosing to risk its life, it is clearly important for the autonomy rights of children that they should be treated as capable of giving a valid consent before they are subject to the full rigours of contract law.
[28] *Gough* v. *NCB* [1954] 1 QB 191 (riding on unmanned colliery trucks).
[29] *Moon* v. *Towers* (1660) 8 CBNS 611, 615 *per* Willes J. This contrasts with the position in France where parents must show that they could not have prevented a child's wrongful act in order to avoid liability (Civil Code Art 1384 al 4 and al 7). In Germany parents are only liable if they were at fault in their supervision, but the burden is on parents to establish a lack of fault (§832 BGB).

by a parent or when acting as a parent's agent. But while parenthood does not entail *vicarious* liability for the torts of children, parents and those with temporary responsibility for looking after children, may also owe *direct* duties to third parties to control or supervise those children.

On supervision, there is a strong series of cases supporting duties to take reasonable care to prevent children misusing dangerous objects, particularly airguns.[30] Such duties may be owed not only by parents who permit their children to possess such objects but also by anybody who supplies such objects to children[31] and anybody who stores such objects where children may be expected to find them.[32] The extension of liability to storers was justified in *Williams* v. *Eady*[33] on the basis that schoolmasters are "bound to take notice of the ordinary nature of young boys, their tendency to do mischievous acts, and their propensity to meddle with anything that came in their way".

Suppliers' and storers' liability tend to shade into a further group of cases which treats the misbehaviour of children as a natural hazard which will not excuse defendants who have created dangers capable of being set off by meddling children.[34] Even the meddling child may have an action in such a case.[35]

A parent's responsibility to control is wider than a duty to take reasonable care to ensure safe use of dangerous objects. In *Smith* v. *Leurs*,[36] a case involving a thirteen-year-old's use of a catapult, Dixon J expressed the broader duty as requiring "a parent who maintains control over a young child to take reasonable care so to exercise that control as to avoid conduct on his part exposing the person or property of others to unreasonable danger".[37] On the facts, however, it was held that warning the child about the danger of the catapult and an instruction to use it only towards a wall was all that could reasonably be expected of parents with regard to a device which was "a common object in boyhood life". There is no fixed age at which children cease to have to be

---

[30] *Bebee* v. *Sales* (1916) 32 TLR 413; *Hawley* v. *Alexander* (1930) 74 SJ 247; *Donaldson* v. *McNiven* [1952] 2 All ER 691; *Newton* v. *Edgerley* [1959] 3 All ER 337 (concerning a .410 gun rather than an air gun); *Gorely* v. *Codd* [1966] 3 All ER 891; *Jauffur* v. *Akhbar* [1984] TLR 51 (concerning candles).

[31] *Burfitt* v. *A & E Kille* [1939] 2 KB 743 (sale of blank cartridge pistol and blank cartridges to a 12-year-old without warning about necessity for regular cleaning); *Ricketts* v. *Erith BC* [1943] 2 All ER 629 (principle accepted, but does not apply to sale of one-penny bamboo bow and arrow).

[32] *Williams* v. *Eady* (1893) 10 TLR 41 (jar of phosphorus); *Jackson* v. *London CC* (1912) 28 TLR 359 (building materials in school playground).

[33] *Ibid*, at 42, *per* Lord Esher MR.

[34] *Haynes* v. *Harwood* [1935] 1 KB 146 (policeman injured by a horse which the defendant had left untethered and which may have runaway because it was pelted with stones by children). *Clark* v. *Chambers* (1878) 3 QBD 327 uses similar reasoning to hold liable a defendant who left a chevaux-de-frise in a street from where it was moved by persons unknown to the position where it injured the plaintiff.

[35] *Lynch* v. *Nurdin* (1841) 1 QB 29 (7-year-old injured falling from cart left in street—"he merely indulged the natural instinct of a child in amusing himself with the empty cart and deserted horse"). *Evans* v. *Souls Garages Ltd*, *The Times*, 23 Jan 2001 (garage selling petrol to a 13-year-old who sniffed it while smoking liable for burns). But compare *Mangan* v. *Atterton* (1866) LR 1 Ex 239.

[36] (1945) 70 CLR 256 (High Court of Australia).

[37] *Ibid*, at 262.

supervised. In *North* v. *Wood*[38] the King's Bench Division upheld a decision to treat a father as not required to supervise his seventeen-year-old daughter's control of her bull terrier since she had "arrived at her years of discretion".

This duty to take reasonable care in controlling children has also been extended beyond parents to others who exert quasi-parental control. Thus in *Carmarthenshire County Council* v. *Lewis*[39] an education authority was held liable to the widow of a lorry driver killed while swerving to avoid a four-year-old boy who had strayed from a nursery school.[40] It was treated as significant that the child was not old enough to be responsible. Indeed Lord Goddard thought that the child was so young that he could be presumed to be unable to take any care for his own safety and was "from the standpoint of reasoning powers . . . much the same as a sheep".[41] Cases such as *Home Office* v. *Dorset Yacht Co.*,[42] however, suggest that duties to control are not limited to situations where children are too young to be liable themselves: there is a duty to control teenagers when there is a supervisory relationship and they are known to be in a situation where they will probably cause damage if left unsupervised.[43]

Summary

In principle, children are liable in the same way as adults, but in applying the ordinary rules of tort law to children allowance is made for their reduced levels of foresight and skill. There is no general vicarious liability of parents for the acts of their children, but it seems that parents may owe direct duties to supervise and control, particularly when the children have access to dangerous things or are known to be incapable of preventing themselves from constituting a risk to others. These duties are not only owed by parents but also by others who may control access to dangerous things or have responsibility for confining children.

OBLIGATIONS OWED TO CHILDREN

"In theory, a child has the same opportunities of seeking tort compensation as does an adult. . . . In practice, few children seek tort compensation. According to our survey

[38] [1914] 1 KB 629 (the daughter's dog had a known and peculiar antipathy to Pomeranian dogs and savaged one which had recently won first prize at a Birmingham dog show).

[39] [1955] AC 549.

[40] While Devlin J ([1953] 1 All ER 1025) and the Court of Appeal ([1953] 2 All ER 1403) had found one of the teachers careless a majority in the House of Lords found carelessness in the failure to ensure that a gate onto the road could not be opened by young children.

[41] To be fair to Lord Goddard his remark should be put in context. The House of Lords had relatively recently concluded that an occupier was not required to fence his land in order to prevent farm animals straying onto the highway: *Searle* v. *Wallbank* [1947] AC 341. The modern law as to animals straying onto the highway is contained in Animals Act 1971, s. 8.

[42] [1970] AC 1004.

[43] Five of the seven borstal trainees who escaped had a record of previous escape and the yachts presented the most obvious means of escaping from the island.

about one per cent of children injured after birth, as compared with about seven per cent of injured adults, obtain any reparation or payment through tort".[44]

The reasons for this disparity are obscure. One factor which has been suggested[45] is the difficulty of proving fault where the main witness is a child.[46] But the authors of another empirical study concluded that the low number of child claims "stems primarily from a low propensity to *think* about compensation or to seek legal advice, rather than any special difficulty in proving a case once a claim has been made".[47] An alternative factor may be the types of accidents which children suffer. For children up to the age of five the vast majority of accidents occur in the home.[48] Common causes of death are burns, suffocation, drowning, falls and poisoning, while falls are the most common form of non-fatal accident requiring medical treatment.[49] In such cases the parents of the child will often be the most obvious defendants and consequently it is readily understandable why few claims are made. Between the ages of five and fourteen most accidents occur on the roads. It seems, however, that many of these may result from lack of pedestrian skills in young children.[50] If parents often accept that injuries incurred in crossing roads were not caused by the carelessness of the drivers involved, then this could partly explain the low number of claims. A further relevant factor may be the fact that most injured children will not have lost earnings and will have received free medical care. Consequently parents may not see any need to claim unless their child has suffered a permanent injury which is likely to require ongoing medical costs or to cause prejudice in the employment market.[51]

[44] Royal Commission on Civil Liability and Compensation for Personal Injury (Chairman: Lord Pearson) (1978) Cmnd 7054–I, para 1494.

[45] *Ibid*, para 1495.

[46] The difficulty would have been magnified during the times when young children were treated as incompetent to give evidence or competent but requiring corroboration. The modern law of evidence is more accommodating: Children Act 1989, s. 96.

[47] D Harris and others, *Compensation and Support for Illness and Injury* (Oxford, Clarendon Press, 1984), p 61. This study found that 70% of those aged 0–15 who contacted a lawyer received damages, but only 6% of those aged 0–15 who were injured in an accident contacted a lawyer (p 64).

[48] Ninety % of injuries and over half fatalities: A Kravitz, "Accident Prevention Research" (1973) 2 *Paediatric Annals* 47–53, quoted in B Gillham and J A Thomson (eds), *Child Safety: Problem and Prevention from Preschool to Adolescence* (London, Routledge, 1996), p 71.

[49] H Roberts, "Child Accidents at Home, School and Play" in B Gillham and J A Thomson (eds), *supra* n 48.

[50] J Thomson calculates that children between the ages of 5 and 7 are forty times more vulnerable than adults between the ages of twenty and fifty to being injured as pedestrians: J Thomson, "Child Pedestrian Accidents: What Makes Children Vulnerable?" in B Gillham and J A Thomson (eds), *supra* n 48. The same author reports that children only approach adult skill levels at age 11, and that even then they do not employ their skills as effectively as adults.

[51] Almost all modern cases involve claims for catastrophic injuries, amputations (particularly of fingers) or damage to eyes. H Roberts, *supra* n 49 reports that 2% of children treated in accident and emergency departments suffer permanent disability.

Parents

One exception to the proposition that children are provided by the law of torts with the same protection as adults is provided by the right of parents to discipline their children: "It is clear law that a father has the right to inflict reasonable personal chastisement on his son".[52] This right could be delegated to schoolmasters[53] and clearly protects from suit behaviour which would otherwise amount to trespass to the person. It seems that the Government's response to a finding by the European Court of Human Rights that the United Kingdom is failing in its duty to protect children from inhuman and degrading punishment will be to clarify the right of reasonable chastisement rather than abolishing it.[54]

Subject to this exception, however, it is clear that children who are assaulted by their parents (or others)[55] can sue for damages for a trespass to the person. This has been recognised in England as the appropriate cause of action for a child who has suffered sexual abuse[56] though some have suggested that incest should be treated as a separate and distinct wrong.[57] In cases of sexual abuse by officials employed to care for children the question of the employer's vicarious liability will often arise. In Canada the Supreme Court has developed an approach to this which explicitly considers whether the employment involved the creation of relationships between adults and children which would materially increase the risk of sexual abuse.[58] The leading English authority, however, treats employees given quasi-parental authority as subject to the same vicarious liability rules as other employees.[59] Consequently, unless the employee-abuser has personal wealth the victim will often not obtain compensation through tort law.

---

[52] *Cleary* v. *Booth* [1893] 1 QB 465, 468 *per* Collins J.

[53] Several cases considered the extent of the authority that it was to be presumed that parents delegated by sending their children to school, e.g. *Cleary* v. *Booth, ibid*; *Mansell* v. *Griffin* [1908] 1 KB 160. See now Education Act 1996 s. 548.

[54] Department of Health, *Protecting Children, Supporting Parents* (2000), para 2.14 responding to *A* v. *United Kingdom* (1999) 27 EHRR 611.

[55] Though children may also be unable to sue for injuries suffered in non-hostile horseplay (*Wilson* v. *Pringle* [1986] 2 All ER 440), particularly if the contact is such as is generally acceptable between children in everyday life (*Collins* v. *Wilcock* [1984] 1 WLR 1172).

[56] *Stubbings* v. *Webb* [1993] AC 498.

[57] J W W Neeb and S J Harper, *Civil Action for Childhood Sexual Abuse* (Toronto, Butterworths, 1994). This suggestion was rejected by the Supreme Court of Canada in *M (K)* v. *M (H)* [1992] 3 SCR 6, though La Forest J held, at 24, that "Incest is both a tortious assault and a breach of fiduciary duty".

[58] *The Children's Foundation* v. *Bazley* (1999) 174 DLR (4th) 45, which applied this to hold the employer liable for sexual abuse of an employee in a residential care home. The same court split five to four on whether an employer should be liable for sexual abuse by the programme director of a recreational facility for children with the majority holding that the "mentoring" relationship was insufficiently parent-like: *Jacobi* v. *Girls' and Boys' Club of Vernon* (1999) 174 DLR (4th) 71.

[59] *Trotman* v. *North Yorkshire CC* [1999] LGR 584.

While there is strong authority for parents owing duties to control their children to third parties courts have been more reluctant to hold that parents owe similar duties to the children themselves to take reasonable steps to control them in order to prevent them being injured.[60] There are several reasons of public policy for being concerned about the possibility of tort actions between children and parents. Most obviously such actions could disrupt family harmony. Adversarial litigation between family members would be antithetical to such harmony,[61] and might be particularly inappropriate where the defendant parent was likely to shoulder the principal burden of caring for the injured child. Further, the recovery of substantial damages might lead to tensions over inequality in the allocation of "family resources" between family members. Even where a parent was sympathetic to a child's claim, for instance because it would be covered by insurance, there might be worries that the possibility of such claims would stimulate fraud.[62] It seems that these reasons are regarded in England as insufficient in cases where parents positively injure their children. It has consequently been accepted that parents owe at least the same duties to their children as a stranger would owe: for instance, parents owe a duty to their children when passengers to drive with reasonable care.[63]

In cases where what is alleged is careless parental supervision there is the further problem that it is not easy for courts to set standards of "reasonable parenting" in many contexts: to set and apply such standards requires investigation of the normally private details of family life, and controversial decisions about how far such standards should accommodate differences in, for instance, views on the value of fostering child-independence. But despite this additional difficulty tort law has recognised a parental duty to take care to prevent a child falling into danger if he or she has specifically assumed responsibility for doing so or has led the child into danger.[64]

Recent litigation has considered how far parents and other agencies[65] may be under private law duties to protect children against deliberate wrongdoing by

---

[60] Generally cases have not involved the child suing its parent directly but defendants who have negligently injured a child claiming a contribution from parents on the basis that the parent's breach of a duty owed to the child was a contributory cause of the injury: in England, see Civil Liability (Contribution) Act 1978.

[61] Although leaving victims without the compensation necessary to purchase proper rehabilitative equipment and support is also not conducive to the maintenance of family relationships.

[62] In the United States of America many insurance companies exclude claims between family members from the risks insured in states which permit such claims.

[63] An extraordinary modern case has held that similar policy reasons are a significant part of the justification for holding that a child does not owe a duty to its parent to take care not to injure itself in such a way as to cause the parent to suffer a psychiatric injury: *Greatorex* v. *Greatorex* [2000] 1 WLR 1970. If this decision is correct then it tends to support the proposition that a parent does not owe her child a duty to take care not to drive so as to injure herself and thereby cause a psychiatric injury to her child witnessing the event.

[64] *Hahn* v. *Conley* (1971) 126 CLR 276 (High Court of Australia), at 283 and 285 *per* Barwick CJ; *McCallion* v. *Dodd* [1966] NZLR 710 (New Zealand Court of Appeal), at 724–5 *per* Turner J, at 729 *per* McCarthy J.

[65] The responsibility of state agencies is considered below, pp 137–141.

others. Canadian courts have found in this context that parents owe both a private law duty of care to take reasonable steps to protect a child in their care against known or reasonably foreseeable threats[66] and a fiduciary obligation which "betokens loyalty, good faith, and avoidance of a conflict of duty and self-interest".[67] This has led to children in Canada successfully claiming damages from a parent who failed to intervene to protect them from child abuse.

While the previous paragraphs demonstrate that the courts have recognised and extended tort law obligations owed by parents to children, the decisions also demonstrate judicial determination not to extend the law of tort too far into family settings. A common theme has been that "the moral duties of conscientious parenthood do not as such provide the child with any cause of action when they are not, or badly, performed or neglected".[68] This raises the difficulty of distinguishing between situations where the parental duty is enforced by the law of torts and where the duty is merely moral. In *Surtees* v. *The Royal Borough of Kingston Upon Thames*[69] Stocker LJ suggested that there would be a clear case in negligence if a mother left a two-year-old toddler alone in a room with a bowl containing scalding water.[70] But in New York a very similar case was held to fall within the "parental supervision" immunity recognised in that state.[71]

Although many of the moral duties of conscientious parenthood cannot support tort claims such duties are relevant in assessing the scope of the duties that strangers owe to a child. Thus in *O'Connor* v. *British Transport Commission*[72] the Court of Appeal held that a train operator was required to make provision for the safety of children of tender years but was entitled to do so on the basis that they would be accompanied by someone capable of looking after them. Similarly, in *Ryan* v. *Camden LBC*[73] Cumming-Bruce LJ suggested that landlords were not liable even though the heating pipes in many of their flats posed a risk to crawling children without the intellectual capacity to appreciate the risk because such landlords might reasonably expect parents to devise means of safeguarding their children.

---

[66] For example, *M (M)* v. *F (R)* (1999) 52 BCLR (3d) 127 (British Columbia Court of Appeals), a difficult case since the defendant foster-mother claimed that her unusual innocence about sexual matters explained her failure to appreciate that the plaintiff was being abused.

[67] *J (LA)* v. *J (H)* (1993) 102 DLR (4th) 177 (Ontario Ct (GD)).

[68] *Hahn* v. *Conley* (1971) 126 CLR 276 (High Court of Australia), at 283, *per* Barwick CJ; *Cameron* v. *Commissioner for Railways* [1964] Qd R 480 (Supreme Court of Queensland); *DJ Collett* v. *Hutchins* [1964] Qd R 495 (Supreme Court of Queensland).

[69] [1992] PIQR P101.

[70] *Ibid* at 105. A majority of the Court of Appeal upheld the judge's finding of fact that the claimant child had not been left in the vicinity of scalding water but had climbed onto a basin and accidentally turned the hot water tap.

[71] *Zikely* v. *Zikely* 98 AppDiv 2d 815 (SC of NY, Appellate Division, 1983), 467 NE 2d 892 (NY Court of Appeals, 1984), applying *Holodook* v. *Spencer* 324 NE 2d 338 (NY Court of Appeals, 1974).

[72] [1958] 1 All ER 558.

[73] [1982] TLR 640.

In England the policy questions concerning claims between parents and children have been addressed by Parliament in the context of possible claims between mother and child arising out of behaviour during the pregnancy. By statute an unborn child is owed a duty by its mother when she drives during pregnancy[74] but the mother does not owe any wider duty of care to the unborn child. The same statute also provides that persons other than the mother can be sued if they break a legal duty owed to one of the unborn child's parents and this leads to the child being born with disabilities.[75] This means that the child can potentially claim for disabilities resulting from its father's actionable carelessness towards its mother. Parliament's decision to make the child's claim parasitic on breach of a duty owed to one of its parents altered the common law. This had eventually accepted that a child could sue if born with injuries which could be attributed to the breach of a "potential" or "contingent" duty owed to it by a third party before its birth.[76] In Canada, where there is no equivalent of the English statute, the common law recognises duties owed by third parties to the unborn child but the Supreme Court has refused to impose tort duties between mother and unborn child. The reasons for this were the difficulty in articulating a judicial standard of conduct for pregnant women and concerns that such a duty would interfere with the privacy and autonomy rights of women.[77]

The state

Several appellate decisions have considered the question how far the state's obligations to protect and provide for children can give rise to damages claims in tort. In this context it is particularly important to note that English tort law does not treat failure to fulfil a statutory duty, or even careless failure, as a wrong which automatically gives rise to a right to claim damages. Instead, a claimant must establish either that Parliament intended the statutory duty to give rise to claims for damages if broken, or, that a common law duty of care exists alongside the statutory duty.[78] If the latter is established then there can be a claim in negligence for the breach of that common law duty. Similarly, where the allegation is of carelessness in the exercise of statutory powers the claimant must establish a common law duty of care.

The English courts have been overwhelmingly reluctant to impute to Parliament any intention to create private law rights to damages for failures in fulfilling statutory duties relating to social welfare.[79] Their approach to the

[74] Congenital Disabilities (Civil Liability) Act 1976, s. 2.

[75] *Ibid*, s. 1.

[76] *Burton* v. *Islington HA* [1993] QB 204; *cf Walker* v. *Great Northern Railway Co of Ireland* (1891) 28 LRIr 69.

[77] *Dobson* v. *Dobson* (1999) 174 DLR (4th) 1 (Supreme Court of Canada).

[78] *X (Minors)* v. *Bedfordshire CC* [1995] 2 AC 633, 730–5.

[79] *Ibid* at 747–8. See also, *Phelps* v. *Hillingdon LBC* [2000] 3 WLR 776, at 789–90.

imposition of common law duties for the benefit of children, however, has been inconsistent. It is consequently necessary to consider separately and sequentially cases involving the state as a protector against physical and sexual abuse, the state as a substitute parent, and the state as an education provider.

The state as a protector against physical and sexual abuse

It is in this context that the English courts have proved most reluctant to recognise common law duties to protect children. Where the manner of performance of any relevant statutory duties or exercise of statutory powers requires decisions about matters of policy, such as how to allocate limited resources between competing demands, it has been suggested that such decisions are non-justiciable and that imposition of a common law duty is inappropriate.[80] Even where this difficulty can be overcome, judges have expressed concern about the effect of imposition of common law duties on morale, resources, co-operation between agencies, and the delicate interplay between protecting the child and preserving the family. Taken together these concerns convinced the House of Lords in *X (Minors)* v. *Bedfordshire CC* that it would not be in the public interest to recognise a common law duty of care owed by local authorities to those children in need of protection.[81]

This conclusion, however, is being challenged before the European Court of Human Rights. The challenge proceeds on two fronts. First, it is acknowledged that the state owes positive obligations to protect children against violations of their human rights, in particular their right to life,[82] right to be free from inhuman and degrading treatment,[83] and right to respect for private life.[84] Where the state fails to fulfil such a positive obligation there is a strong argument that the most appropriate remedy is the payment of damages.[85] It seems likely, however, that the positive obligations imposed by the European Convention on Human Rights will be defined narrowly[86] and that the damages payable may be less than those which would ordinarily be available in the tort of negligence.

The second front to the challenge alleges that a refusal to impose a common law duty of care may amount to a violation of the right to a fair trial.[87] The reasoning seems to be that where a person is arguably a reasonably foreseeable victim of the defendant's carelessness and arguably in a sufficiently proximate

---

[80] *X, op cit* n 78, at 737–8. It is now clear that it is not the case that all decisions involving a discretionary element are non-justiciable: *Barrett* v. *Enfield LBC* [1999] 3 WLR 79.

[81] *Op cit* n 78, at 749–51.

[82] European Convention for the Protection of Human Rights and Fundamental Freedoms (Rome, 4 November 1950; TS 71 (1953); Cmd 8969) [ECHR], Art 2.

[83] ECHR, Art 3.

[84] ECHR, Art 8.

[85] ECHR, Art 13. See also Human Rights Act 1998, s. 8.

[86] In *Osman, infra* n 88, the police were held to be under a positive obligation to do what could be reasonably expected of them to protect life only if they knew (or ought to have known) of a real and immediate risk to the life of an identified individual or individuals: para 116.

[87] ECHR, Art 6.

relationship with the defendant, then that person has a right to have the court consider whether the merits of his individual claim are such that it should be permitted despite any generalised public policy concerns about the effect of such claims.[88] Moreover, it seems that this will often require an assessment of the facts behind the claim.[89]

The state as a substitute parent

The House of Lords responded to this second front of the challenge in *Barrett* v. *Enfield LBC*,[90] an appeal from the striking-out of a claim against a local authority for negligence in looking after a child in its care. Although Lord Browne-Wilkinson[91] expressly queried the reasoning of the European Court of Human Rights he held that until that reasoning was clarified it was impossible to describe *Barrett's* claim as unarguable. He also warned that courts had to be careful in striking-out claims on public policy grounds before the facts had been established. The House of Lords generally thought it would only become clear if the decisions about *Barrett's* upbringing were justiciable once the facts were established. Consequently, the case had to proceed to trial.

Quite apart from the influence of *Osman*, however, *Barrett* was distinguishable from *X* because in *Barrett* the local authority had taken on the role of a substitute parent. Although, as was said in the previous section, courts have been reluctant to treat the duties of conscientious parenthood as actionable in tort the House of Lords thought that it should be easier to sue a local authority *substitute* parent. Lord Hutton suggested that this was partly because some of the decisions that the local authority had to make were very different from those that a natural parent would normally have to make[92] and partly because the local authority employed expert staff and advisers to assist it in taking such decisions.[93] The distinction from *X* was important because, as Lord Slynn expressly stated, the policy concerns found to be influential in *X* might not have the same force in the circumstances of *Barrett's* case.[94] Thus the need for a multi-disciplinary approach, the need to balance the parents' interests, the risk of over-caution and the efficacy of alternative remedies, might all be diminished in a situation where the child claimant was already in care and the local authority was exercising the functions of a substitute parent. Lord Hutton went even further than Lord Slynn and stated that he was already

---

[88] *Osman* v. *United Kingdom* judgment of 28 October 1998, Reports of Judgments and Decisions 1998–VIII p 3124 (1998) 29 EHRR 245, para 139.

[89] *Ibid*, paras 151–2.

[90] [1999] 3 WLR 79.

[91] Lords Nolan and Steyn agreed with the reasons of Lord Browne-Wilkinson and with the reasons of Lord Hutton who expressly held that it was unnecessary to discuss *Osman*.

[92] He gave as an example whether to place a child for adoption, or with foster parents or in a residential home: [1999] 3 WLR 79, at 112. Lord Slynn made the same point, at 98–9.

[93] [1999] 3 WLR 79, at 112.

[94] *Ibid*, at 93.

satisfied that the policy concerns could not preclude a duty of care in this context.[95]

A similar approach to that in *Barrett's* case was taken by the House of Lords in *W v. Essex CC*,[96] refusing to strike-out claims by foster carers and their children for negligence by a local authority in placing with their family a fifteen-year-old boy who had previously committed acts of sexual abuse. Again, the function of the local authority and its relationship with the injured children can be distinguished from the circumstances in *X*, though here the authority's role was as an adviser of the real parents rather than as a substitute parent.[97]

The state as an education provider

Confirmation that the tide has turned against courts treating the policy concerns relied on in *X* as sufficient to preclude the state owing duties of care to children is arguably provided by a recent decision of the House of Lords concerning the state as an education provider. In *Phelps* v. *Hillingdon LBC*[98] the House of Lords held that professionals involved in education, including psychologists and teachers, owed duties not to injure pupils by failing to maintain standards of professional skill and competence. Where such duties were broken local education authorities would usually be vicariously liable. Importantly, such liability includes liability for failure of a pupil to reach the standard of educational attainment that he or she would have reached but for the breach of duty, and for any consequential psychological damage, loss of earnings, or expenditure on training to redress the attainment deficit. Thus the decision comes close to recognising an appropriate education as an interest which pupils have a private law right to against the state. Indeed Lord Clyde expressly relied on an analogy between the rights of pupils benefiting from the services of state-employed professionals and the rights of pupils entering contracts to receive similar services.[99]

The co-existence of *X* and *Phelps* might be thought to suggest that the English law of torts regards a child's interest in receiving an appropriate education as more worthy of protection that a child's interest in being protected from physical or sexual abuse. This would, however, be a misconception. The difference between the two decisions is principally explicable by the different assessments of the public policy consequences of recognising private law duties in each case. Despite the change in judicial attitude to public policy concerns between the two cases the House of Lords in *Phelps* was not willing to castigate the previous case as wrongly decided. Instead, it pointed out that the tensions between public officials and parents were likely to be far more difficult to manage in a child abuse

---

[95] [1999] 3 WLR 79, at 113.

[96] [2000] 2 WLR 601.

[97] *T* v. *Surrey CC* [1994] 4 All ER 577, where the local authority gave a mother careless advice about the suitability of a child-minder, provides a simpler example of this sort of relationship.

[98] [2000] 3 WLR 776.

[99] *Ibid*, at 807–8

investigation than in an assessment of appropriate educational provision. Another relevant factor might be that the state's role is secondary to the parents' in protecting against abuse, while the state is the primary provider of school education. Thus the question how far the state's obligations to protect and provide for children can give rise to damages claims in tort does not have a straightforward answer. The answer in any particular context depends on variables such as the importance of the interest for the child, the degree of dependence of the child on the state for protection of that interest, and the public policy consequences of using tort law to redress any culpable failure by the state.

Drivers

Drivers owe a duty of care to children as they do to adult pedestrians. But while drivers in an area where children are known to play in the streets should appreciate the risk that a child may rush into the road they need not drive in such a way as to be sure not to injure such a child.[100] The position in English law, where an injured child must prove the fault of the driver and is vulnerable to the defence of contributory negligence can be contrasted with French law where liability is strict and there is no defence of contributory negligence available against a victim under the age of sixteen.[101] The Pearson Commission[102] recommended a no-fault motor vehicle compensation scheme for England, with no defence of contributory negligence against a child under twelve, but this was not implemented.

Landowners

In England a landowner's duties to a visitor depend on the legal status of the visitor. At common law a landowner was permitted to insist that those who came onto his land without invitation or licence did so at their own peril. Initially, a landowner was even permitted to set traps to injure trespassers,[103] though later law insisted that there was a duty not to cause injury intentionally or with a disregard "so reckless as to amount to malicious acting".[104] Many of the victims left uncompensated by this doctrine were children, since, as judges recognised, "children at play are always likely to trespass".[105] In order to save a few straying

[100] *Moore (an infant)* v. *Poyner* [1975] RTR 127.
[101] Law 5 July 1985 (no. 85–677).
[102] Royal Commission on Civil Liability and Compensation for Personal Injury (Chairman: Lord Pearson) (1978) Cmnd 7054–I, ch 18, especially para 1077.
[103] *Ilott* v. *Wilkes* (1820) 3 B & Ald 304. This decision was moderated to some extent by *Bird* v. *Holbrook* (1828) 4 Bing 628. See also Spring Guns Act 1827.
[104] *Excelsior Wire Rope Co Ltd* v. *Callan* [1930] AC 404, 411 *per* Viscount Dunedin.
[105] *Adams* v. *Naylor* [1944] 2 All ER 21, 30 *per* Morton J (trespass on minefield to retrieve a tennis ball).

infants from the doctrine's harshness some judges were willing to detect an implied licence to be on the land if children were known by the owner to frequent a place and were not actively excluded.[106] But active exclusion did not have to be effective: to confirm persistent children as trespassers the landowner merely had to do enough to bring home to the minds of the children concerned that they had no business to be where they were.[107] It was only in *British Railways Board* v. *Herrington*[108] that it was established that a landowner might owe a duty to take active steps, such as fencing, to prevent children from trespassing.[109]

Although it was better for a child to be classed as licensee rather than a trespasser, even a child who succeeded in attaining the higher status was only entitled to reasonable protection against hidden dangers or traps.[110] Thus in *Dyer* v. *Ilfracombe UDC*[111] a four-year-old who fell from a slide in a public playground was unable to recover because it was held that the danger was not hidden: "a boy of that age knows that if he falls from a height he is likely to hurt himself". In children's cases the most important variety of trap was the thing which was alluring and inherently dangerous. This variety of trap was of particular importance because it was readily acknowledged that what was alluring was to be considered from the position of a child, not an adult.[112] Although it was recognised that "a child can get into mischief and hurt itself with anything if it is young enough" a trap by allurement required a sufficient combination of temptation and retribution.[113] Although the doctrine of allurement initially applied only to licensees,[114] it was extended to prevent children who were initially licensees from becoming trespassers as soon as they did something they knew to be unauthorised,[115] and was eventually treated as a source of a duty separate from being a licensee.[116]

Another strand of cases which sought to protect straying infants insisted that a child's status as a trespasser was irrelevant where the defendant's duty arose not from his occupation of land but from his doing of a dangerous act.[117] This

---

[106] *Cooke* v. *Midland Great Western Railway of Ireland* [1909] AC 229, 239 *per* Lord Atkinson.

[107] *Hardy* v. *Central London Railway Co.* [1920] 3 KB 459, CA.

[108] [1972] AC 877.

[109] Under the modern statute which applies to trespassers it will not necessarily be sufficient merely to bring home to a child that he will be a trespasser if he enters: Occupiers' Liability Act 1984, s. 1(5).

[110] A good example of a trap is provided by *Williams* v. *Cardiff Corp* [1950] 1 KB 514, CA, where the defendant's land was used as a tip for sweepings and the 4-year-old plaintiff cut her nose on broken glass after rolling down a grassy bank.

[111] [1956] 1 WLR 218, CA.

[112] *Robert Addie & Sons (Collieries) Ltd* v. *Dumbreck* [1929] AC 358, 376 *per* Viscount Dunedin.

[113] *Latham* v. *R Johnson & Nephew Ltd* [1913] 1 KB 398, 416 *per* Hamilton LJ (a pile of broken paving stones in broad daylight insufficient).

[114] *Walder* v. *Hammersmith BC* [1944] 1 All ER 490, following Viscount Dunedin in *Robert Addie, supra* n 112.

[115] *Gough* v. *NCB* [1954] 1 QB 191.

[116] In *British Railways Board* v. *Herrington* [1972] AC 877, Lord Reid treated allurement as "in a sense inviting children to meddle" and as separate from licence by acquiescence.

[117] *Mourton* v. *Poulter* [1930] 2 KB 183, 191 *per* Scrutton LJ, explaining *Excelsior Wire Rope Co Ltd* v. *Callan* [1930] AC 404.

strategy was most plausible when the defendant was not the occupier of the land and consequently had no control over visitors[118] but has been discredited so far as it also purported to impose duties on occupiers as to their activities.[119]

Statute has improved the position of children against landowners. The Occupiers' Liability Act 1957 removed the distinction between licensees and invitees and imposed on occupiers a common duty to their lawful visitors to take such care as is reasonable to see that those visitors are reasonably safe. With regard to the standard of care occupiers are instructed to "be prepared for children to be less careful than adults".[120] This does not mean, however, that occupiers must necessarily make their land safe for unaccompanied children. In judging what precautions are reasonable a landowner may "have regard to the fact that it is the habit, and also the duty, of prudent people to look after their little children".[121] Moreover, where a child is expressly permitted by a parent to play in a particular place that may be compelling evidence that the place was reasonably safe.[122]

The Occupiers' Liability Act 1984 has replaced the common law on occupiers' duties to trespassers. It imposes a duty only if three conditions are met.[123] First, the occupier must be are aware of the danger (or have reasonable grounds to believe that it exists). Secondly, the occupier must know (or have reasonable grounds to believe) that some other may come into the vicinity of the danger. Thirdly, the risk must be one that he may reasonably be expected to offer the other some protection against. In *Ratcliff* v. *McConnell*[124] it was held that this third condition excluded risks that the plaintiff should have been fully aware of.

Summary

Children must primarily turn to their parents for protection against the risks inherent in childhood but their tort rights against their parents are limited because of concerns about disrupting family relationships and undermining parental autonomy. Courts have been reluctant to make the state pay damages for failure to protect children from physical or sexual abuse, but this orthodoxy is under challenge. Moreover, a recent decision of the House of Lords has

---

[118] *Buckland* v. *Guildford Gas Light & Coke Co* [1949] 1 KB 410 (maintainer of high-voltage power-lines). Similar reasoning was relied on in *Davis* v. *St Mary's Demolition* [1954] 1 WLR 592, but in that case the decision that the demolition contractors were not occupiers seems vulnerable.

[119] *Commissioner for Railways* v. *Quinlan* [1964] AC 1054, 1075, PC. See also Occupiers' Liability Act 1957, s. 1(1) and Occupiers' Liability Act 1984, s. 1(1)(a).

[120] Occupiers' Liability Act 1957, s. 2(3)(a).

[121] *Phipps* v. *Rochester* [1955] 1 KB 450, 471 *per* Devlin J Confirmed after the 1957 Act by *Simkiss* v. *Rhondda BC* (1983) 81 LGR 460, 467.

[122] *Simkiss, supra* n 121, at 471. The observations in *Simkiss* should probably not be followed if either it is not reasonable to think that the parent has had the opportunity to assess the safety of the place or the risks of the place are not such as would have been obvious to a reasonable parent.

[123] Occupiers' Liability Act 1984, s. 1(3).

[124] [1999] 1 WLR 670, CA, especially paras 36–8.

extended the responsibility of the state for errors by educational professionals leading to underachievement by pupils. Judicial creativity and statute have both played a part in increasing the obligations of occupiers to protect children on their land but their duties are still limited and qualified by a general understanding that they can usually expect parents to take primary responsibility.

OBLIGATIONS OWED TO PARENTS RELATING TO CHILDREN

Common law allowed a master to claim damages arising from an injury done to a servant.[125] In 1867 Willes J stated that he felt "no difficulty in holding that, upon authority, as well as in good sense, the father of the family, in respect of such service as his daughter renders him from her sense of duty and filial gratitude, stands in the same position as an ordinary master".[126] On the basis of this analogy claims were permitted by fathers for physical injuries to their children,[127] seduction of daughters (leading to pregnancy), and enticement of daughters.[128] Such actions appear to treat children as a form of valuable property, and to thus confirm a popular view about how parents thought about their children during the nineteenth century.[129] It can be argued, however, that this appearance disguises the real practical function of such actions in the nineteenth century. In any case the actions depended on service *within the family* rather than any contributions to the family economy.

Although the form of action meant that it had to be asserted that the child was a servant of the father this would be presumed without evidence if the child lived in his father's family.[130] And even where some service was expressly mentioned it could be minimal: "Even making tea has been said to be an act of service".[131] The value of the services lost was virtually irrelevant. Damages were not calculated to compensate for loss of tea-making or other services. Often damages were sought for costs which the father incurred as a result of the injury. For instance, in the case of physical injuries to children the father might incur medical expenses which could not be recovered by the child.[132] Actions for

---

[125] For a history of this action see, G H Jones, *"Per Quod Servitium Amisit"* (1958) 74 *LQR* 39.

[126] *Evans* v. *Walton* (1867) LR 2 CP 615, 622.

[127] *Jones* v. *Brown* (1794) Peake 233; *Hall* v. *Hollander* (1825) 4 B & C 660 (claim failed on the facts).

[128] *Evans* v. *Walton* (1867) LR 2 CP 615; *Lough* v. *Ward* [1945] 2 All ER 338.

[129] H Cunningham, *Children and Childhood in Western Society Since 1500* (London, Longman, 1995), p 177, "For the great majority of [children] the major change of the first half of the twentieth century was that they lost any productive role within the economy, and increasingly gained a new role as consumers. This undoubtedly altered the way in which children were viewed by their parents. It was not that children had previously been valued above all for the contribution that they could make to the family economy; rather that contribution had been understood as a norm. Once it was removed, parents had to adjust to a new valuation of children".

[130] *Jones* v. *Brown* (1794) Peake 233, *per* Lord Kenyon.

[131] *Carr* v. *Clarke* (1818) 2 Chit R 260, 261 *per* Abbott CJ.

[132] *Collins* v. *Lefevre* (1858) 1 F & F 436. In *IRC* v. *Hambrook* [1956] 2 QB 641, 664, Denning LJ suggested that the action was "confined to the members of the household who rendered services to the head of it and *who had to be kept by him in sickness and in health*" (emphasis added).

seduction were not permitted unless pregnancy had resulted, and the damages could cover the injury to the daughter/servant[133] and expenses incurred by the father.[134] Importantly, damages for seduction included compensation for the father's "wounded feelings"[135] and exemplary damages were similarly available in actions for enticement.[136] Pollock started his discussion of these actions with the statement that "next to the sanctity of the person comes that of the personal relations constituting the family"[137] and it seems that such awards may have drawn on a sense that the defendant had wronged a family's honour.

Despite the fact that the purpose of these actions in the family context was not the protection of the value of the services, many decisions reflected the statement of Kelly CB that "It has been truly said that the action for seduction is founded on a fiction; but for that fiction there must be some foundation, however slender, in fact".[138] Thus claimants were non-suited if the allegation of service was wholly implausible, for instance, because the child injured was too young to perform any acts of service,[139] the daughter was clearly in the service of someone other than the claimant father,[140] or the daughter was "in truth the head of the family".[141] The fiction regularly stymied the practical usefulness of the actions.

The parents' actions were abolished by the combined effect of the Law Reform (Miscellaneous Provisions) Act 1970, section 5 and Administration of Justice Act 1982, section 2. The action for seduction was an anachronism in a world which attached less importance to family honour and where other legal provisions sought to ensure affiliation and support for illegitimate children. Further, in suitable circumstances a victim could now claim for the cost of providing family services that she or he had previously provided.[142] An attempt to

---

[133] *Fores* v. *Wilson* (1791) Peake 55, *per* Lord Kenyon (explaining why so little evidence of service was required in an action for seduction).

[134] Hence the disappointment of the father in *Grinnell* v. *Wells* (1844) 7 M & G 1033 who sued for the cost of supporting a seduced daughter who had previously been able to support herself when told that he could not succeed unless he could allege service to him at the time of the seduction. The reporter added the curt note that the fiction of service protected the rich man whose daughter made tea, but not the poor man whose daughter was sent to earn her bread elsewhere.

[135] *Howard* v. *Crowther* (1841) 8 M & W 601, 604 *per* Lord Abinger CB (explaining why a right to sue for seduction was not an action for injury to property and hence could not be assigned on bankruptcy). See also *Terry* v. *Hutchinson* (1868) LR 3 QB 599, 602 *per* Cockburn CJ, "the action is substantially for the aggravated injury that the father has sustained in the seduction of his child" and *Beetham* v. *James* [1937] 1 KB 527, 533 *per* Atkinson J, "It is the insult to the parents' pride and honour that matters".

[136] *Lough* v. *Ward* [1945] 2 All ER 338 (£500 for enticing a 16-year-old to leave her parents and join a religious community).

[137] F Pollock, *Law of Torts* (1951, 15th ed by P A Landon).

[138] *Hedges* v. *Tagg* (1872) LR 7 Ex 283, 285.

[139] *Hall* v. *Hollander* (1825) 4 B & C 660 (two-and-a-half-year-old).

[140] *Carr* v. *Clarke* (1818) 2 Chit R 260 (daughter in the service of a relative other than the claimant father); *Whitbourne* v. *Williams* [1901] 2 KB 722 (daughter in the service of the seducer).

[141] *Manley* v. *Field* (1859) 7 CBNS 96.

[142] Thus an injured mother can claim damages to cover the cost of hiring a substitute mother for her children. See below, pp 146–147.

develop a fictionless action for interference with parental rights was rejected by the Court of Appeal in *F* v. *Wirral MBC*.[143]

In summary, until recently fathers (later parents) were permitted to bring actions arising from certain wrongful events involving their children which caused the family to incur costs or dishonour. Although these actions asserted loss of the child's services this was a fiction and in most cases recoupment of the value of the child's services was not the purpose of the claim. Such actions should not be treated as providing any recent evidence of treatment of children as quasi-property,[144] though they do reveal an attitude to family honour that today might be considered anachronistic.

ASSESSMENT OF DAMAGES

Claims by injured children

The same general principles are used to assess damages to compensate both injured children and adults but in cases involving children the exercise is often more speculative. For example, in *Cassel* v. *Hammersmith and Fulham HA*[145] assessment of a loss of earnings claim by a child severely injured at birth involved attributing to the claimant, on the basis of his family background, the likelihood of employment with a medium-sized firm of solicitors or accountants. In some circumstances a claim may be so speculative that the judge feels compelled to assess its value as nil.[146] Claims for pain, suffering and loss of amenity are greatly increased when a child is aware of its condition[147] and awards often take account of the psychological disturbance which such awareness may cause at puberty.[148]

Claims by children following torts to parents

"It is plain beyond argument that an infant child, deprived of his mother's care as a result of her being tortiously injured, cannot recover damages against the tortfeasor".[149] Instead, English law awards damages to the injured mother to cover

---

[143] [1991] Fam 69. At 119 Stuart-Smith LJ said that "The extent of such [parental] rights at common law was strictly limited . . . Such as they were, they were abolished by statute in 1970 and 1982." Purchas LJ, by contrast, attached more importance to the idea that tort actions were not the appropriate route for challenges to exercises of statutory powers by local authorities.

[144] The nineteenth century position can be contrasted with the role of similar actions in protecting the economic value of feudal wards in medieval times: See, D J Ibbetson, *A Historical Introduction to the Law of Obligations* (Oxford, Oxford University Press, 1999), pp 66–7.

[145] [1992] PIQR Q1.

[146] *Connolly* v. *Camden and Islington AHA* [1981] 3 All ER 250 (claim for loss of earnings in lost years by child injured when 5 years' old).

[147] For example, *Taylor* v. *Bristol Omnibus Co Ltd* [1975] 1 WLR 1054.

[148] For example, *S* v. *Distillers Co. (Biochemicals) Ltd* [1969] 3 All ER 1412.

[149] *Buckley* v. *Farrow and Buckley* [1997] PIQR Q78, Q80 *per* Simon Brown LJ.

the cost of providing substitute services.[150] By contrast, where a young child's mother is tortiously killed a claim may be brought under the Fatal Accidents Act 1976 for the child's loss.[151] Difficulties have arisen over how to assess that loss where a relative (or other) has taken over the task of providing the care previously provided by the mother. Section 4 of the Act instructs judges to disregard benefits accruing to the child as a result of the death when assessing damages, and in *Stanley* v. *Saddique*[152] the Court of Appeal took this to mean that a child could claim for loss of a mother's services even when superior services were being provided by a step-mother. By contrast, in *Hayden* v. *Hayden*[153] a differently constituted Court of Appeal held that where a child's father had given up work to provide the necessary care the claim should be limited to the difference between the mother's care and what the father could provide, with an allowance for the risk that the father would not continue to provide such care.[154] In *R* v. *Criminal Injuries Compensation Board, ex parte K (Minors)*,[155] where three children were cared for after their mother's death by their uncle and aunt, Brooke LJ followed *Stanley*, but left open the question whether a different result should be reached where the substitute carer had a parental obligation before the death.[156] Despite these difficulties there has been constant agreement that awards under the Fatal Accidents Act 1976 cannot include any sum to compensate bereaved children for loss of "parental love" or "the joys of a happy home" because "these losses cannot be assessed in monetary terms".[157] Children who lose one or both parents are not entitled even to claim the fixed sum for bereavement.[158]

Claims following the death or injury of children

The parents of a legitimate[159] minor may claim a fixed sum[160] for bereavement. The award was introduced in 1982 at the same time as the abolition of actions for loss of a child's services and of the right to damages for loss of expectation

---

[150] *Daly* v. *General Steam Navigation Ltd* [1981] 1 WLR 120. It seems that following *Hunt* v. *Severs* [1994] 2 AC 350 these damages would now be held on trust for the provider of the substitute services.

[151] Fatal Accidents Act 1976, s. 3(1).

[152] [1992] QB 1.

[153] [1992] 1 WLR 986.

[154] In this case the father was also the tortfeasor. *Hunt* v. *Severs* [1994] 2 AC 350 clearly holds that a tortfeasor should not have to pay damages for the cost of care that he is in fact providing voluntarily. If, however, s. 4 excludes such services from the assessment of damages under the Fatal Accidents Act 1976 then a contrasting result may be reached in cases involving death.

[155] [1999] QB 1131.

[156] As in *Hayden*. The argument is that where a substitute carer had a pre-existing parental obligation then the care provided after the death might not be a benefit accruing "as a result of" the death, and hence might not be excluded from the assessment by s. 4 of the Fatal Accidents Act 1976.

[157] *Hay* v. *Hughes* [1975] QB 790, 810–11 *per* Buckley LJ.

[158] Fatal Accidents Act 1976, s. 1A. The Law Commission has recommended that children should be able to claim for bereavement on the death of a parent or a sibling and that the fixed sum award should be increased: *Claims for Wrongful Death* (LC 263, 1 November 1999), para 6.3.

[159] Only the mother of an illegitimate child can claim.

[160] Currently £7,500. If both parents claim then the sum is divided between them.

of life. Until 1982 the claim for loss of expectation of life survived for the child's estate, and thus parents could use such a claim to obtain an indirect solatium. While a claim on behalf of the child's estate for damages for pain and suffering before death is possible, in *Hicks* v. *Chief Constable of the South Yorkshire Police*[161] the House of Lords upheld a decision that awarded no damages where unconsciousness followed swiftly on physical injury and asserted that no damages could be recovered for experiencing terror.[162]

Parents who witness an accident involving their children, or the immediate aftermath of such an accident, may be able to claim for any recognised psychiatric illness triggered by the shock.[163] A distinction is drawn, however, between such illnesses and acute grief. Compensation is denied for grief, sorrow and deprivation because they are "ordinary and inevitable incidents of life".[164] Similarly, parents have no action for the suffering involved in caring for a severely injured child.[165]

Summary

Although no special principles are used when assessing damages for injured children, the lives of their parents are often used as a basis for speculating how their lives would have progressed but for the injury. Where a parent is tortiously killed a dependent child can recover for the loss of financial support and parental services but not for grief. Where a parent is injured then the child has no claim but the injured parent can recover lost income and the cost of providing substitute parental services. Where a child is tortiously killed its parents will recover only a modest sum for their bereavement. Grief, for both the child who loses a parent and the parent who loses a child, is treated as an ordinary and inevitable incident in human life which cannot ground compensation.

CONCLUSIONS

What conclusions can we reach about how the law of torts treats children? We can start by stressing that children are not treated as non-persons. Thus they are regarded as capable of owing and being owed legal duties. But in considering

---

[161] [1992] 2 All ER 65.
[162] "It is perfectly clear law that fear by itself, of whatever degree, is a normal human emotion for which no damages can be awarded" 69, *per* Lord Bridge.
[163] *McLoughlin* v. *O'Brien* [1983] 1 AC 410. But not if the child was responsible for the accident: *Greatorex* v. *Greatorex* [2000] 1 WLR 1970.
[164] *Alcock* v. *Chief Constable of South Yorkshire* [1992] 1 AC 310, 416 *per* Lord Oliver.
[165] *Taylor* v. *British Omnibus Co Ltd* [1975] 1 WLR 1054, 1058 *per* Lord Denning MR, "They have devoted their lives to him and will continue to do so. Yet they are not entitled to recover any damages for all their grief and suffering". Compare *S* v. *Distillers Co (Biochemicals) Ltd* [1969] 3 All ER 1412, 1422, where Hinchcliffe J held that the mother of a child injured by thalidomide was entitled to £5,000 because the fun and joy of motherhood had been partly destroyed.

when they will be responsible for injuries caused to others, or to themselves, judges make allowances for youthful inexperience and the "irresponsibility of childhood",[166] and do not equate children with adults. No fixed ages are significant, however. Instead, reliance is placed on looser concepts such as "tender years" and "years of discretion". The effect of this approach is that, to an extent at least, everyone in society must take the risk of being injured by children behaving like children. In practice, of course, children most often succeed in injuring other children. Thus, although children who cause harm do not have to bear the costs of childhood mishaps, the children they injure often do: Barry Watson is not held to an unrealistic standard of behaviour, nor is his father, but Susan McHale recovers nothing for her injured eye.[167]

The risk of harm being caused to others or to themselves by children behaving like children is limited to some extent by the imposition of duties on those who control children and the dangers which children may trigger. Tort law treats parents as having the primary role in both controlling and protecting their children. This protective role is relied on to reduce the obligations that others, such as occupiers of land, might otherwise owe children. The law of torts has also been willing, however, at least to some extent, to juridify the relationship between parent and child, though in practice this gives rise to few claims. The obligations of parents to control and protect have also been extended to other people taking on quasi-parental roles, such as school-teachers when children are at school and local authorities when children are in care. But although the parental role is primary the law of torts has also imposed obligations to control and protect on others, including in particular the suppliers and storers of objects which can be dangerous for children, and occupiers of land. With regard to occupiers of land, tort law can justly be accused of having relied for too long on doctrine stressing the legal status of visitors to land and ignoring how children perceive property and space.

The role of the state in protecting and providing for children is still an area of controversy within tort law. During the last decade English law has gradually become more willing to treat failures of the social welfare system as giving rise to claims for damages. Courts have been willing to impose tort duties on the state where it acts as a substitute parent or provides advice for parents. Importantly, it has also recently been held that educational professionals are liable in tort for injuries caused by failure to meet professional standards of skill and competence. This development has extended the range of interests vital to children which are protected through tort law. Currently, however, the state is not liable in tort for failing to protect children against physical or sexual abuse.

From the perspective of protected interests, one interest which is particular to children and is protected by tort law is a child's interest in the life and health of its parents. Statute allows children to claim for loss of financial and other dependency

---

[166] *Wilson* v. *Pringle* [1986] 2 All ER 440, 448 *per* Croom-Johnson LJ.
[167] *McHale* v. *Watson, supra* n 11.

following the death of a supporting parent. Indeed some cases suggest that the current English statute over-protects the economic dimension of this interest. Where a supporting parent is injured the same interest is still protected, but indirectly since it is up to the injured parent to claim for the cost of providing substitute care and support. A child's interest in its parents is not fully protected, however, since compensation will not be paid for grief or loss of the emotional bond. The reason for this is not that tort law regards the financial role of parents as more important than the emotional role, but a more general concern that tort law does not have the capacity to try to redress most forms of distress and emotional harm.

9

The Medical Treatment of Children

PENNEY LEWIS

THE LAW GOVERNING the medical treatment of children is characterised by an ostensible respect for the autonomy of the appropriate decision-maker. This decision-maker can be the child herself, in the case of a child with sufficient intelligence and maturity to make her own decisions, or the party with parental responsibility, most often the parents. Courts, however, have been reluctant to allow these decision-makers complete autonomy, and have retained an absolute power to override any decision involving the medical treatment of a child on the grounds of the child's "best interests".

The primary decision-maker, though, will be either the child herself or those with parental responsibility. The identity of the primary decision-maker is determined on the basis of the child's competence. Only decisions involving conflict between the child, those with parental responsibility, and/or the medical team involved in providing treatment, will be brought before a court.

One caveat to this fairly simple scheme should be noted. A child can be detained and treated compulsorily for a mental disorder under the Mental Health Act 1983 regardless of her competence and without the consent of either the child (if she is competent) or those with parental responsibility.[1]

COMPETENCE

As to capacity, section 8 of the Family Law Reform Act 1969 necessarily implies that there is a rebuttable presumption of lack of capacity to consent to medical treatment for children under sixteen.[2] The standard by which one can establish

---

[1] Mental Health Act 1983, ss. 2, 3, 63. However, many doctors prefer not to use the powers of detention under the 1983 Act with child patients either on the basis of perceived "stigma" attached to their use, or because of philosophical opposition by medical staff. See *Re C (Detention: Medical Treatment)* [1997] 2 FLR 180 at 194; *Re W (A Minor) (Medical Treatment: Court's Jurisdiction)* [1993] Fam 64 at 83. This preference can be accommodated because there are other means of imposing compulsory treatment on competent minors without resorting to the powers of the 1983 Act, unlike the situation with competent adults. See *infra*, text accompanying nn. 20–36.

[2] S. 8(1) provides:

"The consent of a minor who has attained the age of sixteen years to any surgical, medical or dental treatment which, in the absence of consent, would constitute a trespass to his person, shall be as effective as it would be if he were of full age; and where a minor has by virtue of this section

that a child under sixteen has the capacity to consent is governed by the House of Lords decision in *Gillick* v. *West Norfolk & Wisbech AHA*.[3] In that case, Lord Fraser stated that:

> "[p]rovided the patient, whether a boy or a girl, is capable of understanding what is proposed, and of expressing his or her own wishes, I see no good reason for holding that he or she lacks the capacity to express them validly and effectively and to authorise the medical man to make the examination or give the treatment which he advises."[4]

Lord Scarman held that the "parental right yields to the child's right to make his own decisions when he reaches a sufficient understanding and intelligence to be capable of making up his own mind on the matter requiring decision".[5]

Thus if the patient is under the age of sixteen, she will be presumed incompetent, and her competence will be tested using the test found in *Gillick*.[6] If she is sixteen or seventeen, then her competence is presumed,[7] but can still be questioned in the same way as can an adult's competence.[8]

A higher standard of competence

There is some evidence that a higher standard of competence is applied to children than to adults. In *Gillick*, Lord Scarman required that the child "understand *fully* what is proposed" and "have a sufficient *maturity* to understand what is involved".[9] Ian Kennedy and Andrew Grubb have suggested that full

given an effective consent to any treatment it shall not be necessary to obtain any consent for it from his parent or guardian".

   [3] [1986] AC 112.
   [4] *Ibid* at 169.
   [5] *Ibid* at 186. See J Montgomery, "Children as Property" (1988) 51 *MLR* 323.
   [6] *Supra* n 3. This test may be further fleshed out using the tests found in *Re C* and *Re MB*, see *infra* n 8. For examples of competence assessments in adolescents, see *Re B (A Minor) (Treatment and Secure Accommodation)* [1997] 1 FCR 618 at 625; *Re C (Detention: Medical Treatment)* [1997] 2 FLR 180 at 196.
   [7] Family Law Reform Act 1969, s. 8.
   [8] The current test of competence is based on the test set out by Thorpe J in *Re C (Adult: Refusal of Medical Treatment)* [1994] 1 WLR 290. To meet the test of competence, the patient must be able to comprehend and retain the necessary information, believe it, and weigh the information, balancing the risks and needs, to arrive at a true choice. This test was approved in a form slightly modified by the Court of Appeal in *Re MB (Medical Treatment)* [1997] 8 Med LR 217 at 224. Butler-Sloss LJ wrote:

> "A person lacks capacity if some impairment or disturbance of mental functioning renders the person unable to make a decision whether to consent to, or to refuse, treatment. That inability to make a decision will occur when: (a) the patient is unable to comprehend and retain the information which is material to the decision, especially as to the likely consequences of having, or not having, the treatment in question; (b) the patient is unable to use the information and weigh it in the balance as part of the process of arriving at the decision. If, as Thorpe J observed in *Re C*, a compulsive disorder or phobia from which the patient suffers stifles belief in the information presented to her, then the decision may not be a true one."

   [9] *Gillick, supra* n 3 at 189 (emphasis added).

understanding could not be taken to mean complete understanding as such a standard would be impossible and unworkable.[10] Perhaps Lord Scarman was simply asserting that the standard of competence for a child under sixteen would be the same as for an adult? The reference to maturity could be similarly understood: Lord Scarman was simply flagging the "care to be taken in complying with the standard" in the case of children whose maturity cannot be (rebuttably) presumed as in the case of adults.[11] With particular regard to the provision of contraceptive advice and treatment, Lord Scarman incorporated additional higher requirements into the general test of ability to understand the nature and purpose of what is proposed. The relevance of these additional factors in circumstances other than the provision of contraceptive advice and treatment may be doubted, but where contraceptive advice and treatment is sought, according to Lord Scarman, before it is given the doctor must be satisfied that the patient is able to understand the relevant "moral and family questions, especially her relationship with her parents; long-term problems associated with the emotional impact of pregnancy and its termination; and . . . the risks to health of sexual intercourse at her age, risks which contraception may diminish but cannot eliminate".[12] As Michael Jones has noted, "[t]he 15 year old who could satisfy this test would be a mature young woman indeed".[13]

Following *Gillick*, cases accumulated in which a higher standard appeared to be applied to children. In *Re R (A Minor) (Wardship: Medical Treatment)*, Lord Donaldson MR stated that *Gillick* competence requires:

> "not merely an ability to understand the nature of the proposed treatment . . . but a full understanding and appreciation of the consequences both of the treatment in terms of intended and possible side-effects and equally important, the anticipated consequences of a failure to treat".[14]

In *Re S (A Minor) (Consent to Medical Treatment)*, the court held that the fifteen-and-a-half-year-old who was refusing life-saving blood transfusions was not competent as she did not understand the full implications of what would happen to her, was hoping for a miracle and failed to comprehend the manner in which death would occur and the associated pain and distress.[15] Similarly, in *Re E (A Minor)*, Ward J held that a fifteen-and-a-half-year-old Jehovah's Witness with acute leukaemia was not competent to refuse blood transfusions. He set out the level of competence required:

---

[10] I M Kennedy and A Grubb, *Medical Law: Text with Materials* (London, Butterworths, 2nd ed, 1994), pp 148–9.

[11] "The Doctor, the Pill, the 15-year-old Girl" in I M Kennedy, *Treat Me Right* (Oxford, Clarendon, 1991), p 105.

[12] *Gillick, supra* n 3 at 189.

[13] M Jones, "Consent to Medical Treatment by Minors after Gillick" (1986) 2 *Professional Negligence* 41 at 44.

[14] [1992] Fam 11 at 26.

[15] [1994] 2 FLR 1065.

"I am quite satisfied that A does not have any sufficient comprehension of the pain he has yet to suffer, of the fear that he will be undergoing, of the distress not only occasioned by that fear but also—and importantly—the distress he will inevitably suffer as he, a loving son, helplessly watches his parents' and his family's distress. They are a close family, and they are a brave family, but I find that he has no realisation of the full implications which lie before him as to the process of dying. He may have some concept of the fact that he will die, but as to the manner of his death and to the extent of his and his family's suffering I find he has not the ability to turn his mind to it nor the will to do so. Who can blame him for that?"[16]

Indeed, it would be difficult to "blame" any person unable to come to terms with the manner of his or her death and the suffering associated with it. This is an exceedingly high standard to impose.[17] Perhaps these cases simply reflect the judicial reluctance to allow a child to "martyr himself".[18] The law of competence is thus distorted in order to provide a covert tool allowing the judge to avoid the consequences of the child's decision.

COMPETENT MINORS

Although from *Gillick* one would have logically inferred that a *Gillick* competent child was competent both to consent to and refuse medical treatment,[19] subsequent decisions have indicated that a *Gillick* competent child's refusal of medical treatment can be overridden by a consent given by a person with parental responsibility. In *Re R,* Lord Donaldson held that as long as either the *Gillick* competent child or the proxy has consented then the doctor is protected.[20] Although his colleagues did not rule on this issue in the case of parental proxies, in *Re W (A Minor) (Medical Treatment: Court's Jurisdiction)*, Lord Donaldson's later doubts were conclusively laid to rest by a majority of the Court of Appeal which held that a *Gillick* competent child's refusal of medical treatment is valid subject to being overridden by the parents.[21] The child's refusal is a very important factor to be weighed but is not conclusive.[22] As long

[16] *Re E (A Minor)* (1990) 9 BMLR 1. See also *Re L (Medical Treatment: Gillick Competency)* [1998] 2 FLR 810.

[17] See A Grubb, "Treatment without Consent: Child" (1996) 4 *Medical Law Review* 84 at 86 ("It is too much to expect of individuals that they come to terms with dying and its processes before they can be said to be competent to make decisions at the end of life").

[18] *Re E, supra* n 16.

[19] See Lord Scarman in *Gillick, supra* n 3 at 186: "as a matter of law the parental right to determine whether or not their minor child below the age of 16 will have medical treatment terminates if and when the child achieves a sufficient understanding and intelligence to enable him or her to understand fully what is proposed". Also, "the parental right yields to the child's right to make his own decision when he reaches a sufficient understanding and intelligence to be capable of making up his own mind on the matter requiring decision". See also McHugh J in *Department of Health & Community Services (NT)* v. *JWB and SMB* (1992) 66 ALJR 300 at 340.

[20] *Supra* n 14.

[21] *Supra* n 1 at 84 *per* Lord Donaldson, at 86 *per* Balcombe LJ, at 94 *per* Nolan LJ *(dubitante)*.

[22] *Re W, ibid* at 84. See, for example, *Re M (Medical Treatment: Consent)* [1999] 2 FLR 1097 (refusal of heart transplant by 15½ year old girl overruled).

as the person with parental responsibility acts within the limits of her power, that is, in the best interests of the child, she can overrule a competent child's refusal to consent to treatment. Moreover, a court can also overrule a competent child's refusal to consent to treatment.[23]

In *Re R*, Lord Donaldson supported this conclusion by arguing from the existence of the court's duty to override parental decisions where necessary, that the court must also have the ability to override decisions by *Gillick* competent children.[24] Gillian Douglas has pointed out the logical flaw in this argument:

"A court may override a parent because it acts as a protector to ensure that persons other than the ward act in his or her best interests. This is quite different from saying that it should act to prevent a *mature* ward from taking decisions which may objectively not be in his or her welfare".[25]

The issue is not simply a straightforward articulation of judicial power to intervene. To approach the problem of refusals by competent minors in this way is to fail to appreciate the distinction between a competent decision-maker who makes a decision about his or her own medical treatment, and a proxy decision-maker who makes a decision about the medical treatment of another (incompetent) person. In the latter case, in which the patient is insufficiently autonomous to make his or her own decisions, the aim must be to make the *best* decision for the patient, on whatever standard is adopted. Using the best interests test, the issue is therefore whether the decision by the proxy *best* enhances the patient's interests. If not, then the court may intervene.[26] With regard to the competent, autonomous patient, while third parties (family members, the court) may believe that a different decision would *better* promote the patient's interests, the patient's decision is respected because he or she is irrebuttably presumed to be the *best* judge of his or her interests. It is this conclusion, inherent in the philosophy embedded in *Gillick*, that the Court of Appeal in *Re R* and *Re W* was unwilling to accept.

In addition to the philosophical conflict with *Gillick*, Lawrence Gostin has also suggested that *Re R*:

"runs counter to the philosophy of the *Children Act 1989*, . . . portions [of which] respect a competent child's right to self-determination. For example, where a child

---

[23] *Re R, supra* n 14; *Re W, ibid* at 81 *per* Lord Donaldson, at 88 *per* Balcombe LJ, at 91 *per* Nolan LJ; *Re K, W and H (Minors) (Medical Treatment)* [1993] 1 FLR 854; *Re C (Detention: Medical Treatment), supra* n 1; *Re L, supra* n 16 (in *obiter*). See *contra, Region 2 Hospital Corporation* v. *Walker* (1994) 116 DLR (4th) 477 at 489 (NBCA) (holding that the right of self-determination underlying the mature minor rule includes both the right to consent to and to refuse medical treatment).

[24] *Supra* n 14 at 25.

[25] G Douglas, "The Retreat from *Gillick*" (1992) 55 MLR 569 at 573.

[26] This of course assumes that the system accepts that the court can be a *better* decision-maker than the proxy. See A Grubb, "Treatment Decisions: Keeping It in the Family" in A Grubb (ed), *Choices and Decisions in Medical Care* (Chichester, Wiley, 1993), p 37 at pp 48–54.

subject to a supervision order has sufficient understanding to make an informed decision on proposed treatment, the court cannot order him to undergo it unless he consents".[27]

The Children Act 1989 came into force shortly after *Re R* was decided and yet the significance of those provisions cited by Gostin was dismissed by Lord Donaldson in *Re W*, on the grounds that the "provisions all concern interim or supervision orders and do not impinge upon the jurisdiction of the court to make prohibited steps or specific issue orders".[28] The development undermines the decision in *Gillick*, fails to respect the proposition that a competent child should be taking responsibility for herself embodied in both *Gillick* and the Children Act 1989, and demonstrates a distinct lack of respect for the child's right of self-determination and bodily integrity.[29]

Some limits have been imposed on this power to overrule a competent minor. In *Re W*, Nolan LJ stated that the power should only be exercised if "the child's welfare is threatened by a serious and imminent risk that the child will suffer grave and irreversible mental or physical harm".[30] Balcombe LJ restricted the power to cases where the child's refusal "will in all probability lead to the death of the child or to severe permanent injury".[31]

Detention and force

In *Re W*, the Court of Appeal upheld the trial judge's order that a competent sixteen-year-old anorexic patient could be moved to a specialist clinic and treated there despite her refusal to consent. More recently in *Re C (Detention: Medical Treatment)*,[32] Wall J applied *Re W* to the case of another sixteen-year-old anorexic and determined that he had the power to authorise her *detention* in a clinic for the purposes of treatment. Although this question had not been specifically considered by the court in *Re W*, Wall J held that the existence of this inherent power could be inferred from the fact that the trial judge in *Re W* had authorised W's removal to the specialist unit and her treatment there. More

---

[27] L Gostin, "Consent to treatment: the incapable person" in C Dyer (ed), *Medicine, Patients and the Law* (Oxford, Blackwell, 2nd ed, 1992), p 72 at p 76. (But see *South Glamorgan County Council v. B* [1993] 1 FCR 626 at 635 in which Douglas Brown J held that the power to overrule a competent child remained part of the court's inherent jurisdiction regardless of the wording of s. 38(6) of the Children Act 1989 which purported to give the competent child the right to refuse to submit to a medical assessment).

[28] *Re W, supra* n 1 at 82.

[29] I M Kennedy and A Grubb, *Medical Law* (London, Butterworths, 3rd ed, 2000) at 984–9. There has been trenchant criticism of *Re R* and *Re W*: see A Bainham, "The Judge and the Competent Minor" (1992) 108 *LQR* 194 at 196–7; J Bridgeman, "Old enough to know best?" (1993) 13 *Legal Studies* 69; J Montgomery, "Parents and children in dispute: who has the final word?" (1992) 4 *JCL* 85.

[30] *Re W, supra* n 1 at 94.

[31] *Re W, supra* n 1 at 88.

[32] *Supra* n 1. See P Lewis, "Case Comment on *Re C (A Minor)*" 7(3) *Dispatches* 5.

generally, Wall J relied on the statement of Lord Donaldson MR in *Re W* that "the inherent powers of the court under its *parens patriae* jurisdiction are theoretically limitless".[33] Wall J also considered the question of whether he could authorise the use of reasonable force, concluding based on recent cases[34] that he undoubtedly had the power under the inherent jurisdiction "not only to direct that [C] reside in the [c]linic but also to authorise the use of reasonable force (if necessary) to detain her in the [c]linic".[35] This power would also extend to the authorisation of the use of reasonable force in order to administer medical treatment, but as the clinic was opposed to the forcible administration of treatment, such authorisation was unnecessary.[36]

These holdings follow from the application of *Re W*. Logically, if the court has the power to overrule a competent minor's refusal of medical treatment, such power must include the power to detain that minor for treatment, and to use reasonable force against her if necessary for the detention or the provision of treatment. Otherwise, the competent minor's refusal would effectively be respected, despite it having been overruled by the court.[37]

Moving forward

It is perhaps too easy to criticise *Re R*, *Re W* and their progeny as failing to pay adequate respect to the competent child's autonomy. Having done so, we are left facing the problem encountered by the Court of Appeal in *Re R* and *Re W*. While it may well have been possible to resolve those particular cases by finding that in each case the patient was not *Gillick* competent,[38] doubts about competence may be less profound in other cases. Gillian Douglas suggests[39] that when faced (as the High Court was in *Re E*)[40] with a fifteen-year-old Jehovah's

---

[33] *Re W, supra* n 1 at 81.

[34] The question of whether reasonable force can be used on an incompetent adult patient when treatment is authorised in her best interests had been left open by Wall J in *Tameside and Glossop Acute Services Trust* v. *CH* [1996] 1 FLR 762. However, it was affirmatively decided by Johnson J in *Norfolk and Norwich Healthcare (NHS) Trust* v. *W* [1996] 2 FLR 613 and *Rochdale Healthcare (NHS) Trust* v. *C* [1997] 1 FCR 274 on the basis of the necessity principle in *Re F (Mental Patient: Sterilisation)* [1990] AC 1 (CA and HL). See P Lewis, "Case Comments on *Tameside and Glossop Acute Services Trust* v. *CH* and *Norfolk and Norwich Healthcare (NHS) Trust* v. *W*" 7(1) *Dispatches* 4 at 4–6. This position was later confirmed in *Re MB, supra* n 8 at 225 by Butler-Sloss LJ:

> It would . . . follow . . . from the decision that a patient is not competent to refuse treatment, that such treatment may have to be given against her continued objection if it is in her best interests that the treatment be given despite those objections.

[35] *Re C (Detention: Medical Treatment), supra* n 1 at 189. See also *A Metropolitan Borough Council* v. *DB* [1997] 1 FLR 767 at 777.

[36] *Re C (Detention: Medical Treatment)*, ibid.

[37] See P Lewis, "Feeding Anorexic Patients Who Refuse Food" (1999) 7 *Medical Law Review* 21 at 29.

[38] Kennedy and Grubb, *supra* n 29 at 988–9.

[39] Douglas, "The Retreat from *Gillick*", *supra* n 25 at 574.

[40] *Supra* n 16.

Witness who is refusing a blood transfusion, we should apply the Rawlsian approach suggested by Michael Freeman:

> "what sorts of action or conduct would we wish, as children, to be shielded against on the assumption that we would want to mature to a rationally autonomous adulthood and be capable of deciding our own system of ends as free and rational beings? We would choose principles that would enable children to mature to independent adulthood".[41]

Douglas assumes that if this approach is applied, the patient can be held to be "not mature" and her decision overridden.[42] Such an assumption appears equivalent to an approach simply based on the patient's status as a child. Under such an approach a *Gillick* competent child would *never* be permitted to reject medical treatment if that would prevent him or her from reaching "independent adulthood".[43] This then, would be consistent with the approach taken by Nolan and Balcombe LJJ in *Re W*.[44]

Could we contemplate an approach more respectful of a *Gillick* competent minor's autonomy? A more nuanced view of Freeman's approach would be to consider whether the fifteen-year-old can *already* be considered to be "capable of deciding [her] own system of ends as [a] free and rational being"? Is this not what *Gillick* competence would require in this situation?[45] Even if this requirement were to go beyond what is required for *Gillick* competence, it is possible that a *Gillick* competent fifteen-year-old could meet such a test. If she can, then "the retrospective inquiry is . . . redundant".[46]

Along these lines, Margaret Brazier and Caroline Bridge suggest an expansion of the concept of *Gillick* competence to include a deeper analysis focusing on whether a choice is "maximally autonomous", rather than simply competent:

> "If the law is to operate a truly functional test of autonomy, and not rely on outcome to vitiate decisions society judges imprudent, a presumption has to be made that adults not afflicted by mental disability possess the strength of character to make their own choices, to prioritise their own interests. The younger the individual the less that presumption may accord with reality. . . . As long as minority necessarily imposes a degree of dependency on the minor, and until, in the vast majority of cases, the hormonal disturbances of adolescents are safely in the past, society might well adopt a more sceptical approach to autonomy. Rather than presuming autonomy, decision makers should satisfy themselves that a choice truly is maximally autonomous".[47]

---

[41] M Freeman, *The Rights and Wrongs of Children* (London, Frances Pinter, 1983), p 57.

[42] Douglas, "The Retreat from *Gillick*", *supra* n 25 at 574.

[43] Indeed, this is Douglas' alternative proposal: "Parliament could lay down a fixed age for deeming maturity to determine life-threatening decisions, where probably 18 would be better than 16". *Ibid*.

[44] See *supra*, text accompanying nn. 30–1.

[45] See *Re S*, *supra* n 15 and accompanying text.

[46] Bainham, *supra* n 29 at 196.

[47] M Brazier and C Bridge, "Coercion or caring: analysing adolescent autonomy" (1996) 16:1 *Legal Studies* 84 at 109. See also, C Bridge, "Religious Beliefs and Teenage Refusal of Medical Treatment" (1999) 62 *MLR* 585 at 592–4.

Such an investigation would encompass problems of dependence, undue influence and voluntariness. It would range beyond the cognitive analysis focusing on understanding embodied in *Gillick*, and examine the extent to which the decision furthers the child's own goals and is consistent with the child's own values. It may be that in a small minority of cases, an adolescent will be able to make a competent, maximally autonomous choice to refuse life-saving treatment. Respecting such a choice will be difficult, but it is preferable to arbitrary discrimination on the basis of age alone.

INCOMPETENT MINORS

If the child patient does not meet the test of competence, then she can be treated in her best interests with the consent of a person with parental responsibility or the court.[48] If the person with parental responsibility consents to the recommendations of the medical team, it is unlikely that any concerns will arise.[49] If, however, the persons with parental responsibility refuse the recommended treatment, or demand treatment which is not recommended, then the medical team may take steps to bring the issue before a court if the consequences of the refusal or demand are thought serious enough to warrant such a step (which will undoubtedly have negative repercussions for the relationship between those with parental responsibility and the medical team). In a series of such cases, courts have considered the appropriate ambit of the autonomous decision-making of those with parental responsibility.

The first important case was *Re B (A minor) (Wardship: Medical Treatment)*, in which the parents of a neonate with Down's Syndrome refused consent to an abdominal operation. The child would have died without the operation, which was likely to be successful and to allow the child to live a normal life with Down's Syndrome. Templeman LJ described the approach of the Court of Appeal:

"at the end of the day it devolves on this court in this particular instance to decide whether the life of this child is demonstrably going to be so awful that in effect the child must be condemned to die, or whether the life of this child is still so imponderable that it would be wrong for her to be condemned to die. There may be cases, I know not, of severe proved damage where the future is so certain and where the life of the child is so bound to be full of pain and suffering that the court might be driven to a different conclusion, but in the present case the choice which lies before the court is this: whether to allow an operation to take place which may result in the child living for 20 or 30 years as a mongoloid or whether (and I think this must be brutally the

[49] Although consent to experimental treatment or to research may pose more difficult problems. See R Nicholson (ed), *Medical Research with Children: Ethics, Law and Practice* (Oxford, OUP, 1990); Kennedy and Grubb, *supra* n 29 at 1718, 1727–31; JK Mason and A McCall Smith, *Law and Medical Ethics* (London, Butterworths, 5th ed, 1999), pp 471–6.

result) to terminate the life of a mongoloid child because she also has an intestinal complaint. Faced with that choice I have no doubt that it is the duty of this court to decide that the child must live".[50]

Dunn LJ concurred, also focusing on the predictions of the child's future quality of life. The operation should proceed "because there is no evidence that this child's short life is likely to be an intolerable one. There is no evidence at all as to the quality of life which the child may expect".[51]

The court's attitude was fleshed out further in *Re J (A minor) (Wardship: Medical Treatment)*, which concerned a severely brain-damaged baby who was not terminally ill.[52] All three judges upheld the decision of the trial judge that it would be in the child's best interests to withhold mechanical ventilation should he suffer a further respiratory collapse. The court rejected the absolutist approach based on the sanctity of life that treatment must be given to any child who is not dying. Instead, each judge adopted a balancing approach looking to the child's quality of life.[53] Lord Donaldson suggested that "account has to be taken of the pain and suffering and quality of life which the child will experience if life is prolonged. Account has also to be taken of the pain and suffering involved in the proposed treatment itself".[54] According to Taylor LJ, referring back to the criterion of intolerability proposed by Dunn LJ in *Re B*, "the correct approach is for the court to judge the quality of life the child would have to endure if given the treatment and decide whether in all the circumstances such a life would be so afflicted as to be intolerable to that child".[55]

Courts have also been faced with refusals by those with parental responsibility based on religious convictions. In a series of cases, the courts have consistently overruled the refusals of Jehovah's Witness parents who have refused life-saving blood transfusions for their children. In *Re E (A Minor)*, Ward J relied upon the oft-cited statement of Rutledge J in the United States Supreme Court case of *Prince* v. *Massachusetts*:

"Parents may be free to become martyrs themselves, but it does not follow that they are free in identical circumstances to make martyrs of their children before they have reached the age of full and legal discretion when they can make choices for themselves".[56]

In *Re S (A Minor) (Medical Treatment)*, the parents of a four-and-a-half-year-old child suffering from T-cell leukaemia had refused to allow doctors to transfuse the child. Without transfusions, the child's only hope of cure would be removed. Thorpe J asked:

[50] [1981] 1 WLR 1421 at 1424.
[51] *Ibid.*
[52] [1991] Fam 33.
[53] *Ibid* at 46–7 *per* Lord Donaldson, at 52 *per* Balcombe LJ, at 55 *per* Taylor LJ.
[54] *Ibid* at 46.
[55] *Ibid* at 55.
[56] 321 US 158 at 170 (1944), cited in *Re E (A Minor)*, *supra* n 16.

"are the religious convictions of the parents to deny their child a 50% chance of survival? Are those convictions to deny him that 50% chance and condemn him to inevitable and early death? [Counsel for the parents] realistically saw that this was an extreme case and one in which is it difficult to pursue the argument that the religious convictions of the parents should deny the child the chance of treatment".[57]

The cases discussed up to this point have all involved parental *refusal* of life-saving treatment on behalf of the child. In the recent case of *Re C (Medical Treatment)*, the parents were seeking an order *requiring* the medical staff to *provide* treatment. Judicial opposition to such orders is clear.[58] The Orthodox Jewish parents refused to consent to the withdrawal of their seriously ill sixteen-month-old baby from a ventilator, unless the medical staff would agree in advance to re-ventilation in the event of a further respiratory collapse. The child suffered from spinal muscular atrophy, which is a terminal illness. The parents' religious views prevented them from consenting to any course which might have the effect of indirectly shortening life. Sir Stephen Brown P overruled the parents' objection on the grounds that it was in the child's best interests to withdraw ventilation in order to prevent her from suffering.[59]

The cases involving quality of life determinations and the religious objection cases illustrate the certainty with which the court sees itself as the arbiter of the child's best interests. The views of the parents are considered, but they do not appear to have significant weight. This attitude was challenged by the Court of Appeal in *Re T (A minor) (Wardship: Medical Treatment)* which involved an eighteen-month-old boy who, after an earlier unsuccessful operation, needed a liver transplant in order to survive beyond the age of two-and-a-half.[60] The boy's parents refused to consent to the operation, despite the unanimous clinical opinion that the transplant would be in the child's best interests. Reviewing *Re B* and *Re J*, Butler-Sloss LJ held that it was clear that "the welfare of the child is the paramount consideration".[61] The court held that the trial judge had misdirected himself in focusing on the reasonableness of the mother's decision, rather than on the welfare of the child. While the parents' decision would constitute an important consideration, and the extent to which it was considered would depend on its reasonableness, nevertheless the court retained the power to overrule the decision of a reasonable parent in the best interests of the child.

The controversy which has attached to the case stems not from the use of the best interests or welfare test, but from the way in which the three judges applied that test to the facts of the case, each concluding that to order the transplant

[57] *Re S (A Minor) (Medical Treatment)* [1993] 1 FLR 376. See also, *Re O (A Minor) (Medical Treatment)* (1993) 19 BMLR 148, *Re R (A Minor)* (1993) 15 BMLR 72.
[58] See *Re J (A Minor) (Child in Care: Medical Treatment)* [1993] Fam 15 at 27, 29, *Re J, supra* n 52 at 41, *Re R, supra* n 14 at 22, 26.
[59] *Re C (Medical Treatment)* [1998] 1 FLR 384 at 390–1. See J Fortin, "A Baby's Right to Die" 10 *CFLQ* 411.
[60] [1997] 1 WLR 242. See P Lewis, "Proxy Refusals Of Medical Treatment" (1997–98) 8 *KCLJ* 101; M Fox and J McHale, "In Whose Best Interests?" (1997) 60 *MLR* 700.
[61] *Ibid* at 250.

over the mother's refusal would not be in the child's best interests. Much of the guidance given in earlier cases did not figure in the court's analysis. Taylor LJ's admonition in *Re J (A minor) (Wardship: Medical Treatment)* that "the court's high respect for the sanctity of human life imposes a strong presumption in favour of taking all steps capable of preserving it, *save in exceptional circumstances*"[62] was eschewed in favour of the more general statement of Lord Donaldson MR in *Re J* that "[t]here is without doubt a very strong presumption in favour of a course of action which will prolong life, but . . . it is not irrebuttable".[63] The more stringent criterion that the child's life post-treatment be "intolerable", adopted by Taylor LJ in *Re J* from *Re B*[64] was not discussed, and must now be taken as having been abandoned, as was indeed advocated by Butler-Sloss LJ in *Airedale NHS Trust* v. *Bland*, relying on the judgment of Lord Donaldson MR in *Re J*.[65]

Instead, the judges considered various case-specific factors, ranging from factors strictly related to the child,[66] to considerations which related first to the mother (and father), with an ensuing impact on the child's welfare. All three judges emphasised the need for the "total commitment of the caring parent" in order for the treatment to be successful. Butler-Sloss LJ emphasised the "unusual facts" of the case, distinguishing this case from *Re B* in which the "simple" operation required would have cured the condition, while this child would "require complicated surgery and many years of special care from the mother", thus signalling the "need for the confidence in and the commitment to the proposed treatment by the principal carer". For Butler-Sloss LJ, it was "the enormous significance of the close attachment between the mother and baby" which made the case unusual and meant that the child's welfare depended upon his mother.[67]

Waite LJ emphasised the medical expert's concern that the child's welfare would be detrimentally affected if the mother was coerced. For him, however, this consideration was not sufficient to warrant automatic respect for the mother's views. The case would have to be one in which there was "genuine scope for a difference of view between parent and judge". In such a case:

"there must be a likelihood . . . that the greater the scope for genuine debate between one view and another the stronger will be the inclination of the court to be influenced

---

[62] *Supra* n 52 at 53 (emphasis added).

[63] *Ibid* at 46.

[64] *Re J, ibid* at 55 *Re B, supra* n 50 at 1424.

[65] *Airedale NHS Trust* v. *Bland* [1993] AC 789 at 819–20.

[66] These were raised primarily by Butler-Sloss LJ, who discussed the "deep-seated concern of the mother as to the benefits to her son of the major invasive surgery and post-operative treatment, the dangers of failure long-term as well as short-term, the possibility of the need for further transplants, the likely length of life, and the effect upon her son of all these concerns". *Supra* n 60 at 250–1.

[67] *Ibid* at 251–3. For Roch LJ, it was the fact that the case involved an organ transplant which made the parents' views of such significance for the success of the procedure, and therefore for the welfare of the child, as well as the "formidable practical difficulties" created by the fact that the family no longer lived in the United Kingdom. *Ibid* at 256.

by a reflection that in the last analysis the best interests of every child include an expectation that difficult decisions affecting the length and quality of its life will be taken for it by the parent to whom its care has been entrusted by nature".[68]

For Waite LJ, it seems that in borderline cases, where there is room for a difference of opinion as to the child's best interests, it is the parents and not the court who should make the decision.

It could be argued that each judge effectively moved the locus of decision-making from the court to the parents in certain circumstances. Unfortunately, the court gave little guidance as to when these circumstances might arise in the future. Furthermore, whatever guidance was given was far from consistent. In particular, the approaches of Butler-Sloss and Waite LJJ may well conflict in some cases. For the former, where the parent's total commitment is needed, the refusing parent's good faith would apparently be sufficient to require respect for his or her decision, because it will not be in the best interests of the child to proceed without the parent's consent. How often this "unusual" situation will occur remains to be seen. The latter, however, envisaged some inquiry into the reasonableness or rationality of the refusing parent's decision, although he was content to leave this for another case, referring only to "the clear case where parental opposition to medical intervention is prompted by scruple or dogma of a kind which is patently irreconcilable with principles of child health and welfare widely accepted by the generality of mankind".[69]

Granted, this was a difficult case with heartbreaking facts. The judges may well have placed too great an emphasis on the need for the mother's commitment, and on the practical difficulties associated with granting the order. Moreover, the Court of Appeal squandered an opportunity to state the criteria which must inform the best interests test, and failed to articulate clearly those circumstances in which the court's view should cede to that of the parents. It appears that the resistance to religious objections remains, at least according to Waite LJ. Unconventional medical beliefs have also been treated unsympathetically.[70] Beyond this, we must wait and see how subsequent courts respond to *Re T*, to discover whether there will be a wholesale move towards greater respect for parental decision-making, or whether the decision will be effectively side-lined as aberrant (as indeed many commentators thought it was).[71] This case may be the first decision in a move away from the otherwise steadfast position that the court is the ultimate and omniscient guardian of a child's best interests, whether competent or incompetent.

---

[68]   *Ibid* at 254.

[69]   *Ibid* at 254.

[70]   *Re C (HIV test)* [1999] 2 FLR 1004 (order that a baby be tested for HIV despite her HIV-positive mother's refusal on the basis of her doubts about the validity of the generally accepted theories on HIV and AIDS).

[71]   See for example, A Bainham, "Do babies have rights?" [1997] *CLJ* 48, S Michalowski, "Is it in the best interests of a child to have a life-saving liver transplantation? *Re T (Wardship: Medical Treatment)*" (1997) 9:2 *CFLQ* 179.

10

The Minor as (a) Subject: The Case of Housing Law

DAVID COWAN AND NICK DEARDEN*

"There are two meanings of the word *subject*—subject to someone else by control and dependence, and tied to his own identity by a conscience or self-knowledge. Both meanings suggest a form of power which subjugates and makes subject to".[1]

INTRODUCTION

THERE IS A cruel irony about the minor—a person under eighteen[2]—as a subject of housing (law). The rule is that the minor is unable to hold a legal estate in land.[3] On the one hand, the law has been set up to protect the minor, on the basis that the minor "is easily exploited by reason of lacking, to a marked degree, the social and intellectual advantages of the average citizen".[4] On the other hand, this protection acts against the interests of the minor because it is used, in an unconvincing fashion, to justify the exclusion of the minor from accessing social and other types of housing. A number of mortgage lenders will not lend money to minors to purchase property; private sector landlords tend to shy away from renting to minors;[5] and age is the second most

---

* The authors are grateful to Paddy Hillyard who, while he has not read this paper, was the inspiration for many of the ideas contained in it.

[1] Michel Foucault, "The subject and power" in H Dreyfus and P Rabinow (eds), *Michel Foucault: Beyond Structuralism and Hermeneutics* (Chicago, Chicago University Press, 1982), p 212.

[2] Originally, the relevant age was 21, but this was reduced in the Family Law Reform Act 1969, s. 1, as a result of the report of the Latey Committee, *Report of the Committee on the Age of Majority*, Cmnd 3342 (London, HMSO, 1967), paras 382–91.

[3] Law of Property Act 1925, s. 1(6).

[4] P Birks, *An Introduction to the Law of Restitution* (Oxford, OUP, 1989), p 216.

[5] M Bevan, P Kemp and D Rhodes, *Private Landlords and Housing Benefit* (York, Centre for Housing Policy, University of York, 1995), p 51 *et seq*. Indeed, as housing benefit regulations reduce the available amount for under 25s, any landlord-prejudice against minors is exacerbated: see A Marsh *et al*, *Harassment and Unlawful Eviction of Private Rented Sector Tenants and Park Home Residents* (London, DETR, 2000).

common reason for local authorities excluding minors altogether from their accommodation.[6]

What then do we mean when we seek to identify the minor as a subject of housing law? In order to answer this question, we need to have a closer look at how children have been constructed by legal discourse, discursive processes which position children (for example, the allocations process), and the prevailing structuring framework which, through law, dis/allows and regulates minors' subjectivity.

Minors are legitimately discriminated against in the allocation of real property. The rationale for this discrimination lies in the desire and need of real property lawyers for certainty (or as the Latey Committee put it, "there must be no room for uncertainty").[7] Without certainty, the conditions of possibility for the transference of capital are not met:

> "Any uncertainty as to the effect of land transactions on various types of real property right has the effect of inhibiting purchasers and of stultifying dealings in land. No purchaser wants to risk his money if there is any real danger that the land purchased may be subject to adverse rights vested in others which render his title effectively or substantially worthless".[8]

In fact, we argue that this apparent legitimisation is a shroud, which obfuscates the reality about much housing decision-making. As Hale J has argued, while considering whether succession to public sector tenancies only applies to the legal estate, "The fact that leases or tenancies are capable of being legal estates does not mean that they must be . . . the concept of an equitable term of years is well known to the law".[9] In other words, the lawyer's need for certainty is not affected by rules about the legal estate in land. Legal discourse is the medium through which capital's call for certainty is operationalised; how individuals are positioned within property/housing law is, therefore, primarily a function of capital. The way in which minors are subjected to capital's interests is (usually) by exclusion from the regulatory framework which facilitates property transactions. As outsiders, minors' relation to the housing market or the allocations process becomes mediated by the state (through social services and other state agencies) or by a more enfranchised subject of the discourse (e.g. a

---

[6] S Butler, *Access Denied* (London, Shelter, 1998), p 20; see also I Anderson, "Young single people and access to social housing" in J Rugg (ed), *Young People, Housing and Social Policy* (London, Routledge, 1999). Less is known about Registered Social Landlords' and other housing associations' exclusions. The Housing Corporation, which regulates RSLs, is not particularly clear about whether RSLs are entitled to exclude minors (although RSLs are entitled, in certain circumstances to exclude those "unable to meet the conditions of the occupancy agreement without additional support": *Performance Standards* (London, Housing Corporation, 1997), p 46). The actual practice varies between different RSLs, although many operate a test about whether the applicant is capable of independent living—see D Cowan *et al, Allocation of Social Housing to Sex Offenders—An Examination of Practice* (York, Joseph Rowntree Foundation, 1999).

[7] *Op cit* n 2, para 382.

[8] K Gray, *Elements of Land Law* (London, Butterworths, 1993), pp 74–5.

[9] *Kingston-upon-Thames Borough Council* v. *Prince* (1999) 31 HLR 794, at 798.

parent). Later we look at whether there are any conditions under which minors can acquire subjectivity.

In this chapter, we concentrate on decision-making in social housing, specifically analysing the housing application process. Our reason for this concentration is that for most minors, independence in the housing market will involve going through this process at some stage because the private sector often will not be open to them. This process also gleans considerable insights about the way in which minors are treated within the housing system and the reasons for this treatment. Our argument is that the norm set by property law—that under eighteen's are not entitled to hold a legal estate—is reinforced through the procedures and attitudes within the housing system, which all serve to facilitate the marginalisation of minors.

The old argument propagated by social housing managers—that as minors are unable to hold a tenancy they should not therefore be successful in the social housing process—is underpinned by a set of beliefs about what minors should not do and where they should live. We relate our discussion to two interconnected themes which have gained prominence in social theory: risk and responsibility.[10] Arguing that risk and responsibility form the centrepiece of access to social housing is somewhat unusual because hitherto it has been the position that social housing is allocated on the basis of *housing need*.[11] The concept of housing need is superficially attractive, but housing management has, since its inception under the auspices of Octavia Hill, graded households according to their suitability and not on the basis of housing need.[12]

Among social housing professionals, minors (and particularly *vulnerable* minors) are widely regarded as being partly responsible for the decline of certain estates.[13] Once an estate has "tipped" and becomes known as an undesirable place to live, vulnerable people, including minors, who are willing to accept any form of accommodation move in to the area.[14] This issue of perception is the first point of exclusion, in the sense that minors are regarded as occupying the spaces of exclusion. The second point arises in the following way: social

[10] See A Giddens, *The Consequences of Modernity* (Cambridge, Polity, 1990); U Beck, *The Risk Society* (London, Sage, 1992).

[11] See for example, DoE, *Our Future Homes—Opportunity, Choice, Responsibility*, Cm 2901 (London, HMSO, 1995), ch 6.

[12] See for example, Central Housing Advisory Committee, *Council Housing Purposes, Procedures and Priorities* (London, HMSO, 1969), ch 3. Under the Housing Act 1996, certain asylum-seekers and other "persons from abroad" are automatically excluded from social housing precisely because of their immigration status, which challenges the notion of allocation according to need because these people include some of the most needy on any objective view. The Immigration and Asylum Act 1999 includes provision to remedy this defect, but through the Home Office bureaucracy. For discussion of this subject, see D Cowan, *Housing Law and Policy* (Basingstoke, Macmillan, 1999), ch 10.

[13] See A Benjamin, "Working with young residents: the problem" (1999) March/April *Roof* 36.

[14] On the development of "residential crime careers", see A Bottoms and P Wiles, "Environmental criminology" in R Morgan and R Reiner (eds), *The Oxford Handbook of Criminology* (Oxford, OUP, 1997).

landlords are required to pare down housing management costs;[15] housing disputes and evictions are labour intensive, costly, and housing managers regard them as symbols of housing management failure;[16] disputes and evictions can be minimised through the allocations processes. In this way, the housing allocations process becomes a tool of risk management, as opposed to one for addressing housing need. In this context, risk relates to the use to which the housing applicant, if successful, would make of the accommodation offered to them. One method of gauging this risk (a calculation of future possibilities) is to consider the level of responsibility shown by the applicant (a calculation based upon past housing outcomes) or by relating the decision to knowledge of the consequence of past allocations to the client group. Hence, a strategy or policy of offering otherwise hard to let property appears to discharge a local authority's duty simultaneously allowing it to reserve the more desirable stock to those assessed as low risk, in terms already outlined. Nevertheless, this model of housing allocation is not without its tensions: at this point, the identity category of minor is recognised because capital needs another market for its provision of housing, which, on tipped/sink estates, is essential if the void is to be eradicated. The cost of letting to a minor would be assessed in terms of the minor's ability to assume responsibilities against the risk of not meeting them.

Thus, to adopt the pre-modern term, we are concerned with a political economy which places at its forefront "exercising towards its inhabitants, and the wealth and behaviour of each and all, a form of surveillance and control as attentive as that of the head of a family over his household and his goods".[17] Whereas Foucault was concerned to place his analysis of power beyond analyses of the state, "seep[ing] into the very grain of individuals",[18] we nevertheless retain a concept of state and sovereignty in this chapter. As Stenson suggests, "The concern with bringing the writ of sovereign law, backed by the coercive apparatus of the state, to the rookeries of the poor in the nineteenth century has its modern counterpart in attempts to regain control over perceivably disorderly housing estates and the illegal economies which sustain them".[19] State sovereignty and the pre-modern use of political economy can clearly be seen in recent reforms to the system governing the procedures relating to the discharge of

---

[15] This has particularly arisen since local authorities' housing expenditure has been ring-fenced, after the Local Government and Housing Act 1989: see D Cowan, *Housing Law and Policy* (Basingstoke, Macmillan, 1999), ch 4.

[16] See Centre for Housing Management, *The Nature and Effectiveness of Housing Management* (London, HMSO, 1989).

[17] M Foucault, "Governmentality" in G Burchell, C Gordon and P Miller (eds), *The Foucault Effect—Studies in Governmentality* (London, Harvester Wheatsheaf, 1991), p 92.

[18] M Foucault, "An interview" (1977) 16 *Radical Philosophy* 10, at 10.

[19] K Stenson, "Crime control, social policy and liberalism" in G Lewis, S Gewirtz and J Clarke, *Rethinking Social Policy* (London, Sage, 2000), p 240; see also the rapidly burgeoning literature on anti-social behaviour, which shows the state exercising its sovereign might (however inadequately) including S Scott and H Parkey, "Myths and reality: anti-social behaviour in Scotland" (1998) 13 *Housing Studies* 325; D Cowan, *Housing Law and Policy, supra* n 12, ch 18.

responsibility to those minors being "looked after" by the state. The Consultation Paper was prefaced by Frank Dobson, then Secretary of State for Health, in the following way:

"In developing the new arrangements I asked everyone involved to look at things from the point of view of the young people and to ask, 'Would this have been good enough for me when I was a child?' or 'Would this be good enough for my own children?' I am determined that young people living in and leaving care will in the future get the same support, as far as possible, as other young people who are living at home and leaving home. This means a home to live or return to, a shoulder to cry on, encouragement with work or school or college, someone to take you out for a meal or out for a drink, someone to help you with a bit of cash when you need it, somewhere to get the washing done".[20]

We see the housing application process as a form of submission to the state's sovereignty, through the tool of law, which reinforces the power of the state to discipline and punish its subjects in terms of who is recognised/rewarded/disciplined (those who make the appropriate or necessary performances which enable the prevailing structure to work) and who is marginalised/punished because they cannot or will not contribute to that (re-)production. Although this requires testing empirically, the social housing application process is the housing system's equivalent of the *confession* in which the applicant is required to confess their housing histories in the hope that absolution will be provided through rehousing.[21] Applying for social housing, like the sexual confession, can be seen as a "disquieting enigma"[22] within a housing system which prioritises the norm of ownership.[23] As Hillyard and Watson put it:

"The poor, the unemployed, the sick, the immigrant, the criminal and the homeless are constantly being surveyed or monitored and asked to declare or disclose to a social researcher, police officer or social administrator something which has previously been kept secret and which is often (pre)-judicial to themselves".[24]

The homelessness legislation, with its emphasis on fault and comparative vulnerability, and the housing waiting list, with its restricted access, both form part of this.

We pursue our argument below in the following sections: first, we briefly outline the relevant methods of accessing social housing; in the second section, we discuss the risks posed by allocating accommodation to minors drawing attention to two particular strands, legal and responsibility risks. It is commonly

---

[20] Department of Health, *Me, Survive, Out There? New Arrangements for Young People Living in and Leaving Care* (London, DoH, 1999).

[21] The confession is part of the "wider domain of disciplinary power" and "at the heart of the power-knowledge nexus": P Hillyard and S Watson, "Postmodern social policy: a contradiction in terms?" (1996) 25 *Journal of Social Policy* 321, at 329.

[22] M Foucault, *The History of Sexuality* (London, Penguin, 1990), p 35.

[23] See C Gurney, "*Pride and Prejudice*: discourses of normalisation in public and private accounts of home ownership" (1999) 14 *Housing Studies* 163.

[24] P Hillyard and S Watson, *op cit* n 21 at 329.

argued that the legal risks of allocating accommodation to minors are too great—an argument which, at least, influences the development of social landlords' exclusion policy. As already indicated, we argue that these legal risks are, at worst, minimal. On the other hand, responsibility risks, which are commonly obfuscated by reliance on legal risks, form an important rationale for exclusion.

ACCESSING SOCIAL HOUSING

Housing legislation

The homelessness legislation[25] and the housing register[26] govern the selection and allocation process of local authority housing. Previous research has found that these methods give legitimacy to the exclusion of a significant proportion of minors from social housing.[27] To a large extent, they also govern the allocation of Registered Social Landlord ("RSL") accommodation, as most RSLs are locked into agreements (forced upon them by the Housing Corporation) to accept nominations from the local authority for a percentage of their annual allocations.[28] Little is known about allocations processes operated by RSLs, although their regulatory guidance requires them to prioritise similar persons to those prioritised by local authorities.[29] In any event, what is clear is that as funding becomes ever more problematic, RSLs are having to function more like businesses, with the attendant mode of risk assessment.[30]

Homelessness

A minor is only entitled to make a homelessness application if they have sufficient capacity to accept an offer of accommodation as well as undertake the responsibilities that are involved in taking a lease.[31] Once over this "capacity" hurdle, in order to qualify for temporary rehousing (for a two-year period) through the homelessness legislation, a household must be found to be eligible, homeless, in priority need, and not intentionally homeless.[32] If the household

---

[25] Housing Act 1996, Part VII.

[26] Housing Act 1996, Part VI.

[27] See D Cowan, *Homelessness: The (In-) Appropriate Applicant* (Aldershot, Dartmouth, 1997), ch 3; S Butler, *Access Denied* (London, Shelter, 1998); P Carlen, "The Governnance of Homelessness: Legality, Lore and Lexicon in the Agency-Maintenance of Youth Homelessness" (1994) 41 *Critical Social Policy 18*, where housing providers' approaches are referred to as "denying" the status of homelessness, and deterring minors from making applications as homeless.

[28] See *Performance Standards*, pp 41–3; in some areas, where supply outstrips demand, nominations are rarely made as social housing providers compete for new households.

[29] *Performance Standards*, p 35 *et seq*.; see more generally D Cowan, *supra* n 12, ch 9.

[30] See D Cowan, *supra* n 12, pp 109–16.

[31] R v. *Bexley LBC ex p Bentum* [1993] 2 All ER 65, 72; for a critique of this test, see D Cowan and J Fionda, "New angles on homelessness" (1993) *JSWFL* 403.

[32] A person becomes intentionally homeless " . . . if he deliberately does or fails to do anything in consequence of which he ceases to occupy accommodation which is available for his occupation and which it is reasonable for him to continue to occupy" (s. 191, Housing Act 1996).

has no "local connection" with the local housing authority, the latter has a discretion to refer the applicant to an authority with which a local connection exists. Single persons can only be in priority need if they are vulnerable for some particular or special reason. Vulnerability tends to be related to difficulties in finding and keeping accommodation.[33] In other words, homelessness to certain people renders them more "at risk"/vulnerable than other homeless persons and this is sufficient to enable them to fulfil this criterion. Risks that affect homeless minors may soon be relevant to this decision, although hitherto this has certainly not been the case. An amendment to the Code of Guidance, to which authorities will be required to have regard, makes the following point: "The Secretary of State considers that homeless 16 and 17 year olds are likely to be *at risk* as a result of their age and circumstances and he would normally expect authorities to find that such applicants are vulnerable".[34]

The housing register

The second method of selection and allocation is through the housing register, colloquially known as the waiting list. Local authorities are entitled to exclude certain persons from appearing on the register and minors are the second most common exclusion. Once entitled to appear on the register, the legislation requires reasonable preference to be given to households who fall within one or more categories.[35] Each of the categories is essentially a method of prioritising those whom central government believes are at some form of risk because of their housing circumstances and/or socio-economic position. For example, the first category relates to "people occupying insanitary or overcrowded housing or otherwise living in unsatisfactory housing conditions"—the central rationale for prioritising such people derives from the (physical) health risks which come from occupying such housing.[36] The most preferred category (in the sense that additional preference attaches to someone within it) relates to "households consisting of or including someone with a particular need for settled accommodation on medical or welfare grounds".[37]

Proposals for the future

The Green Paper on Housing was published in April 2000,[38] and a Housing Bill is anticipated in the near future. Arguably its most radical suggestions for

---

[33] R v. *Waveney District Council ex p Bowers* [1983] QB 238; cf R v. *Kensington & Chelsea Royal Borough Council ex p Kihara* (1996) 29 HLR 147.

[34] DETR, *Code of Guidance for Local Authorities on the Allocation and Accommodation and Homelessness* (London, DETR, 1999), para 14.10 (emphasis added).

[35] S. 167 Housing Act 1996.

[36] Indeed, much of the early public health legislation which attempted to rectify housing standards had this as its basis.

[37] S. 167(2)(e) Housing Act 1996.

[38] DETR, *Quality and Choice: A Decent Home For All* (London, DETR, 2000).

reform appear in chapter 9, concerned with housing allocation—or rather housing lettings as it will become. The most positive suggested change is that minors
will *automatically* have priority need, provided they are unintentionally homeless.[39] Additionally, the power to create blanket exclusions will be withdrawn,
although there will be a power "temporarily to reduce the priority or suspend
the applications of households on an individual basis".[40] However, mainstream
allocations will operate through a revamped waiting list which will prioritise
applications essentially through the length of time they have waited on the list.[41]
This latter point seems to be a throwback to the types of policies which existed
in the 1950s and which were heavily criticised at that time for producing discrimination against new arrivals;[42] clearly, this could also operate to discrimi-
nate against minors.

Social services legislation

By virtue of the Children Act 1989 (CA), certain minors "in need"[43] are entitled
to accommodation.[44] Indeed, it is the duty of the local authority to provide such
accommodation (the Act does not prescribe any particular tenure).[45] The definition of local authority is important, for, unless the authority is unitary, the
obligation is placed upon the county council and thus the social services department. Their stock of accommodation being what it is, it is likely that they will
need help from a housing provider. The Act, foreseeing this problem, entitles the
social services department to "request the help" of, *inter alia*, the housing
department. The latter cannot refuse the request unless "it is [in]compatible

[39] Para 9.56.
[40] Para 9.13—such suspensions are expected to be "exceptional and that other ways of managing problems or risk may be more appropriate": para 9.15. The Homes Bill 2001 contains these provisions.
[41] Paras 9.20–3.
[42] See Cullingworth Committee, *Council Housing Purposes, Procedures and Priorities* (London, HMSO, 1969).
[43] As defined by s. 17(10).
[44] Fortin identifies the privatisation of family life as an effect of the Children Act 1989, presumably with the concept of parental responsibility being one of the Act's chief tools of risk allocation: "Rights brought home for children" (1999) 62 *MLR* 350. The net effect is to place the child in a relationship as child, leaving the responsibility for the child's actions with a less risky adult, either as parent, someone with parental responsibility, or simply a trustee. In this section, though, we refer to the use of the 1989 Act as a means of giving the minor rights to accommodation independently of their carer.
[45] S. 20 Children Act 1989 states:

"(1) Every local authority shall provide accommodation for any child in need within their area who appears to them to require accommodation as a result of . . .
   (c) . . . the person who has been caring for him being prevented (whether or not permanently, and for whatever reason) from providing him with suitable accommodation or care . . .
   (3) Every local authority shall provide accommodation for any child in need within their area who has reached the age of sixteen and whose welfare the authority consider is likely to be seriously prejudiced if they do not provide him with accommodation. . ."

with their own statutory or other duties and obligations and does not unduly prejudice the discharge of any of their functions".[46]

In *R v. Northavon DC ex parte Smith*,[47] the House of Lords had to deal with a particularly knotty scenario. The Smith family had been found intentionally homeless by the housing authority; the social services department assessed one of the Smith children as being "in need of accommodation" under section 20 CA, and requested the assistance of the housing authority under section 27 CA. Not unnaturally, the housing department refused "clearly assert[ing]" that to provide accommodation would unduly prejudice the discharge of their obligations. Lord Templeman argued that, if the social services department had been successful, this would have caused a blurring of functions between housing and social services. Furthermore:

> "Every social services authority will understandably seek to exercise their powers under section 27 in order to transfer the burden of the children of a person intentionally homeless from the social services authority to the housing authority. Every refusal by a housing authority to comply with a request under section 27 will be scrutinised and construed with the object of discovering grounds for judicial review. *The welfare of the children involved, the welfare of children generally and the interests of the public cannot be advanced by such litigation*".[48]

Once again, paternalistic arguments are used to justify the avoidance of obligations to minors, but such paternalism is infused by concerns about the proper role of judicial review (subsequently, Lord Templeman argues that "judicial review is not the way to obtain cooperation" between local authority departments).[49] Housing obligations on Social Services departments have been reinforced by provisions in the Children (Leaving Care) Act 2000.[49a] The final section of this chapter discusses the concerns generated by the interaction and interrelationship between these statutory authorities, locating the rationales for the disputes in terms of risk.

WHY EXCLUDE MINORS?

In this part, we consider the various rationales for excluding minors from accessing social housing (indeed, making the access laws seem distinctly Orwellian). We deal with two rationales for such exclusion, seeking to develop the notions of risk adverted to in the introduction to this chapter. The first risk

---

[46] S. 27.

[47] (1994) 26 HLR 659. The case is discussed in its various judicial stages by D Cowan and J Fionda "Usurping the Housing Act 1985, Part III" (1994) *CLJ* 19; "Housing homeless families—an update" (1995) 7 *CFLQ* 66.

[48] (1994) 26 HLR 659 at 664—emphasis added.

[49] *Ibid* at 666.

[49a] S. 2 inserts s. 23B into the Children Act 1989, subss. (8)–(10) of which create rehousing obligations in respect of certain minors who are leaving or have left care.

relates to the supposed problems arising from the grant of a legal tenancy to a minor. It is argued that these legal problems are hardly relevant and, in any event, easily sidestepped (indeed, it has been common practice to sidestep them). The second risk relates to what we have termed "responsibility risks". These responsibility risks explicitly draw upon the notions of morality which imbue the decision-making process in the allocation of social housing. Here we trace a shift in the discourse around minors and tenancies from a nineteenth-century perspective of liberal paternalism, concerned with the welfare of children (seen particularly in the contractual position), to one of late twentieth-century risk assessment.

Legal risks

In this section, we are concerned to analyse the legal problems—the "stinging nettles"—caused by the grant of a tenancy to a minor. The legal "stinging nettles" can be divided into two parts: the grant of tenancies, on the one hand, and enforcing obligations, on the other. It will be argued that while there are real problems in both these areas, there are sufficiently numerous methods of circumventing them—"dock leaves"—to alleviate, if not completely remove, the pain. Indeed, these methods are well-known and have been reaffirmed in the important case of *Kingston upon Thames Borough Council* v. *Prince*.[50]

Granting a tenancy

The hallowed principle of the law of property that a minor cannot be granted a legal estate in land is the derivation of the considerable problems which arise in this area. For, if one does attempt to grant a legal estate to a minor, such a grant splits the legal and equitable interest. The minor does take the equitable interest; but the legal estate remains vested in the grantor. This process creates traps for the unwary. Unless there was an explicit trust for sale created, such a situation used to fall neatly within the definition of a "settlement" under the Settled Land Act 1925 (SLA).[51] The effect of this was that the tenancy ". . . operated only as an agreement for valuable consideration to execute a settlement by means of a principal vesting deed and a trust instrument in favour of the [minor], and in the meantime to hold the land in trust for the [minor]".[52] Thus, the social housing landlord still retained the legal estate under a contract to create a SLA settlement—a rather different result from the altruistic purposes of the initial grant. On the minor gaining majority, the legal estate could then pass

---

[50] [1999] 31 HLR 794..

[51] S. 1(1)(ii)(d) Settled Land Act 1925 ("SLA").

[52] S. 27(1) SLA. This provision only applied to a conveyance, but presumably includes informal creation where the tenancy is for less than three years.

although the minor could disclaim the interest.[53] The landlord remained the legal owner but with added fiduciary responsibilities.[54] Where a tenancy was granted to a minor together with a person with the requisite capacity to hold a legal estate, the latter would take the tenancy as the legal owner with both holding the beneficial interest.

Since the implementation of the Trusts of Land and Appointment of Trustees Act 1996 (TLATA), these particular problems have all been thrown into focus. That Act provides for a new system of landholding called the Trust of Land (replacing the old familiar concepts). Minors now take as beneficiaries behind a trust of land, whatever the situation.[55] However, the legal estate is not disposed of and thus remains with the grantor, unless one of the grantees is over eighteen (in which case, that person takes as trustee). Pre-existing grants to minors (those subject to section 27 SLA) are also brought within this system.[56] Thus, what might have ameliorated the situation from the landlord's perspective unfortunately appears to retain the same problems: the non-disposal of legal estate and take-up of fiduciary responsibilities. However, in terms of our analysis, legal subjectivity of a minor is regulated by TLATA until the child becomes an adult, at which point subjectivity becomes constituted by the prevailing structures of property ownership, reproducing that order of social power and the knowledge that minors should not hold legal estates.

However, the non-disposal of the legal estate does not cause any insuperable practical difficulty. Under the SLA, its relative obscurity and machinery might have caused some problems, but these have disappeared with the post-1996 system. A question might arise over whether a fiduciary social housing landlord can seek a possession order against their minor tenant. In such cases, it can be argued that the fiduciary relationship does not affect the landlord's broader housing management responsibilities, nor its public law responsibilities to the wider community, both of which have gained great prominence in recent times.[57] Where there is a breach of agreement by the minor, sufficient to justify a possession order, then the fiduciary relationship must give way to the breach of obligation by the minor. In other words, the fiduciary relationship refers to the grant and continuation of the property interest, but not to its end through legal processes; the economic interests therefore are preserved and only momentarily interrupted as they override the fiduciary duties.

Until recently, it has certainly been arguable that tenancies granted to minors attract no security of tenure until the minor takes the legal estate,[58] although "it

---

[53] See R Megarry and H Wade, *Modern Law of Real Property* (London, Stevens & Sons, 1984), p 1019.

[54] See for example, *Davies v. Benyon-Harris* (1931) 47 TLR 424.

[55] Sch 1, s. 1(b).

[56] Para 1(3).

[57] See for example, C Hunter "Hanging about on street corners: is it a crime?" (1998) *JHL* 83; C Hunter, T Mullen, and S Scott, *Legal Remedies for Neighbour Nuisance: Comparing Scottish and English Approaches* (York, Joseph Rowntree Foundation, 1998).

[58] See N Goss, "Can children be tenants of their own homes?" (1996) May *Childright* 5, at 6.

is universally assumed that a contract operating as an equitable tenancy under the doctrine of *Walsh* v. *Lonsdale* should also be protected.[59] Megarry's *Rent Acts* assumes that a minor could take statutory protection for their interest under the Rent Act 1977[60] and the same would surely be true under the 1988 Act regime. Counsel's opinion to the Housing Corporation appears to have assumed that minors do have the benefit of the 1988 Act and suggests:

> "[Housing Associations] should normally grant assured shorthold tenancies, with the Assured Shorthold Tenants' Guarantee, to young persons aged 16/17 until they have reached their 18th birthday when they should normally be granted an assured periodic tenancy with the Tenants' Guarantee for Assured Periodic Tenants".[61]

In *Kingston upon Thames Borough Council* v. *Prince*, the question arose as to whether a minor could succeed to a statutory tenancy under the Housing Act 1985, section 87. Hale J held that the succession provisions applied equally to equitable and legal tenancies. They therefore catered for the succession of a minor, notwithstanding that the minor could not hold the legal estate. Such a conclusion was reinforced by the fact that a minor could be assigned a tenancy by virtue of matrimonial and child care legislation without the loss of security. By way of conclusion, the judge argued that "The modern tendency of the law was to recognise that children were indeed people. It simply could not be assumed that they were omitted from legislation unless the contrary was expressed". It follows that equitable tenancies granted to minors also fit within the statutory security regime. At first glance, the scope of this judgment would seem to facilitate the enfranchisement of children as independent subjects of law. Such a move would see law as a discourse of productive power "generating forces, making them grow, and ordering them, rather than one dedicated to impeding them, making them submit, or destroying them".[62] However, it is often the case that local authority practice fails to acknowledge the needs of minors as minors, thereby denying the minor subjectivity and positioning the child as child within the system (that is, as an object of power, as opposed to young adult engaged in a process of empowerment) and renders the child subject to the authority's project of minimising exposure to risk.

Practical solutions

While the division of interest inherent in a grant to a minor operates as a trap for the unwary, there are plenty of eminently suitable mechanisms used by the wary. First, the minor could be granted a licence with or without exclusive possession. No trust mechanism is required for this purpose. Licences with

---

[59] See P Sparkes, "Co-tenants, joint tenants and tenants in common" (1989) 19 *Anglo-American Law Review* 151, at 158.
[60] Page 229, cited in Sparkes *ibid.*
[61] HC Circ R3-05/96, para 5.3.
[62] M Foucault, *Power/Knowledge* (New York, Pantheon, 1980), p 136.

exclusive possession are personal interests and also attract security of tenure under the Housing Act 1985,[63] although not under the Housing Act 1988. Second, the tenancy could be granted to a parent, relative, social worker, or other person on behalf of the minor. This is a common practice, although some statutory agencies have concerns about the obligations involved in such a grant. In such cases, the effect of the Children Act 1989, section 20(1), containing the duty of social services departments to provide accommodation to children "in need", will provide some negotiating position for the social landlord. Furthermore, in respect of those leaving care, there is now a recognition that the state has a continuing obligation to such persons.[64] Third, if the private sector is to be used to provide accommodation, it is now regarded as good practice for local authorities to provide rent and deposit guarantees, although these might be stretched by the recent limitations on housing benefit to the under twenty-fives.[65] Thus, there are workable mechanisms which enable the grant of some type of interest to minors without major difficulty for the landlord, whose prime concern becomes rental income streams, voids and dilapidations liabilities.

Obligations

We now turn to a reiteration of some basic principles concerning the enforcement of contractual obligations against minors. In relation to protection of minors, the law in this area has had to wrestle with the competing interests of (both) parties to any contract and manifests itself in two ways. First, and foremost, laws have evolved around protection against inexperience (the nineteenth-century paternalism). Second, adults who deal with minors should not be prejudiced by such dealings. The law broadly protects both parties, and the interest of the landlord in rental income and dilapidations is not adversely affected by the fact that the occupant is a minor.

The obligation to pay rent is binding, unless the minor repudiates the contract.[66] It appears that the right of repudiation subsists throughout minority but is lost a reasonable amount of time after the date on which the minor attains majority.[67] In terms of how this contractual discourse positions the minor then, we see a form of enfranchisement here, where the minor calls the shots in terms of the future of the relationship with the landlord. As long as the minor pays the rent and meets the other obligations in the lease, contract law will recognise the agreement. In this respect, the minor is a subject of the discourse. The minority here is irrelevant because the landlord's right to sue, terminate and evict render

---

[63] *Westminster CC* v. *Clarke* [1992] 1 All ER 695.

[64] Social Exclusion Unit, *Bringing Britain Together: A National Strategy for Neighbourhood Renewal*, Cm 4045 (London, HMSO, 1995), p 23.

[65] DoE, *Our Future Homes*, Cm 2901 (London, HMSO, 1995) p 23.

[66] *Keteley's Case* (1613) 1 Brown 120; *Davies* v. *Benyon-Harris, supra* n 54.

[67] Law Commission, *Law of Contract: Minors' Contracts* (Law Com No 134, 28 June 1984), para 5.15; K Gray, *Elements of Land Law* (London, Butterworths, 1993), p 684.

it so. In *Lowe* v. *Griffith*,[68] it was held that only if the subject matter of the lease could be classified as a necessary would the minor be liable for the rent (the policy argument being that, unless contractual obligations could be enforced against minors, minors would not be able to acquire goods and services regarded as necessary for their existence). However, this decision does not reflect the law in this area. Treitel states that "[this] requirement is not elsewhere stated and is probably not law. On the contrary, it seems that a lessee who is under age is liable unless he repudiates even though the lease is disadvantageous to him".[69] In any event, a lease to a minor by a social landlord on the basis of the minor's housing need could not be regarded as anything other than a necessary.

What then is the effect of repudiation in these circumstances? It is not entirely settled as to whether obligations incurred prior to such repudiation are extinguished. However, as counter-restitution would be impossible, as a matter of principle it is generally accepted that any prior liability should continue. The minor's future liabilities are certainly relieved, but then the social landlord will also be free to re-allocate the accommodation.

As for dilapidations, depending on the state and condition of the property at the date of repudiation and the repairing obligation in the lease, repudiation may well not assist the minor. The property could have been in dilapidated state prior to the date of the lease, or the unwitting lessee might have caused or somehow suffered damage to the rented property. As the authorities relating to whether, for example, internal plastering amounts to the structure of a building, go either way,[70] this potential liability is not inconsiderable. In that case, similarly, the landlord is technically not prejudiced in law. Whether the minor has the wherewithal to pay for dilapidations liability is a different matter, a perennial problem for landlords (although one which might be solved in part by a deposit guarantee). At this point then, we move to the later concept of responsibility risks, which call for an assessment of whether a child is more or less likely than the adult subject of (housing) law to cause a problem to the landlord.

Responsibility risks

There are a number of responsibility risks associated with providing accommodation to a minor. These risks are both internal to the minor—or imputations derived from the decision-maker's view of the minor—as well as external to the minor, in the sense that the minor has little or no impact upon the decision to be made.

---

[68] (1835) 4 LJ.CP 94.
[69] G H Treitel, *The Law of Contract* (London, Sweet & Maxwell, 1995), p 501.
[70] See for example, *Staves and Staves* v. *Leeds City Council* (1990) 23 HLR 107; *Irvin* v. *Moran* (1990) 24 HLR 1.

The internal responsibility risk relates to a moral position of what the characteristics of an *appropriate* application from a minor should be. What this means is that minors must conform in some way to the decision-maker's value system which, in this sense, relates to whether an applicant is *capable of independent living*. In other words, the applicant must be able and willing to pay the rent and generally look after the property and not cause nuisance to others in the locality.[71] Applicants who are not so capable (from the decision-maker's perspective) are regarded as wasting valuable resources of both the decision-maker and any accommodation offered. It is this decision which may well provide the central focus of most of the decisions concerning access to social housing because the financial and social pressures of housing management require it to be made (despite the fact that it does not appear explicitly or implicitly in any legislation). We suggest that this is the case even despite the disparate circumstances in which social housing providers find themselves. Consider the following comment made by a London borough's housing needs manager:

> "The point of the allocation process is that they are ready to accept a permanent tenancy and to take on, to a large extent, independent living. If there is evidence that there is clearly a risk then we wouldn't accept them for a permanent tenancy because we feel that more care and support was needed and it was not appropriate that we just put them into a bed-sit and let them get on with it".[72]

What this person is saying is that the allocations process is designed to weed out those applicants who are unable to take on the obligations of a tenancy. The allocations process is, therefore, a process of weeding out those persons who are too risky in terms of the housing management prerogatives and is being used as a risk management tool, rather than one which addresses need.

Exactly the same decisions need to be made in respect of minors but here the internal risks are less concrete (particularly where the minor has no history of living independently). The potential for the minor to be evicted from the accommodation, for example for non-payment of rent, and then reapply as homeless (the revolving door "syndrome") makes this a crucial question. Rather than relating it to past housing circumstances, the essential questions are based on hypothetical or pre-determined questions with the emphasis on the future, as with all risk-based questions (will the applicant pay their rent when housed? Will the applicant live up to the agreement?). When it comes to making a decision about a minor, particularly those with no housing history, there are narrow limits to the information that can be gleaned about the individual. This may also mean that the rationale for the decision is based upon a more general morality or broader understanding of the risks posed by those deemed to be attached to

---

[71] Cf the comment of Lord Griffiths in R v. *Bexley LBC ex parte B, Oldham MBC ex parte G* that applicants must have "the capacity to understand and respond to an offer [of accommodation] and if they accept it to undertake the responsibilities that will be involved": [1993] 2 All ER 65, 72; for discussion, see D Cowan and J Fionda, "New angles on homelessness", *supra* n 31 at 403.

[72] See D Cowan *et al*, Housing Sex Offenders: an examination of current practice (Coventry: Chartered Institute of Housing, 1999); D Cowan *et al*, "Risking housing need" (1999) *JLS* 403.

a particular class or identity of applicant (or perhaps we should say to those "others" excluded from the particular class/identity/subjectivity recognised by the allocations process). The extent to which the minor acquires subjectivity is the extent to which the minor becomes disciplined or regulated by the process; the more obedient, the more incorporated the individual becomes and the fact of minority is secondary. The minor does not become housed as a minor but as an appropriate applicant; there is no call on the allocations system to recognise any identity here (which would take the system dangerously close to requiring an understanding of and response to need). Nowhere has this been better expressed than in the following comment from a homelessness officer in a small rural-based local authority in the South of England:

> "[Minors who want to apply as homeless] have to work at living in supportive accommodation first and make the effort, otherwise why should we help. They must show they want to get on, look for a job, putting a basis down for a future. The possibilities of us trying to help them are then fairly good. Where 17 or 18 year olds are concerned, who are more mature, we have actually provided them with housing after deeming them to be more vulnerable when we are satisfied that they can live on their own, show a mature attitude to life, able to hold their own—it works very well and we haven't had any management problems".

One wonders why the word "vulnerable" is even used here, when need is clearly irrelevant, but risk management is the overriding aim.

Discussion of these internal responsibility risks neatly leads to the report of the Social Exclusion Unit ("SEU") on teenage pregnancies.[73] The notion of teenagers becoming pregnant to "get a council house" has been a particularly vivid metaphor in the development and regression of the homelessness legislation.[74] The SEU faces this question head-on, and found that "this is an unprovable assertion", but that "a number of factors make it seem improbable".[75] Furthermore, seven out of ten mothers under sixteen, and fifty per cent of mothers between sixteen and eighteen, stay at home.[76] Indeed, qualitative research has found, not surprisingly, that teenage mothers knew little if anything about housing and other benefits before becoming pregnant.[77] Despite all of this, Blair in introducing the Report, has argued:

> "I don't believe leaving a 16 year old girl with a baby in her own flat, often halfway up a tower block, benefits her, the baby or the rest of us. It gives her too much and yet not enough".

[73] Social Exclusion Unit, *Teenage Pregnancy*, Cm 4342 (London, SO, 1999).
[74] For discussion, see D Cowan, "Reforming the homelessness legislation" (1998) 57 *Critical Social Policy* 435; D Cowan and J Fionda, "Homelessness", in S Bright and J Dewar (eds), *Land Law: Themes and Perspectives* (Oxford, OUP, 1998) pp 268–9.
[75] Paras 4.7–8, original emphasis. Factors include the following: benefit payments are not generous; relatively few lone parents live in council flats; and in the era of council housing surpluses, young people may be able to get a tenancy fairly readily.
[76] Para 9.15.
[77] I Allen and S Dowling, *Teenage Mothers: Decisions and Outcomes* (London, PSI, 1997).

"It could send out a signal to young teenagers that having a baby is a fast track to their own flat and the symbols of adulthood. It can certainly deny them the help and support they will need as single parents".[78]

The patrician concerns of New Labour are, as he argues, that children should be given a chance to be children;[79] this policy would also appear to be applied to their mothers. As a result the DETR is planning to amend its homelessness and allocations Code of Guidance by 2003.[80]

External responsibility risks relate to factors outside the control of the applicant. The most important such factor is the way organisations interact or otherwise. It is a fundamental characteristic of a generic organisation, such as those responsible for the provision of housing, that they must rely on other organisations for at least part of the data upon which they must make their decisions and where appropriate for such agencies to provide any necessary services. In particular, given their responsibilities to minors, joint working has been encouraged between housing and social services departments.[81] Almost immediately, however, the relationship proved problematic. This was partly because of funding—social services prioritisation of child protection meant that housing issues were marginalised[82]—and partly because of inter-agency antipathy. Research conducted by CHAR found that, while most social services departments assessed minors under the 1989 Act, "those young people who are homeless and roofless are still strongly perceived as having just a housing problem and as such are not seen as requiring social services intervention".[83] As the *Smith* case had exposed, relationships between the departments were straining:

"The research found that professional hostilities are clearly still operating. Working under different legislative frameworks, with different styles and ways of working, both departments have unclear and limited perceptions of their respective roles. Communication between departments can often be strained and difficult, with a lack of trust".[84]

It became commonplace initially for social services departments to refer housing obligations to housing departments and, as time wore on, some joint agreements became shelved and ignored.[85] This occurred partly because of the

---

[78] T Blair, "Why we should stop giving lone teenage mothers council homes", *Daily Mail*, 14 June 1999. It should be noted that safety generally dictates that babies and children are rarely placed in tower blocks.

[79] See also Home Office, *Supporting Families* (London, Home Office, 1998).

[80] SEU, para 11.15. Given the current legislation, there must be grave doubt as to whether this could be done simply by Guidance, particularly given the prescriptiveness of the new policy.

[81] Department of Health, *The Children Act 1989 Guidance and Regulations*, Vol 3 (London, HMSO, 1990), paras 9.81–3.

[82] Prioritisation is itself based upon risk—see H Kemshall, N Parton, M Walsh and J Waterson, "Concepts of risk in relation to organizational structure and functioning within the personal social services and probation" (1997) 31 *Social Policy and Administration* 213.

[83] J McClusky, *Acting in Isolation* (London, CHAR, 1994), p 21.

[84] *Ibid*, p 39.

[85] What follows is a summary taken from D Cowan, *Homelessness: The (In)Appropriate Applicant*, *supra* n 27, pp 75–94.

"firefighting" tactics adopted by some housing departments, for example referring applicants back to the social services departments. These tactics were used because of the potential that applicants could overturn decisions made by the housing department, and because of the potential large numbers of households which could use the system in this way. Some housing departments referred to the non-effect of the 1989 Act as "an open secret". Early inter-departmental antipathy then became watered-down to a mutual respect for the resource limitations ("rather than continually battling it out, they ignored each other").[86]

Lord Templeman's argument in the *Smith* case suggests that reliance should be upon goodwill and a real policy of joint working between local authority departments. Not only is this, we argue, wishful thinking and not borne out in practice, but it ignores the shifts we have detailed from responsibilities around satisfying housing need to risk avoidance strategies employed in the public sector (as apparent in 1993 as today).[87] More recent research similarly relates how minors requiring accommodation fall between two stools and reveals that authorities working within the same legislative framework, and the voluntary sector, similarly have strained relations.[88]

CONCLUSIONS

In *The Downing Street Years*, Thatcher argued that housing welfare legislation should not encourage those under twenty-five to leave home in search of the bright city lights.[89] Somewhat ironically, statistics suggest that the norm appears to be males under twenty-five are more likely to live with their parents than not, although the reverse is true for women (35 per cent living with their parents between the ages of twenty and twenty-four).[90] This has led to an assumption within the policy discourse that minors should remain with their parents until they become "non-dependent", and legislation is structured accordingly. This is evident from housing law which commonly denies minors the status of being homeless, denies the selection of minors from the housing register, and denies minors a full panoply of welfare benefits. Minors who do not fit within the (assumed or legislatively prescribed) norm become the subjects of prejudice and complex, ill-meshing legislation. Thus, statistics feed the "art of government" in a cycle which justifies such penality. As Foucault suggests, what has emerged "into prominence is the family considered as an element internal to population, and as a fundamental instrument in its government".[91]

[86] D Cowan, *Homelessness: The (In)Appropriate Applicant*, *supra* n 27, p 89.

[87] See McClusky, *op cit* n 83.

[88] See D Quilgars and N Pleace, "Housing and support services for young people" in J Rugg (ed), *Young People, Housing and Social Policy* (London, Routledge, 1999) who argue, at p 125, that there has been "something of a policy disarray around responses to young people's housing need . . ."

[89] M Thatcher, *The Downing Street Years* (London, Harper Collins, 1993), p 603.

[90] Office for National Statistics, *Social Trends* 29 (London, TSO, 1999), p 46.

[91] M Foucault, "Governmentality", in G Burchell, C Gordon and P Miller (eds), *supra* n 17, p 99.

11

The Child in Family Law

MICHAEL FREEMAN

INTRODUCTION

THE LAW UNTIL relatively recently took little interest in children. If it was interested in their delinquency this was because adults were the victims of this. It is, I think, notable that, as Helmholz has shown,[1] English law reacted to abuse of parents by children long before it ever awoke to the phenomenon of child abuse.

Childhood is a social construction. Understanding of it is not constant either in space or time. And even within a given system it has different meanings in different contexts. Thus, to take one, perhaps, crude, example English law endows sexual citizenship two years before it accords political citizenship.[2] Children are treated differently by different branches of law. Criminal responsibility almost certainly antedates the acquisition of Gillick competence.[3] Some "children's legislation" treats the young (or does so in part) as consumers (the Children Act 1989 is a paradigm example). While in other areas (education law is a prime example) they would appear to be little more than objects.

No less problematic than childhood is the concept of family law. This may mean different things to academics and practitioners. Otto Kahn-Freund was famously once asked whether there was a law of marriage! It certainly means different things to civilians and common lawyers. We would never classify questions of capacity or of nationality as within the remit of family law, but they are readily subsumed within the law of persons as this is categorised in civilian systems.

This chapter examines the ways English family law, as currently and conventionally defined, looks at children. The emphasis is thus on children at the millennium, though inevitably the eye is cast back to earlier constructions. And the differences are great, even if one goes back only a generation.

---

[1] "And were there Children's Rights in Early Modern England? The Canon Law and 'Intra-Family Violence' in England, 1400–1640" (1993) 1 *International Journal of Children's Rights* 23.

[2] On sexual citizenship see David T Evans, *Sexual Citizenship: The Material Construction of Sexualities* (London, Routledge, 1993), ch 8.

[3] Criminal responsibility is now fixed at the age of 10. Gillick competence is, of course, not attached to any age, but the assumption among decision-makers is that most 10-year-olds would not be Gillick competent.

A FEW SNAPSHOTS OF THE PAST

Specialist family law reports (they were called Probate and Divorce reports) only began in 1865, though cases are, of course, also reported in Chancery Appeals.[4] The first volume contains no less a gem than *Hyde* v. *Hyde and Woodmansee* and thus perhaps the most famous sentence in all family law.[5] But there are at most five cases, indexed, interestingly under the heading "children" and not, as would later be the case, "infants", which are about children and may give us some clue as to how "family law" perceived children at the beginning of the modern era. Two of the cases are legitimacy petitions.[6] Though such applications still occur,[7] they are now marginal concerns of a family law in which the significance or otherwise of legitimacy is minuscule. Where it remains of significance, in the law of nationality[8] and domicile,[9] it is in areas traditionally pigeon-holed outside family law. Over a third of children born today are illegitimate,[10] but it is their fathers who bear the consequences of this.[11]

The other cases reported in 1865 have a more modern ring. Unlike the two legitimacy petitions, where property was the primary concern, they concern the welfare of children. The most interesting is *Chetwynd* v. *Chetwynd*.[12] The court transferred custody of children aged ten and eight from parents who were not deemed fit to care for them to two other members of the family. We are offered tantalisingly few facts. It is not even clear who these members of the family are beyond that they are relatives of the father—though they are titled. Nor is it possible to judge the "fitness" or otherwise of the parents. It would, however, seem that unfitness is identified with immorality. Perhaps the parents were also bad parents. This is not so stated: the implication is that, if immoral, parents were also incapable or uncaring. It is possible that property is at the root of this case too. This would certainly be one reading of unspoken facts.

---

[4] There are no cases in 1865 but two in 1866. *Re Newbery* (1866) 1 Ch App 263 bars the widow of a Church of England clergyman from bringing up their children as Plymouth Brethren. It was urged that the children (who were young adolescents) ought to be seen to ascertain their views. Knight Bruce LJ thought their views "immaterial" (p 266). *Re Kaye* (1866) 1 Ch App 387 showed the court evincing a reluctance to overturn a trial judge's discretion: it is thus a forerunner of *G* v. *G* [1985] FLR 894.

[5] (1866) LR 1 P&D 130. "Marriage, as understood in Christendom, may be defined as the voluntary union for life of one man and one woman to the exclusion of all others", *per* Lord Penzance. The sentence is at the core of all civil marriage ceremonies even today.

[6] *Ryves and Ryves* v. *Attorney General* (1865) LR 1 P&D 23.

[7] *Watson* v. *Attorney General and Cowen* (1865) LR 1 P&D 27.

[8] British Nationality Act 1981 s. 1(1) and s. 50(9)(b). On legitimation see s. 47.

[9] An illegitimate child takes the domicile of origin of his mother : see *Udny* v. *Udny* (1869) LR 1 Sc & Div 441. This has been criticised by the Law Commission (Law Com. No. 168, 1987) but legislation to follow its recommendation has not been forthcoming and seems unlikely.

[10] See *Social Trends 1998* (London, The Stationery Office, 1999).

[11] They do not have parental responsibility (and therefore parental rights). A recent illustration of the problems this can cause is *Re J* [1999] 2 FLR 653.

[12] (1865) LR 1 P&D 39.

The other two cases do, however, appear to concern the welfare of children. *Mallinson* v. *Mallinson*[13] held that the court had jurisdiction to regulate the custody of a child until he/she reached the age of sixteen. The so-called "age of discretion"[14] (fourteen for boys and sixteen for girls) was to retain significance for a long while yet, and this accordingly may be seen as an early breach of the principle. *In Matter of Chaplin*,[15] the court held that a guardian would not be appointed for a child until it could be shown that he was likely to benefit from such an appointment. The reasoning has a remarkably modern resonance.

By 1900 we had Probate reports—in retrospect aptly so called. There were some family law cases, of course, but remarkably in 1900 no case about children at all. Nor was there a case of any significance in the *Chancery* reports. In 1925, the year of the Guardianship of Infants Act, there were also no reported cases in this major set of "Family" reports on children. There is one only in the *Chancery* reports, hinging on whether an illegitimate child was a child for the purposes of construing a will.[16] More surprisingly still, twenty-five years on in 1950 there were also none. One brief report is in the Chancery reports.[16a] Even in 1960 there was only one. That case (*Francis* v. *Francis*)[17] is still in *Bromley*. Again, it is a case about legitimacy, and it shows how seriously this was taken only a generation ago. The wife was having an affair and the husband always used condoms. The court, emphasising that these did not always work,[18] concluded the husband was the father of the child. The presumption, that a woman's husband was the father of the child, was, it was said, a very strong one. It remains strong but since 1969[19] it has been rebuttable on a balance of probabilities.[20] There are no child law cases in the 1960 *Chancery* reports volume. Even in the late 1960s few cases of interest to lawyers concerned with children were being reported. The *Probate* reports for 1969 contain just three.[21]

By contrast in 1980 the *Family Law Reports*, the first year this specialist publication appeared, has twenty-seven cases which relate to children and forty-seven which do not do so, at least directly. And the range of subject matter is wide: the amount of an affiliation order,[22] the assumption of parental rights,[23]

---

[13] (1866) LR 1 P&D 221.
[14] It flickered as late as the Court of Appeal decision in *Gillick* v. *West Norfolk and Wisbech AHA* [1986] AC112, *per* Parker LJ at 127 and Fox LJ at 141–2.
[15] (1867) LR 1 P&D 328.
[16] *Re Taylor* [1925] Ch 739.
[16a] *Re An Infant* [1950] Ch 629 (a cursory half page judgment on when a child becomes a ward of court).
[17] [1960] P 17. *Bromley's Family Law* (9th edition edited by Nigel Lowe and Gillian Douglas) (London, Butterworths, 1998), p 276.
[18] A good example of judicial notice!
[19] Family Law Reform Act 1969, s. 26.
[20] Despite *Serio* v. *Serio* (1983) 4 FLR 756. See Sir David Cairns at p 763. This decision can be taken as discredited since *Re H* [1996] AC 563 (see Lord Lloyd at p 577).
[21] *B* v. *B&F* [1969] P 37; *B (BPM)* v. *B(MM)* [1969] P 103; *L* v. *L* [1969] P 25.
[22] *Haroutunian* v. *Jennings* (1980) 1 FLR 62.
[23] *M* v. *Wigan Metroplitan Borough Council* (1980) 1 FLR 45.

adoption,[24] the relationship between wardship and care,[25] custody[26] (including the first reported case where the mother's lesbianism was in issue),[27] care proceedings,[28] access.[29] This has a more modern ring though it hardly needs to be said that several of these institutions are no longer and many of the concepts have been replaced or reconstituted. Strikingly also—and in how many other areas of law could this be true—very few of the child cases reported in 1980[30] remains an authority today. The only case with substantive interest (and this diminished because of the impact of child support legislation) is the House of Lords case of *Supplementary Benefits Commission* v. *Jull*[31] which held that even that part of maintenance payments which was intended to be made for the benefit of the child, rather than a parent, was to be fully taken into account and so was to reduce Income Support entitlement pound for pound. The remaining cases are on procedural or evidential matters: judges must give reasons if they refuse to follow the recommendations of welfare reports;[32] an independent welfare office should ascertain a child's views;[33] where there are applications for adoption and access they should be heard concurrently;[34] it may be necessary to enforce a court order for access by transferring custody from a recalcitrant parent;[35] a husband's failure to deny that a child is a child of the family in undefended proceedings will not raise an estoppel, because to do so might invite unnecessary litigation.[36] One 1980 case which provoked a lot of interest at the time is *Dipper* v. *Dipper*.[37] It is primarily a case about clean breaks on divorce and everything said about the meaning of custody is strictly *obiter*. But two of the Lord Justices (Ormrod and Cumming-Bruce) commented on the legal status of custody, bringing out the distinction between custody as a fact (in effect what today would be the consequence of a residence order) and custody as a bundle of rights and responsibilities (today's parental responsibility). The comments would be of little more than historical interest, were it not for a suggestion in the 1994 Court of Appeal decision in *Re G* that, despite the clear wording of section 2(7) of the Children Act 1989, which indicates that where parental responsibility is shared each may "act alone and without the other (or others) in meeting that responsibility", there is a duty to consult, at any rate over long-term decisions.[38] As Cumming-Bruce LJ had put it, in 1980, "the parent is always entitled,

[24] *Re G* (1980) 1 FLR 109.
[25] *M* v. *Humberside Country Council* (1980) 1 FLR 91.
[26] *B* v. *B* (1980) 1 FLR 385.
[27] *S* v. *S* (1980) 1 FLR 143.
[28] *R* v. *Greenwich Juvenile Court, ex parte London Borough of Greenwich* (1980) 1 FLR 304.
[29] *V-P* v. *V-P* (1980) 1 FLR 336; *L* v. *L* (1980) 1 FLR 396.
[30] They have been overtaken by the Children Act 1989.
[31] (1980) 1 FLR 226.
[32] *Re T* (1980) 1 FLR 59.
[33] *Re A* (1980) 1 FLR 100.
[34] *Re G* (1980) 1 FLR 109.
[35] *V-P* v. *V-P* (1980) 1 FLR 336.
[36] *Rowe* v. *Rowe* (1980) 1 FLR 166.
[37] (1980) 1 FLR 286.
[38] [1994] 2 FLR 964.

whatever his custodial status, to know and be consulted about the future education of the children and any other major matters".[39]

THE BIRTH OF MODERN CHILD LAW

Modern child law can be dated in different ways. Much depends on how particular landmarks are identified. The 1925, 1948 and 1969 legislation are all important.[40] The 1975 Act[41] was often described as a children's charter[42] (it bore the birth pangs of the Maria Colwell tragedy).[43] The House Lords decision in *J* v. *C*[44] established the paramountcy of paramountcy. All these are important events but they pale in significance in comparison with the *Gillick* ruling.[45] Before *Gillick* there had been a few references by members of the judiciary to the personality of children and their rights. In 1973 Wrangham J said that access was a child's right.[46] But the general tenor of child law, as the historical snapshots have revealed, was to construct a framework to provide for disputes about children, to regulate the orderly transmission of property and to preserve family ties. Children were thus social problems, rather than social participants.

In an earlier age children had been little more than property. But even in the period leading up to modern child law—and sometimes, as we shall see, even beyond—remnants of this ideology remained. Mia Kellmer-Pringle, writing in 1975, could still detect an attitude that:

"a baby completes a family, rather like a TV set or fridge . . . a child belongs to his parents like their other possessions over which they may exercise exclusive rights".[47]

It was attitudes like this that led, until the mid 1970s, to an unwillingness on the part of social workers and others to remove children who had been physically abused from their parents, and to an over-hasty readiness to return such

[39] *Op cit*, n 37, at 298.

[40] Guardianship of Infants Act 1925, Children Act 1948 and Children and Young Persons Act 1969.

[41] On which see M D A Freeman, *The Children Act 1975: Text With Concise Commentary* (London, Sweet & Maxwell, 1976).

[42] "A nation's children represent a nation's future", *per* David Owen MP introducing the Children Bill (Minister of State in the Department of Health and Social Security) *Hansard* HC vol 893, col 1821).

[43] On which see the Field-Fisher Report, *The Care and Supervision Provided in Relation to Maria Colwell* (London, HMSO, 1974).

[44] [1970] AC 668; see particularly Lord MacDermott at 710–11. A good review of the scope and limits of paramountcy is Jonathan Herring, "The Welfare Principle and the Rights of Parents" in A Bainham, S D Sclater and M Richards (eds), *What Is A Parent?* (Oxford, Hart, 1999), p 89. And see also N Thomas and C O'Kane, "When Children's Wishes and Feelings clash with their 'Best Interests'" (1998) 6 *International Journal of Children's Rights* 137.

[45] *Gillick* v. *West Norfolk and Wisbech AHA* [1986] AC 112.

[46] M v. M [1973] 2 All ER 81. See also *Re H* [1992] 1 FLR 148.

[47] *The Needs of Children* (London, Hutchinson, 1975), pp 69–70.

children to their parents.[48] Such attitudes were commented upon critically in reports of enquiries set up after such children died at the hands of their parents. The Maria Colwell case is the most publicised of examples.[49] One critic at the time, John Howells,[50] was to claim that Maria Colwell was killed by a misplaced emphasis on the blood tie. Where nineteenth-century commentators—and judges aping them—referred to the natural law, counterparts in the twentieth century, right up to the modern period as I have identified it, used science, or rather pseudo-science. So, in one notorious case (*Re C (MA)*) in 1966,[51] the "blood-tie" was used to justify a toddler's transfer from prospective adopters, the only parents he knew, to his middle-aged father, and the father's wife, with whom he had had no contact, because, as Russell LJ argued, "if a father (as distinct from a stranger in blood) can bring up his own son as his own son, so much the better for both of them".[52] Though heavily criticised at the time, and still possibly part of the folk-memory, the decision was not so far out of the line with other pre-modern trends. It was grounded in a father's rights, rather than a child's welfare. Other cases emphasised parents' rights. And sometimes the justification was couched in the language of family autonomy, nowhere more so than in the influential writings of Goldstein, Freud and Solnit.[53] But neither a child's personhood nor any concept of children's rights—a child's right to autonomous parents was about as far as they went[54]—figures prominently in the analysis or prescriptions of Goldstein and his colleagues.[55]

THE BACKDROP TO *GILLICK*

The *Gillick* case must be seen as a watershed, but it would be unrealistic to see it as a unique development. Parental authority was under attack as early as 1970: in *Hewer* v. *Bryant*,[56] Lord Denning MR referred to *Re Agar-Ellis*,[57] said it was "out of date" and concluded that custody was a "dwindling right which the

---

[48]   And see R Dingwall, J Eekelaar and T Murray, *The Protection of Children : State Intervention and Family Life* (Oxford, Basil Blackwell, 1983).

[49]   And see P Reder, *Beyond Blame* (London, Routledge, 1992).

[50]   *Remember Maria* (London: Butterworths, 1974).

[51]   [1966] 1 All ER 838.

[52]   *Ibid* at 863.

[53]   These began with *Beyond The Best Interests of the Child* (New York, Free Press, 1973) and culminated with an integrated volume *The Best Interests of the Child: The Least Detrimental Alternative* (New York, Free Press, 1996).

[54]   See *The Best Interests*, *ibid* at p 90.

[55]   I have written a critique "The Best Interests of the Child? Is *The Best Interests of the Child* in the Best Interests of Children?" (1997) 11 *International Journal of Law, Policy and the Family* 360.

[56]   [1980] 1 QB 357.

[57]   [1883] 24 Ch D 317. See also *Thomasset* v. *Thomasset* [1894] P 295.

courts will hesitate to enforce against the wishes of the child. It starts with a right of control and ends with little more than advice".[58] And, a couple of years before *Gillick*, Lord Brandon in *R v. D* agreed that a child with "sufficient understanding and intelligence" could so consent to being taken away by a stranger as to provide a defence to a charge of kidnapping. He assumed that juries would not "find at all frequently that a child under 14 had sufficient understanding and intelligence to give its consent".[59]

THE IMPORTANCE OF *GILLICK*

The *Gillick* decision builds upon this reasoning. Lord Scarman's judgment is so forward-looking that he himself is unable to grasp how much progress it makes. Thus, he denies that English law has ever treated the child as "other than a person with capacities and rights recognised by law".[60] On a literal level this is true, but legal practice until very shortly before *Gillick* fell short of this norm. *Gillick* accepts that growing up is a process. As Lord Scarman put it:

> "The law relating to parent and child is concerned with the problems of growth and maturity of the human personality. If the law should impose upon the process of 'growing up' fixed limits where nature knows only a continuous process, the price would be artificiality and a lack of realism in an area where the law must be sensitive to human development and social change".[61]

The majority thus reject a status test for one which looks to capacity (or competence). Some, Fortin for example, are critical of this. She says that "the inherent weakness of the concept of *Gillick* competence is its uncertainty".[62] I rather see the reasoning as insightful. Lawyers—perhaps Fortin is one—like to dichotomise—but this does not always work. The dilemma, which the law has ducked, over transsexualism is a salutary lesson to those who wish to divide or to pigeon-hole.[63] The importance of *Gillick* lies in its recognition of adolescence, and in its understanding that not all adolescents are the same. This is not the first example of English laws tying legal capacity or liability to ability: the

---

[58] *Hewer* v. *Bryant, op cit* n 56 at 369. With a flourish that few other judges were capable, Lord Denning added: "Youngsters of 18 and 19 fought the battle of Britain . . . since which time pop singers of 19 have made thousands of pounds a week and revolutionaries of 18 have broken up universities. Is each of them in the custody of his father? Of course not" (*Ibid*).

[59] [1984] AC 778, at 806.

[60] *Op cit*, n 45 at 186.

[61] *Ibid* at 188.

[62] *Children's Rights And the Developing Law* (London, Butterworths, 1998), p 73.

[63] Its insistence that one is either male or female (and that this is categorised at birth). The problems began with *Corbett* v. *Corbett* [1971] P 83. The categorisation has survived challenges in the European Court but, in the light of *Sheffield and Horsham* v. *United Kingdom* [1998] 2 FLR 928 it appears to be on its last legs.

doli incapax presumption,[64] recently jettisoned,[65] was a medieval construction which did just that. And, of course, the concept of the "age of discretion", though using rigid age qualifications, was a recognition that children were capable of some decisions before adulthood. It was inherently flawed by an unrealistic gender distinction.[66]

For the majority in *Gillick* competence hinges on understanding and intelligence. Thus, for Lord Scarman "parental right yields to the child's right to make his own decisions when he reaches a sufficient understanding and intelligence to be capable of making up his own mind on the matter requiring decision".[67] Elsewhere in his judgment he refers to a competent child as one who "achieves a sufficient understanding and intelligence to enable him or her to understand fully what is proposed" and also (and this is often overlooked by commentators on the case) has "sufficient discretion to enable him or her to make a wise choice in his or her own interests".[68] In these terms competence incorporates understanding and knowledge with wisdom. There are dangers in conflating knowledge and wisdom, but this is commonly done. Few adults are *Gillick* competent if competence hinges upon abilities to understand fully what is involved in a decision: but many children who are well below the ages with which we tend to associate *Gillick* competence are competent within the test articulated by Lord Scarman if "wise choice" is genuinely situated within the child's personal experiential knowledge of his or her "own interests". Alderson and Goodwin noted that we tend to value highly "professional, textbook knowledge",[69] whilst discounting personal experiential knowledge. This is surely what happened to the anorexic sixteen-year-old in *Re W*,[70] a case to which I shall return. Once such "wisdom" is ignored, the child is assumed to be ignorant, except insofar as he or she can recount medical or other professional information. It becomes easy then to dismiss the contribution they can make to decision-making. Alderson and Goodwin argue that the non-competent child:

> "who figures in the legal imagination is treated as arational rather than irrational. When children are credited, at least, with misguided rationality, the importance of explaining and correcting misunderstandings is accepted. If children are implicitly treated as arational, then enforced treatment without regard to the child's views is endorsed by the courts".[71]

---

[64] The presumption is medical in origin. In 1994 the Divisional Court described it as an anachronism: C v. *DPP* [1994] 2 ALL ER 190. The House of Lords reinstated it (see [1995] 2 ALL ER 43) but its fate was clearly sealed.

[65] See Crime and Disorder Act 1998 s. 34, following *Tacking Youth Crime* (Home Office Consultation Paper, 1997) and *No More Excuses* (London, The Stationery Office, 1997, Cm 3809, paras 4.3–4.5).

[66] With girls reaching the age of discretion at 16 and boys at 14.

[67] *Supra* n 45, at 184.

[68] *Ibid* at 187.

[69] "Contradictions Within Concepts of Children's Competence" (1993) 1 *International Journal of Children's Rights* 303, at 305.

[70] [1993] Fam 64.

[71] *Supra* n 69 at 305.

The *Gillick* decision sent a strong message to parents. But did they hear it? And, if they did, what were they to make of the emphasis only four years later in the Children Act of the primacy of parental responsibility?[72] Some would have read the message of *Gillick* as extending only to contraceptive advice and treatment or more generally to medical treatment. But it is clear that the support of the decision went much further. John Eekelaar, for example, argued that all parental rights, including the right to decide where the child should live, terminated once an adolescent had acquired competence according to the test in *Gillick*.[73] The outcome of *Gillick* was, in Eekelaar's view, that "Children will now have, in wider measure than ever before, that most dangerous but most precious of rights: the right to make their own mistakes".[74] And the right to do what others think is wrong is, Dworkin famously reminded us,[75] at the root of "taking rights seriously".

Gillick also sent a strong message to the judiciary. They have clearly been uncomfortable with it. This has been obvious in a number of cases concerned with medical treatment, most recently the well-publicised case of the girl in Newcastle who refused to have a heart transplant.[76] But, lest it be thought that the problems (as conceived by the judiciary) only occur in such dramatic cases, I will examine another area first.

THE IMPLICATIONS FOR CHILD REPRESENTATION

Re H[77] is a good illustration of a child being treated in a way that would be quite unacceptable in the case of an adult. He was nearly sixteen, of "above-average ability". Although there was a conflict of opinion between him and his guardian *ad litem*, he continued to be represented by the guardian and a solicitor. He appealed against a care order and the court had to interpret a rule[78] which instructs solicitors to represent children in accordance with instructions received from the guardian *ad litem*:

> "unless the solicitor considers, having taken into account the views of the guardian *ad litem* and any direction of the court . . . that the child wishes to give instructions which conflict with those of the guardian *ad litem* and that he is able, having regard to his understanding, to give such instructions on his own behalf, in which case he shall conduct the proceedings in accordance with the instructions received from the child".

Thorpe J considered that a child "must have sufficient rationality within the understanding to instruct a solicitor. It may well be that the level of emotional

---

[72] See s. 2.
[73] "The Eclipse of Parental Rights" (1986) 102 *LQR* 4, at 8. See also his article "The Emergence of Children's Rights" (1986) 6 *Oxford Journal of Legal Studies* 161, at 180–2.
[74] *Ibid* at 182.
[75] *Taking Rights Seriously* (London, Duckworth, 1977), p 193.
[76] *Re M* [1999] 2 FLR 1097.
[77] [1993] 1 FLR 440.
[78] Family Proceedings Courts (Children Act 1989) Rules 1991 r. 12(1)(a).

disturbance is such as to remove the necessary degree of rationality that leads to coherent and consistent instruction".[79] But we do not question an emotionally-disturbed adult's ability to instruct a solicitor. One wonders whether the consequences of this sort of reasoning and the decisions it leads to have been thought through. The removal of autonomy can lead to the destruction of identity; a feeling of being out of control can exacerbate disturbance. Despite his emotional problems, the adolescent in *Re H* probably had the ability that Lord Scarman captured as "wise choice", even if he may have lacked the sort of professional knowledge that we associate with "rationality".

Another good illustration is *Re S*.[80] An application had been made by S's father for residence and contact orders. S, who was eleven, was made a party to the proceedings and the Official Solicitor was appointed to act as his guardian *ad litem*. The Official Solicitor recommended that S should continue to live with his mother (he had done so since he was five) and should see his father less frequently. It was the father's contention, which S supported, that S should live with him in North America. S contended from the outset of the proceedings that the Official Solicitor should not represent him, and that he should be able to act independently through a solicitor. The Court Rules allow for this but the child must have "understanding". The Court of Appeal gave this a quite restrictive interpretation. In line with *Gillick*, Sir Thomas Bingham MR emphasised understanding rather than age, and he accepted that this increased with the passage of time. He noted that "different children have differing levels of understanding at the same age. And understanding is not an absolute. It has to be assessed relatively to the issues in the proceedings".[81] But he concluded that "where any sound judgement on these issues calls for insight and imagination which only maturity and experience can bring, both the court and the solicitor will be slow to conclude that the child's understanding is sufficient".[82]

It is clear that the Master of the Rolls has both a desire to promote children's capacity for independence, so that it is important to consult them, and a concern to protect them from making mistakes. Thus, he writes of two considerations:

> "First . . . the principle . . . that children are human beings in their own right with individual minds and wills, views and emotions, which should command serious attention. A child's wishes are not to be discounted or dismissed simply because he is a child. He should be free to express them and decision-makers should listen. Second is the fact that a child is, after all, a child. The reason why the law is particularly solicitous in protecting the interests of children is that they are liable to be vulnerable and impressionable, lacking the maturity to weigh the longer term against the shorter, lacking the insight to know how they will react and the imagination to know how others will react in certain situations, lacking the experience to match the probable against the possible. . ."[83]

---

[79] *Op cit*, n 77 at 449.
[80] [1993] 2 FLR 437.
[81] *Ibid* at 444.
[82] *Ibid*.
[83] *Ibid* at 448.

This paragraph has been quoted with approval many times and not surprisingly because it encapsulates the dilemma so well. The court's conclusion, however, which rejected the boy's application, is less satisfactory. True, the boy may have been influenced, even over-influenced, by his father, and he may have been impressionable. But the rules provide for children to be able to make such decisions, and they are, after all, hardly decisions likely to harm them severely or irreparably.[84]

One might have expected Booth J in *Re H*[85] to have come to the same conclusion, but she did not. A fifteen-year-old boy was warded by his parents after the man with whom he was living was charged with sexual offences against another boy. He had been left in England when his parents moved to France. He now wished to stay in England, and ran away each time he was taken to France. He considered that the Official Solicitor who was representing him was not representing his views, and he applied to be allowed to continue to defend the proceedings without the Official Solicitor acting as his guardian *ad litem*, and for the removal of the Official Solicitor from that position. There was a difference of psychiatric opinion. The psychiatrist instructed by the Official Solicitor considered that *H* lacked sufficient understanding to participate in the proceedings because *H* did not appreciate the dangers posed by the suspected sex offender. The psychiatrist treating *H* considered that the views expressed were those of *H*, and that having his own representative would help him feel that justice was being done, and so would assist him to accept and comply with provisions made for him and reduce the risk of rash and unwise decisions. It was this latter opinion which Booth J favoured. She held that *H* had the understanding necessary to instruct his own legal adviser without the services of the Official Solicitor. This is a liberal conclusion, the more so since, if anything, one might have supposed that *H* was in greater need of protection than *S*. She also adopts a broader approach to competence than Sir Thomas Bingham MR did. She noted:

> "The court must be satisfied that *H* . . . has sufficient understanding to participate as a party . . . without a guardian ad litem. [This] . . . means much more than instructing a solicitor as to his own views. The child enters the arena among other adult parties. He may give evidence and he may be cross-examined. He will hear other parties, including in this case his parents, give evidence and be cross-examined. He must be able to give instructions on many different matters as the case goes through its stages and to make decisions as need arises. Thus a child is exposed and not protected in these procedures . . ."[86]

Of course, many adults do not have these abilities.

---

[84] In *The Rights and Wrongs of Children* (London, Frances Pinter, 1983), I argue that interferences with the exercise of a child's autonomy can be justified where the child will be severely and irreparably damaged by the exercise of such autonomy, so as to be unable to reach an autonomous adulthood (see ch 2).

[85] [1993] 2 FLR 552.

[86] *Ibid* at 554–5.

The judiciary has thus trod warily in the footsteps of *Gillick* where issues relating to representation have arisen. Where a child's medical treatment has been contentious, there has been a veritable retreat from the implications of *Gillick*. *Gillick* make it clear that a competent child under sixteen (sixteen being supposedly the age where children acquire the power to make their own medical decisions)[87] could consent to medical treatment. I do not think that anyone at the time contemplated courts subsequently deciding that in effect they could not refuse their consent to treatment, because if they did their refusal would be overridden. Even less could anyone have imagined that statutory provisions (initially the Family Law Reform Act 1969[88] and subsequently the Children Act 1989)[89] would have been outflanked by a judiciary more concerned to protect the medical profession[90] than to recognise the personality of children. It is perhaps all the more dumbfounding because this rejection of autonomy, this imposition of intrusive treatment, has come at a time when the judiciary has been willing to recognise the implications of the principle of self-determination for other medical patients. A chronic paranoid schizophrenic in Broadmoor can refuse to have his gangrenous leg amputated;[91] a woman can refuse a caesarean even if it imperils her baby;[92] a learning disabled woman of twenty-five with renal failure can refuse dialysis.[93] Why then do the courts have such difficulty with children, including those over sixteen, who, for one reason or another, want to reject medical treatment?

In *Gillick*, the question raised—about access to contraceptive advice and treatment without parental consent—was hypothetical. But in the cases which have plagued the courts since, the dilemmas were very real. Thus, in *Re R*[94] a fifteen-year-old girl was refusing psychotic medication; in *Re W*,[95] a sixteen-year-old girl with anorexia nervosa was refusing medical treatment for this condition and there was a danger that she would starve herself to death; in *Re L*,[96] a fourteen-year-old Jehovah's Witness, was refusing a blood transfusion; in *Re M*,[97] a fifteen-year-old girl was refusing a heart transplant (she did not want to have someone else's heart or to take medication for the rest of her life). The judges

---

[87]   Family Law Reform Act 1969, s. 8(1).

[88]   Despite the seeming ambiguity of s. 8(3).

[89]   See s. 38(6) and its interpretation in *South Glamorgan County Council* v. *W and B* [1993] 1 FLR 574.

[90]   This concern is very clear in Lord Donaldson MR's judgments in *Re R* [1992] Fam 11 and *Re W* [1993] Fam 64.

[91]   *Re C* [1994] 1 All ER 819.

[92]   *St. George's Healthcare NHS Trust* v. *S* [1998] 2 FLR 426.

[93]   *Re JT* [1998] 1 FLR 48.

[94]   *Op cit*, n 90.

[95]   *Op cit*, n 90.

[96]   [1998] 2 FLR 810.

[97]   [1999] 2 FLR 1097.

see themselves as staring into the abyss, and it is not a prospect, understandably, that they relish. Nonetheless, their attitudes are so very different when the patient has reached the magic age of eighteen.

It is notable that there is a reluctance to find *Gillick* competence in these cases, and it is striking that it is in the "adult" cases beginning with *Re C* (the "Broadmoor" case) that some attempt has been made to fill out what is meant by competence,[98] and that no attempt has been made to apply the test so developed in the "children" cases. If *R, W, L* and *M* were asked the questions posed by Thorpe J in *Re C*, relating to comprehension and retention of treatment information, believing it, and weighing it in the balance to arrive at a choice, they would have been as likely to be pronounced "competent" as *C* was. Instead, there tends to be a presumption of non-competence. In *Re R*, the consultant child psychiatrist reported that *R* was "of sufficient maturity and understanding to comprehend the treatment being recommended".[99] Lord Donaldson MR's response was to limit *Gillick* to "the staged development of a normal child" and to translate competence into "an assessment of mental and emotional age, as contrasted with chronological age", adding "but even this test needs to be modified, in the case of fluctuating mental disability, to take account of that misfortune".[100] On this test, the learning disabled could never consent or refuse consent. Lord Donaldson MR continued:

> ". . . What is involved is not merely an ability to understand the nature of the proposed treatment . . . but a full understanding and appreciation of the consequences both of the treatment, in terms of intended and possible side effects and, equally important, the anticipated consequences of a failure to treat".

On this criteria she was "not only *Gillick*—incompetent, but actually sectionable".[101] Of course, on this criteria most of the population is not *Gillick* competent. Further, it is clear from later cases (in particular *Re C*) that a person who is sectionable may nevertheless be competent.

In *Re W*, *Gillick* competence was not in issue, since the girl was over sixteen. Relevant or not, Thorpe J found that the girl had sufficient understanding to make an informed decision. The Court of Appeal disagreed. What Thorpe J, it said, had failed to appreciate is that "it is a feature of anorexia nervosa that it is capable of destroying the ability to make an informed choice".[102] That the girl was sixteen and that Parliament had said nothing about the quality of her decision-making were readily dismissed. Sixteen-year-old anorexics are likely to satisfy the *Re C* test without difficulty.

---

[98] The rest was approved by the Court of Appeal in *Re MB* [1997] 2 FLR 426 at 433. The test has been applied in child cases but only where the issue is raised by the child's mental disability, not where developmental maturity is in question: see *Re C* [1997] 2 FLR 180 and *Re B* [1997] 1 FCR 618.

[99] *Op cit*, n 90.

[100] *Ibid* at 25–6.

[101] *Ibid* at 26.

[102] *Op cit*, n 90 at 81.

Re L is not the first case of an under-age Jehovah's Witness who has refused to consent to a blood transfusion, nor obviously will it be the last.[103] *L's* case is different from some of the earlier ones, where the need for blood was a continuing one and where courts acknowledged it could not be enforced upon the adolescent after his/her eighteenth birthday. Here it was needed, at least initially, for burns treatment. Once again, however, the evidence for and against *Gillick* competency is cursorily dismissed. Sir Stephen Brown P says:

> "I base [my view that she is not Gillick competent] upon all the evidence that I have heard. She is certainly not "Gillick competent" in the context of all the necessary details which it would be appropriate for her to be able to form a view about".[104]

This (absence of) reasoning is hardly likely to convince any but those uncomfortable with what *Gillick* stands for.

THE CHILDREN ACT AND CHILDREN'S RIGHTS

The core of child law today is the Children Act 1989, passed contemporaneously with the United Nations Convention on Rights of the Child. It takes a more positive view of children than previous legislation has. Thus, their opportunities for initiating proceedings are greater.[105] They can, for example, seek leave to apply for a residence order in favour of the person with whom they wish to live.[106] This was promptly dubbed "children divorcing parents",[107] though it was nothing of the sort. The child—no age is specified—does require leave to make the application, and the court must be satisfied that s/he has "sufficient understanding".[108] This in itself may be difficult enough to establish, but in *Re SC* Booth J ruled that a court has discretion whether to grant leave even if it has been established that the child has sufficient understanding to make the application.[109] The likely success of the substantive application was also to be considered. It has also been suggested that the welfare principle should operate at the stage of the leave process.[110] Although I previously thought this the right approach,[111] I now recognise it should only be at the trial of the substantive issue that what a court considers to be in a child's best interests should govern. At the stage of

---

[103] *Op cit*, n 96.

[104] *Ibid* at 813.

[105] For example, challenge an emergency protection order (s. 45(8) of the Children Act 1989), seek contact when in care (s. 34(2)), seek the court's leave to obtain a s. 8 order (s. 10(2), (8)).

[106] Children Act 1989, s. 10 (8).

[107] It was the US case of *Kingsley* v. *Kingsley* 623 So 2d 780 (Fla Dist Ct App 1993) which first promoted this media response. On England see Michael Freeman, "Can Children Divorce Their Parents?" in Michael Freeman (ed), *Divorce—Where Next?* (Aldershot, Dartmouth, 1996), p 159.

[108] See s. 10(8) of the Children Act 1989.

[109] [1994] 1 FLR 96.

[110] By Johnson J in *Re C* [1994] 1 FLR 26.

[111] In *Op cit*, n 105, pp 169–70.

leave, it is her wishes that are in issue. Other courts have agreed that such a distinction should be made.[112]

The Act also emphasises the importance of a child's wishes and feelings.[113] But a concern remains that children are not able to put their views to a court as readily as should be the case. Their views will often reach the court only through the filter of a welfare officer's report and may not, as a result, coincide with the child's views, particularly where these are not consistent with what the welfare officer believes is in the child's best interests. The case of *Re M*[114] graphically illustrates the difficulties. *M* was twelve-and-a-half, deemed by the court to be able, intelligent, articulate, with an attractive personality. She wanted to live with her father who had been denied a residence order. But she was not allowed to swear an affidavit supporting her father's appeal. On one level this is understandable: the welfare officer's report had already conveyed to the court what *M*'s views were. But since the welfare recommendation went against these views, it undermines the participatory rights of the person most affected by the decision. Butler-Sloss LJ was clearly concerned to prevent children becoming entangled in their parents' litigation, and alarmed that a child might be manipulated by a parent. But the end result—the silencing of an intelligent adolescent does not augur well for the future of children.

On several occasions since the Children Act judges have positively discouraged children from participating in proceedings which related directly to them. In *Re C*[115] where the views of a girl of thirteen were discounted (she was "too young to carry the burden of decisions about her own future, and too young to have to bear the weight of responsibility for a parent who lacks authority and plays on her feelings of protectiveness"),[116] Waite J commented that "to sit for hours, or it may even be days, listening to lawyers debating one's future is not an experience that should in normal circumstances be wished upon any child as young as this".[117] In *North Yorkshire County Council* v. *G*,[118] magistrates had allowed "a young lad" (he was just short of his seventeenth birthday) to become a party in care proceedings in respect of a younger sibling. The local authority and the guardian *ad litem* were opposed to any such participation, and Douglas Brown J agreed. The boy had been particularly supportive of a mother who spoke little English and was isolated. The court held that he was able to carry out a supportive role by being present or by being a witness. The positive disadvantages, as the judge identified them, in the boy being a party were that he would have sight of all the documentation in the case, and this included psychiatric evidence about

---

[112] See *Re C* [1995] 1 FLR 927.
[113] Children Act 1989, s. 1 (3) (a). See Christine Piper, "The Wishes and Feelings of the Child" in Shelley Day Sclater and Christine Piper (eds), *Undercurrents of Divorce* (Aldershot, Ashgate, 1999), p 77.
[114] [1995] 2 FLR 100.
[115] [1993] 1 FLR 832.
[116] *Ibid* at 840.
[117] *Ibid* at 841.
[118] [1993] 2 FLR 732.

his mother. In *Re W*,[119] the child was much younger (ten) but the case concerned his liberty. The case was a local authority application for a secure accommodation order. For the child it was contended that this is the equivalent of a custodial order in a criminal court and that natural justice dictates that he should be allowed to be in court before an order is made which will have that effect. The judge could not see "any analogy between orders made in this Division and orders made by the criminal court".[120] And he added—in a give-away line—"the purpose of the criminal court is to deal with criminal offences committed *by people or children* (my emphasis) . . .". By contrast "this jurisdiction is . . . Different. It is . . . a benign jurisdiction".[121] There was evidence that she was likely to be unruly, but in criminal proceedings this would not justify exclusion. As Fortin comments:

> "It is unrealistic to expect a child to see a civil secure accommodation order as anything other than a Draconian measure designed to lock her (sic) up. Denying her (sic) the right to attend the hearing because she (sic) is emotionally damaged or to ensure its smooth running reflects an extremely adult view and appears to ignore her (sic) own perspective of the situation".[122]

The judiciary has been hardly more receptive to allowing children to communicate their views in private. Back in 1981 Ormrod LJ said that whether a judge should see a child in private was a personal matter for himself to determine.[123] Earlier still, in 1974, Megaw LJ commented that it was "of course often most desirable . . . that the judge hearing the case should see the children and should see the children otherwise than in open court".[124] But despite the Children Act and the UN Convention (in particular Article 12), there is now an ambivalence, with a greater willingness to see children in public law proceedings than in private law proceedings. Thus, in *Re M*[125] Wall J suggested that "an intelligent and articulate twelve-year-old who had an excellent grasp of the issues and who had discussed the matter fully was entitled to see the judge who was to decide his future". The same judge detected an inherent contradiction in a later case (*B* v. *B*)[126] in seeing children to ascertain their wishes while being obliged to report to their parents anything material they said. The ambivalence also appears when the judiciary allow themselves the jurisdiction to see children in private but deny this to magistrates, who hear the bulk of the cases. Booth J thus thought that it was only in "rare and exceptional cases" that magistrates were entitled to see children privately.[127]

---

[119] [1994] 2 FLR 1092.
[120] *Ibid* at 1096.
[121] *Ibid*.
[122] *Op cit*, n 62, p 181. It is clear that the child is male: is it not rather perverse to use the female pronoun to conform to contemporary fashion?
[123] *D* v. *D* [1981] 2 FLR 74.
[124] *H* v. *H* [1974] 1 All ER 1145 at 1147.
[125] [1994] 1 FLR 749 at 755.
[126] [1994] 2 FLR 489 at 495.
[127] *Re M* [1993] 2 FLR 706 at 709.

Children's rights feature elsewhere in the Children Act. The range of court actions a child may initiate is broad. S/he may challenge an emergency protection order,[128] seek a contact order when in care,[129] ask for a care order to be discharged.[130] Separate representation of children by guardians *ad litem*—the initial breakthrough was in 1975[131] after the Maria Colwell scandal—is extensive (in public law proceedings the norm).[132] The contact order is now expressed as child-centred.[133] The family assistance order may be made in favour of the child.[134] Adopted children are given an enhanced ability to establish contact with their family of origin with the establishment of the adoption contact register.[135]

The statutory checklist in section 1(3), to which reference has already been made, finds echoes elsewhere. So, just as courts must have regard to the ascertainable wishes and feelings of the child, in the light of the child's age and understanding,[136] local authorities,[137] voluntary organisations[138] and persons running registered voluntary homes[139] must also do so before taking any decision in relation to a child looked after by them. Local authorities, voluntary organisations and registered homes must also take steps to ascertain the wishes and feelings of the child before taking any decision with respect to him/her, and in making the decision must give "due consideration" to the child's views (again in the context of the child's age and understanding).[140] Since "due consideration" is not further explicated, this gives the persons concerned considerable discretion. It is very much up to them, for example, how important they consider the child's views in the context of the views of others concerned, whether members of the family or welfare professionals.

The significance of the reconstruction of the parent-child relationship as based on parental responsibility rather than the traditional parental rights must also not be overlooked.[141] Rights are redolent of the ties between a person and property, whereas responsibilities suggest more the relationship between a trustee and the beneficiary of that trust. Children are reconceptualised as persons and thus as participants in the social process rather than as possessions or problems.

---

[128] Children Act 1989, s. 45 (8).

[129] *Ibid* s. 34(2).

[130] *Ibid* s. 39(1).

[131] Children Act 1975, s. 64.

[132] This is in contrast to private law disputes, though the Family Law Act 1996 s. 11 envisages an improvement—if this is ever brought into operation.

[133] Children Act 1989 s. 8 (1).

[134] *Ibid*, s. 16 (2) (c).

[135] Adoption Act 1976, s. 51A, as substituted by s. 88 of the Children Act 1989 and Sched 10, para 20 (2).

[136] Children Act 1989, s. 1 (3) (a).

[137] *Ibid*, s. 22(4) and (5).

[138] *Ibid*, s. 61(2) and (3).

[139] *Ibid*, s. 64(2) and (3).

[140] *Ibid*, s. 61(2), s. 64(2).

[141] See Children Act 1989, ss. 2 and 3. See also S Edwards and A Halpern, "Parental Responsibility : An Instrument of Social Policy" (1992) 22 *Family Law* 113–18.

Lyon and Parton describe the "net effect" of these provisions as enhancing the relevance of the child's views. And they continue:

"In theory it should be more difficult for the court and welfare professionals to regard the child as essentially an *object* of welfare. Children must be allowed to make an independent input to decisions concerning them although their views may be superseded by the views of others and/or overtaken by other considerations. Children are entitled to have a say in matters affecting them but not the final say. The provisions offer children qualified autonomy but fall well short of allowing children full consequences of action".[142]

There is thus a framework if not for a cultural revolution, at least for a rethinking of childhood. But, as we have seen, the opportunities thus presented have been scorned by the judges. In part this is their natural conservatism. In part it is genuine welfarist concerns. But in part also it is the result of an ambiguous message. Neither Parliament nor government is prepared to see through the implications of a new vision of childhood. To take just one example: despite brave efforts at the time to extirpate the institution, corporal punishment—or at least what is now euphemistically called a "safe smack"—was not banned by the Children Act and is likely to survive even a European Court ruling.[143] Indeed, it took sixteen months after the ruling for the Government to put out a promised consultation paper on the subject; fudge—for this was what was anticipated and we were not disappointed—usually takes longer than purposeful and positive action.

CONCLUSION

The child is now at the centre of family law. That was not so a matter of a generation ago. The image of the child in family law has also radically changed. There is little concern today about whether the child is born in or out of marriage and questions of property and succession are marginal. But concerns with new forms of "property" have emerged: conflicts over name and identity have resulted. We have come to accept the personality of the child and to recognise the importance of his/her autonomy. But we remain—and family law reflects this—ambivalent about the consequences of this new status. Certainly, we have shown ourselves more willing to impose criminal—or, in the case of those under ten, quasi-criminal—responsibility on children before granting them participatory rights. The sociology of childhood ("childhood studies") emerged only in the 1990s: the law had taken the lead with *Gillick* but, as it has retreated, social

---

[142] "Children's Rights and the Children Act 1989" in Bob Franklin (ed), *The Handbook of Children's Rights* (London, Routledge, 1995), pp 40–55 at p 42.

[143] A v. *United Kingdom* [1998] 2 FLR 959, discussed by M Freeman, "Children Are Unbeatable" 13 *Children and Society* 130. The Department of Health report *Protecting Children, Supporting Parents* (London, Department of Health, 2000) refuses even to consider making hitting children unlawful.

scientists have begun to map out an image of childhood with children as social actors constructing their own childhood. The implications of this for social policy are profound. How the law will respond—positively or negatively—and how long it will take the law to respond are questions of major importance for all concerned with the future of children.

12

Children's Rights and Education

PAUL MEREDITH

INTRODUCTION

WHILE CHILDREN MAY have a strong moral or political claim or interest in respect of the nature and substance of their education, education law in England and Wales[1] in its present form does little to underpin any such claim or interest, and generally falls far short of conferring on children directly enforceable legal rights in respect of their education. Furthermore, to the very limited extent to which any enforceable legal rights are vested in individuals in respect of the provision of education as correlative to the imposition of legal duties on public authorities responsible for the administration of the education system, these rights tend to vest in parents rather than in children. This is perhaps most graphically illustrated by section 9 of the Education Act 1996, a symbolically important but, in view of its highly qualified terms, an almost entirely unworkable provision requiring the Secretary of State and local education authorities (LEAs) to "have regard to the general principle" that pupils should be educated in accordance with their parents' wishes, so far as compatible with the provision of efficient instruction and training and the avoidance of unreasonable public expenditure. The statutory system of education as it has developed from the Education Act 1944 to the present day has provided virtually no legal or administrative mechanisms for the articulation of the interests or preferences of children independently of their parents.[2] The legal structures have been developed upon the broad and arguably mistaken assumption that the claims and interests of children and those of their parents simply coincide.[3] It may be that educational considerations will feature in judicial proceedings in the family law context concerning the welfare of children under section 1 of the Children Act 1989, requiring the court to have particular regard to the ascertainable wishes and feelings of the child concerned, considered in the light of his or her age and

---

[1] This chapter is confined to the law relating to education in England and Wales, apart from incidental reference to the Standards in Scotland's Schools, Etc. Act, 2000. Education in Scotland and Northern Ireland is provided under different statutory provisions, although there are close parallels in those jurisdictions.

[2] In Scotland, however, provision has very recently been made for the consultation of children by virtue of s. 2(2), Standards in Scotland's Schools, Etc. Act, 2000.

[3] See P Meredith, *Government, Schools and the Law* (London, Routledge 1992), pp 7–9.

understanding;[4] there has, however, been no principled and rational attempt hitherto by the courts in the educational context to draw an analogy with the conferment by the House of Lords in *Gillick* v. *West Norfolk and Wisbech Area Health Authority*[5] of a degree of independent autonomy in older adolescents in respect of contraceptive advice given in confidence by medical practitioners.[6] Indeed, as Andrew Bainham has commented:

". . . the principles of education law show little appreciation of the maturing child's capacity for taking responsibility for her school life or her ability to reach important decisions over her education, without parental interference. Indeed, in some respects, the law seems to have become increasingly blinkered to such an ideal".[7]

The absence of any legally established and recognised independent voice for children in respect of the provision of education has been a consistent feature of education law in England and Wales, and the many radical reforms of the structure, substance and delivery of education by successive governments since 1979 have done nothing to alter this situation. One of the key underlying philosophies which informed educational reform during the tenure of the Thatcher and Major Conservative governments between 1979 and 1997 was the enhancement of accountability by the providers of education (principally LEAs, school governors and teachers) to those who were identified as their "consumers"; and consistently those identified as the consumers of educational services were the *parents* of the children being taught rather than the children themselves. The enhancement of accountability as a central philosophy was manifested in many ways, but perhaps most notably through legislation designed to underpin parental choice of school[8] coupled with the imposition of "open enrolment" procedures upon LEAs and school governors, requiring school admissions authorities to admit pupils, subject to certain statutory exceptions, in accordance with parental preference unless a school had reached its standard number—meaning, in essence, that the school was full to capacity.[9] Very significantly, these provisions were introduced in conjunction with new funding arrangements under which schools were funded primarily on the basis of the number of registered pupils on each school's roll.[10] These related reforms were designed to underpin parental choice and to make schools responsive to

---

[4] Children Act 1989, s. 1(1) and 1(3)(a). See also *Re P (A Minor) (Education)* [1992] 1 FLR 316; and N Harris, *Law and Education: Regulation, Consumerism and the Education System* (London, Sweet & Maxwell 1993), p 19.

[5] [1986] AC 12.

[6] See A Bainham, *Children: the Modern Law* (London, Family Law, 2nd ed, 1998), pp 132–3; P Meredith, *Government, Schools and the Law*, op cit n 3, pp 8–9.

[7] A Bainham, *op cit* n 6, p 132.

[8] Originally introduced in Education Act 1980, s. 6; see now, School Standards and Framework Act 1998, s. 86.

[9] Open enrolment was originally introduced in Education Reform Act 1988, ss. 26 and 27; see now, School Standards and Framework Act 1998, ss. 86(5) and 93.

[10] These funding arrangements were originally introduced as an integral part of the local management initiative in the Education Reform Act 1988, ss. 33–47; see now Education Act 1996, ss. 101–26.

parental demand for places by giving them a strong financial incentive to recruit as many pupils as possible within the limit of their capacity. This essentially enshrined the philosophy of the educational market place in which education was perceived as a commodity offered by a range of different providers within a given area, parents being in theory free to take their custom to whichever provider they wished. Furthermore, the range and variety of the choice enjoyed by parents would be significantly enhanced by increasing the diversity of types of school within a given area: hence the introduction of grant-maintained schools[11] and the encouragement of schools to specialise in particular areas of curricular provision and to introduce the selection of a given percentage of their pupil intake by academic ability.

A striking feature of these reforms is that, although the key interest of children in the best possible standard of educational provision was clearly an essential underlying factor informing the government's thinking, the only individual interests given any statutory protection by these reforms were those of parents. Children themselves—including mature adolescents—were given no procedural protections whatsoever. The legal regime underpinning choice of school serves as a powerful illustration of the absence of legal recognition of children's rights in the educational sphere, and one which is reflected in many other areas of education law including provisions relating to school attendance, the exclusion of pupils from school, and important curricular matters.

The reforms introduced since 1997 by the Labour Government, now enshrined principally in the School Standards and Framework Act 1998,[12] have similarly failed to recognise and establish any enforceable legal rights in the individual child. The 1998 Act has introduced wide-ranging and penetrating measures for underpinning and enhancing standards in schools, including the introduction of LEA education development plans,[13] and of new measures for dealing with schools[14] and with LEAs[15] deemed by Office for Standards in Education (OFSTED) inspectors to be failing. While all these important measures were designed to facilitate achievement of the Government's key goal of raising school standards, with children as the primary beneficiaries, they are by nature structural reforms and mechanisms of intervention and control at institutional level, and do not begin to address the issue of enforceable children's rights at an individualised level.

All of this constitutes striking evidence of the absence of any significant element of autonomy or capacity for self-determination on the part even of older

---

[11] Originally introduced under Education Reform Act 1988, ss. 52–104; these provisions were subsequently consolidated in Education Act 1996, ss. 183–311. Grant-maintained schools are, however, now being brought within the new framework of maintained schools provided for in School Standards and Framework Act 1998, ss. 20–35.

[12] See White Paper, *Excellence in Schools*, Cm 3681 (July 1997). See also P Meredith, "The Fall and Rise of Local Education Authorities" (1998) XX(1) *Liverpool Law Rev* 41.

[13] School Standards and Framework Act 1998, ss. 6–7.

[14] *Ibid*, ss. 14–19.

[15] *Ibid*, s. 8.

children in the context of their education, and is strongly indicative of a pre-dominantly paternalistic approach in this sphere. The more extreme forms of children's liberationist approach, denying paternalistic limitations upon chil-dren's freedom, would appear to have had relatively little impact on educational provision for minor children.[16] Rather, the prevailing approach in the educa-tional context follows the assertion of JS Mill that minor children lack the capacity for personal autonomy enjoyed by adults:

> "It is, perhaps, hardly necessary to say that this doctrine (of personal autonomy) is meant to apply only to human beings in the maturity of their faculties. We are not speaking of children, or of young persons below the age which the law may fix as that of manhood or womanhood. Those who are still in a state to require being taken care of by others, must be protected against their own actions as well as against external injury".[17]

This is consistent with a widely held view that children lack the capacity for rational self-determination and autonomy in relation to decisions affecting their education, in part because they may be tempted by short-term considerations which could operate to harm their best interests in the longer term. Children may need an element of coercion in order to ensure that they are subjected to the best available educational influences in order to optimise their longer-term life chances. This may be in the best interests both of the child and of wider society which arguably has a clear and legitimate interest in a well-educated and well-ordered community.

A paternalistic approach *may* thus perhaps be justified in the context of the education at least of younger children. Many would, however, argue that older adolescents have a legitimate claim to some element of autonomous decision-making capacity in respect of education, just as they may in certain circum-stances do by virtue of the *Gillick* decision[18] in the context of medical advice. This view may have particular force in the light of the potential for conflict between the interests of parents and children, which may arise, for example, over choice of school, continuing school attendance, withdrawal of a child from religious or sex education, or many other aspects of educational provision. Some of these conflicts of interest may arise in a particularly acute way in respect of parents from minority cultural, ethnic or religious backgrounds, in some cases of a fundamentalist persuasion, wishing to shelter their children from exposure to what they in all sincerity view as harmful educative influences prevalent in educational provision in maintained schools. Such parents might argue that a policy of imposed cultural pluralism is fundamentally misconceived and counter-productive, that the maintenance of their own cultural traditions is best achieved by making special or segregated educational arrangements, and

---

[16] See J Fortin, *Children's Rights and the Developing Law* (London, Butterworths, 1998), ch 1.
[17] J S Mill, *On Liberty* (1859), quoted from M Warnock (ed), *Utilitarianism* (London, Fontana Press, 1962), p 135.
[18] See n 4 *supra*.

that their children's educational and social interests would in no sense be harmed thereby. Others might take the view that the pursuit of fundamentalist notions involving the segregation of children would be severely injurious to the children's educational, emotional and social development; and that the interests of other children might be adversely affected through their not being exposed to the enriching experience of diverse cultural and religious influences. There may be little common ground between these opposing views,[19] but what seems clear is that the children involved could find themselves caught in the centre of profoundly conflicting approaches to what is best for their future.

The argument thus far has stressed, first, the paucity of rights as a whole in the context of education; and, secondly, that such individual rights as do exist tend to be vested in parents rather than in the children themselves. This would appear to be all the more remarkable in the light of the fundamentality of education to the child's most vital interests. Beyond the most basic elements of nourishment and physical care, it is arguable that little could be more fundamental to the pursuit of a fulfilled and worthwhile adult life than education; education is central to the development of a child into a fully autonomous adult equipped to the optimum degree to take full advantage of such life chances as are made available to it. In particular, education provides an essential foundation for the enjoyment of other crucial human rights, including in particular such key civil and political rights as freedom of expression and freedom of thought, conscience and religion. Education is critical to the conferment on the individual of genuine freedom of choice in the exercise of those other rights.

It should thus be emphasised at the outset that individual rights in education are residual and impoverished in nature and rarely enforceable in legal terms. Furthermore, this state of affairs has come about not by accident but by the deliberate action of successive governments in constructing the legislative framework of the education system: very rarely do the Education Acts confer enforceable rights of real substance on individuals.[20] Although some statutory rights of a *procedural* nature are conferred on individuals—for instance the right of parents to express a reasoned preference as to choice of school[21]—virtually no enforceable statutory rights of a *substantive* nature are conferred. Rather, the legislation adopts the technique of conferring generously phrased discretionary powers or highly generalised statutory duties upon public authorities; and, where statutory duties are imposed, they are frequently couched in such highly qualified terms that it is very difficult to discern any legally enforceable correlative rights vesting in individuals flowing from such duties.

---

[19] For an incisive discussion of the policy options in this context, see S Poulter, *Ethnicity, Law and Human Rights: the English Experience* (Oxford, Clarendon Press, 1998), pp 10–22.

[20] This comment must now be qualified to some extent by s. 1, Standards in Scotland's Schools, Etc. Act 2000 which does express the child's right to education in positive terms, although the extent of its enforceability remains open to question.

[21] School Standards and Framework Act 1998, s. 86.

The purpose of this chapter will now be to illustrate the impoverished nature of the rights of the child in the context of education by exploring—in a necessarily selective way—some aspects of the substantive content of what is taught in maintained schools where individual interests may often arise in a particularly acute way.

CURRICULAR RIGHTS

Introduction

The maintained school curriculum—the substantive content of what is delivered in state schools by way of educational provision—lies at the very heart of education and of any claims or rights children may have in respect of their education, yet it is extremely difficult to assert that children have anything in the nature of enforceable legal rights in this context. This may come as no surprise, given that the right to education is generally categorised as a social, economic and cultural right of a positive nature whose realisation is dependent upon a wide range of political and economic considerations. On the other hand, the educational interests of children are acute and the potential scope for taking issue with curricular content or presentation is wide: some, indeed, would go so far as to challenge the entire structure and ethos of the National Curriculum as an insidious capitalist conspiracy moulding children into docile conformity with a system whose very basis they would regard as fundamentally flawed; others might accept the general thrust of the school curriculum, but take issue with specific aspects of its aims or contents; others might accept its aims and contents but seek to challenge the nature and perhaps the quality of its presentation and mode of delivery—a challenge rather to educational standards and perhaps also to the standard of the infrastructural support and resources upon which high educational standards so much depend. These present some examples of the wide range of very different types of curricular challenge that could be made: while they are very different, a common element is that each would be extremely difficult to pursue by way of any form of legal challenge, not only by virtue of the absence of procedural mechanisms within the legislative framework of education, but also the almost inevitable absence of consensus as to what ought to be the aims and the substantive content of education.

The absence of consensus as to the aims and substance of educational provision is reflected in the very broad terms of international charters and conventions bearing on education as well as in the phraseology of domestic legislation. Of the several international charters and conventions which seek to promote rights in the context of education, the UN Convention on the Rights of the Child 1989 is perhaps the most specific, but this too remains highly generalised in its terms. Article 29, for instance, provides that the education of the child shall be directed to:

"(a) The development of the child's personality, talents and mental and physical abilities to their fullest potential;

(b) The development of respect for human rights and fundamental freedoms. . .;

(c) The development of respect for the child's parents, his or her own cultural identity, language and values, for the national values of the country in which the child is living, the country from which he or she may originate and for civilisations different from his or her own;

(d) The preparation of the child for responsible life in a free society, in the spirit of understanding, peace, tolerance, equality of sexes, and friendship among all peoples, ethnic, national and religious groups and persons of indigenous origin;

(e) The development of respect for the natural environment".

These highly generalised aspirations are reflected in the terms of the Education Act 1996 which imposes broad duties upon LEAs to "contribute towards the spiritual, moral, mental and physical development of the community"[22] by securing that "efficient education" and "sufficient schools"[23] are available for their area providing "appropriate education" offering for pupils living in their area "such variety of instruction and training as may be desirable" in view of the pupils' different ages, abilities and aptitudes.[24] The Act requires the Secretary of State, local education authorities and school governors to secure that the school curriculum[25] shall be "balanced and broadly based", and that it shall promote ". . . the spiritual, moral, cultural, mental and physical development of pupils at the school and of society".[26]

It is clear that these extremely broad duties placed upon the Secretary of State and other public authorities bear no relation to the types of duties which would create correlative rights enforceable in law in individual pupils, their parents, or others. Similarly, while the substantive content of the programmes of study and assessment arrangements for each foundation subject within the National Curriculum is specified in considerable detail in documents referred to by Orders in Council issued from time to time by the Secretary of State,[27] and while it is clear that the Secretary of State and other public authorities have an onerous statutory duty[28] to ensure that these curricular requirements as laid down are complied with, judicial enforcement of those duties would be a remote prospect. It is true that, in the case of individual curricular complaints, a procedure exists for referral of the complaint to a statutory curricular complaints body established at LEA level:[29] empirical research funded by the Nuffield Foundation has, however, found that there is a strikingly low incidence of

---

[22] Education Act 1996, s. 13(1).
[23] *Ibid*, ss. 13(1) and 14(1).
[24] *Ibid*, s. 14(1)-(3).
[25] In maintained schools in England and Wales.
[26] Education Act 1996, s. 351(1).
[27] *Ibid*, s. 356(4).
[28] *Ibid*, s. 351(2).
[29] Under Education Act 1996, s. 409.

recourse to such bodies.[30] Furthermore, the nature of any remedies available to such LEA complaints bodies is unclear, and it appears that enforcement would entail further complaint to and direction by the Secretary of State.[31]

This is not a regime of statutory duties that could be said, therefore, to give rise to enforceable rights in the individual; indeed, in respect of the obligations imposed on public authorities by virtue of the National Curriculum, it would perhaps be surprising if it were otherwise, given the depth and breadth of the policy, financial and educational considerations which inevitably inform both the formulation and the delivery of the school curriculum. The absence of legal underpinning of individual claims or interests in children—or, indeed, in their parents—in respect of the curriculum, however, arguably fails to recognise that the curriculum is potentially an area fraught with conflict where issues of individual rights may arise in an acute way. Not only is there wide scope for fundamental disagreement as to the very aims and objectives of education but, in more specific and concrete terms, there may be significant scope for challenge in relation to such controversial areas of the school curriculum as sex education, aspects of education raising issues of high political controversy, and religious education and collective worship. Clearly each of these raises wide issues of concern which cannot be explored within the confines of a single chapter: here we shall focus specifically on sex education as illustrative of some of the interests, claims and rights that may arise in this context.

Sex education

Few curricular areas could be of deeper concern than sex education,[32] raising as it does acute issues of personal, moral, cultural and religious conviction. Sex education in maintained schools falls strictly outside the National Curriculum, but forms a key component of what is termed the "basic curriculum" of all maintained schools under the Education Act 1996.[33] Each school governing body is required to formulate and keep up to date a policy on sex education:[34] governing bodies thereby enjoy a wide discretion as to the content and delivery of sex education in their particular school. In the case of primary schools, it is possible for the governors to formulate a policy that there shall be *no* sex education in their school. In the case of secondary schools, however, sex education must be provided for all registered pupils, subject to a parental right of withdrawal.[35]

---

[30] See N Harris, *Complaints About Schooling: The Role of Section 23 of the Education Reform Act 1988*, Nuffield Foundation (1992). See also N Harris, *Law and Education: Regulation, Consumerism and the Education System*, *op cit* n 4, pp 245–51.

[31] Under Education Act 1996, s. 496 or 497.

[32] See N Harris (ed), *Children, Sex Education and the Law*, National Children's Bureau (1996).

[33] Education Act 1996, s. 352.

[34] *Ibid*, s. 404(1)(a).

[35] *Ibid*, s. 405.

Key areas of conflict that may arise in the light of this statutory and administrative framework include, first, challenge by individuals (parents or pupils) to the content or mode of delivery of sex education as provided in a particular school, in respect of which the parental right to withdraw their child may be viewed as only a very partial resolution; and secondly, challenge by children to the exercise by their parents of the parental right of withdrawal, the children asserting that they are being denied a crucial aspect of their education by virtue of that withdrawal.

As argued above, school governors enjoy considerable discretion in formulating their statements of policy on sex education, but this is subject to certain limited statutory constraints: first, it is required under the Education Act 1996 that sex education shall include education about AIDS, HIV and other sexually transmitted diseases;[36] secondly, the Act also requires that the LEA, governing body and the headteacher:

". . . take such steps as are reasonably practicable to secure that where sex education is given . . ., it is given in such a manner as to *encourage those pupils to have due regard to moral considerations and the value of family life*".[37]

These strong exhortations upholding the value of family life have very recently been amplifed by the Labour Government in the form of section 148 of the Learning and Skills Act 2000. This requires LEAs, school governors and headteachers to have regard to guidance issued by the Secretary of State on sex education, and imposes a statutory obligation on the Secretary of State to issue such guidance. Furthermore, it provides expressly that that guidance shall be designed to secure that, when sex education is given to registered pupils at maintained schools,

"(a)   they learn the nature of marriage and its importance for family life and the bringing up of children, and

(b)   they are protected from teaching and materials which are inappropriate having regard to the age and the religious and cultural background of the pupils concerned".[38]

Furthermore, school governors and headteachers may feel constrained (although they themselves are not strictly within the ambit of the provision) by the prohibition imposed *upon local authorities* by the Local Government Act 1988 from promoting the teaching in any maintained school of ". . . the acceptability of homosexuality as a pretended family relationship".[39] In 1994, the then Secretary of State amplified the statutory provisions by issuing an important departmental circular[40] in which it was emphasised that:

[36] *Ibid*, s. 352(3).
[37] *Ibid*, s. 403(1). Emphasis added. This provision was first introduced as s. 46, Education (No. 2) Act 1986.
[38] S. 148(4).
[39] Local Government Act 1988, s. 28.
[40] Department for Education Circular 5/94, *Education Act 1993: Sex Education in Schools*.

"The Secretary of State believes that schools' programmes of sex education should . . . aim to present facts in an *objective, balanced and sensitive* manner, *set within a clear framework of values* and an awareness of the law on sexual behaviour. Pupils should accordingly be encouraged to *appreciate the value of stable family life, marriage and the responsibilities of parenthood* . . . Teachers need to acknowledge that *many children come from backgrounds that do not reflect such values or experiences*. Sensitivity is therefore needed to avoid causing hurt and offence to them and their families; and to allow such children to feel a sense of worth. But teachers should also help pupils, whatever their circumstances, to raise their sights".[41]

Although of no binding effect, the terms of this Circular had a significant influence on governors in formulating their policies on sex education. The Circular issued in 1994 remained in force until it was withdrawn and replaced in July 2000 by the statutorily ordained Guidance referred to in section 148 of the Learning and Skills Act 2000:[42] this Guidance provides that:

"As part of sex and relationship education, pupils should be taught about the nature and importance of marriage for family life and bringing up children. But the Government recognises . . . that there are strong and mutually supportive relationships outside marriage. Therefore pupils should learn the significance of marriage and stable relationships as key building blocks of community and society. Care needs to be taken to ensure that there is no stigmatisation of children based on their home circumstances".[43]

It seems clear from the tenor of the 1994 Circular and of the 2000 Guidance that has now replaced it that both the Major Conservative Government and the Blair Labour Government are strongly of the view that sex education ought to have a strong moral base, emphasising the value of stable family life, marriage and the responsibilities of parenthood. Many would regard this as entirely appropriate and well-balanced. However, a key issue of concern from the viewpoint of children's rights is that it is clearly arguable that the underlying tenor of the Circular and the Guidance is reflective of the views of a highly moralistic sector of society, that it inadequately reflects the reality of individual and family life for very large numbers of children and their parents, in a diverse multicultural society, and that it is thus excessively narrowly focused and insufficiently pluralistic in its approach.[44] Many individuals may argue that the Government's notion of "stable family life" is dangerously and unacceptably narrow, that it has a tendency to reflect and to further the interests of sectors of society that are already disproportionately advantaged, that it signally fails to accord parity of esteem to less advantaged groups and individuals, and that it tends towards the perpetuation of social divisions in society. Above all, it fails to acknowledge the legitimacy of alternative lifestyles, and it tends to stigmatise

---

[41] Department for Education Circular 5/94, *Education Act 1993: Sex Education in Schools,* para 8. Emphasis added.

[42] *Sex and Relationship Education Guidance*, DfEE 0116/2000

[43] *Ibid*, Introduction, para 4.

[44] See P Meredith, "Incorporation of the European Convention on Human Rights into UK Law: Implications for Education" [1998] 2 *European Journal for Education Law and Policy* 7 at 19.

the many children who come from family backgrounds which do not conveniently fit within the Government's perceived ideal model—a tendency which may have profound and lasting detrimental effects upon the educational and social development of the children concerned.

It could clearly be contended, on the other hand, that the 1994 Circular, while emphasising the importance of "appreciating" the value of "stable family life, marriage and the responsibilities of parenthood", also expressly recognised that many children came from backgrounds that did not reflect such values or experiences, that sensitivity was needed to avoid causing hurt or offence, and that such children should be encouraged to feel a "sense of worth". It may be true that the Circular was indeed drafted to take account of the wide diversity of children's backgrounds, but parents and children outside the ideal model might nonetheless feel a sense of alienation and argue that the terms of the circular were deeply patronising, particularly in its exhortation to teachers to help such pupils to "raise their sights". The 2000 Guidance is arguably softer in its tone, emphasising in particular the importance of avoiding stigmatisation of children based on their home circumstances, but nonetheless similarly goes out of its way to uphold traditional family values in the strongest terms.

What has been argued above relating to the insufficiently inclusive and pluralistic tenor of the guidance offered to governors in the sex education Circular and Guidance presents, of course, merely one example of the substantive nature of the many conflicts that may arise between parents (and children) and school governing bodies over the substance and delivery of sex education. Clearly, other key areas of conflict may include such deeply controversial topics as contraception, abortion, and homosexuality, AIDS, HIV and other sexually transmitted diseases. The 1994 Circular did not spell out in detail how these topics were to be approached. It indicated, however, that, at the primary stage:

> ". . .very great care should be taken to match any sex education provided to the maturity of the pupils involved which may not always correspond to their chronological age. . . At the primary stage, the aim should be to prepare pupils to cope with the physical and emotional challenges of growing up, and to give them an elementary understanding of human reproduction. Pupils' questions should be answered sensitively: due consideration should be given to any particular religious or cultural factors bearing on the discussion of sexual issues, and to parents' wishes as to the degree of explicitness of the concepts and presentation to be used".[45]

In respect of secondary schools, the 1994 Circular indicated that sex education should, in addition to factual information concerning human reproduction processes and behaviour, include consideration of the broader emotional and ethical dimensions of sexual attitudes, and that it was *required* to include, at a point appropriate to the age and maturity of the pupils, education concerning AIDS, HIV and other sexually transmitted diseases.[46] It emphasised in particular

[45] DFE Circular 5/94, para 10.
[46] This is required under Education Act 1996, s. 352(3).

that in dealing with these and other sensitive matters, including contraception and abortion, schools should:

> ". . . aim to offer balanced and factual information and to acknowledge the major moral and ethical issues involved. Where schools are founded on specific religious principles, this may have a direct bearing on the manner in which such subjects are presented".[47]

It seems clear from the tenor of the Circular that the Government endorsed the inclusion of *some* major issues of controversy within the sex education curriculum, presented in their moral and ethical context, and with sensitivity for the age and the ethnic, cultural and religious background of the pupils concerned. While explicit mention was given in the Circular of contraception and abortion, however, it is noteworthy that there was no express mention of homosexuality, although this topic might be likely to arise in the context of discussion of AIDS, HIV and other sexually transmitted diseases. In this respect the 1994 Circular differed significantly from its predecessor, issued in 1987, which had stated that:

> "There is no place in any school in any circumstances for teaching which advocates homosexual behaviour, which presents it as the 'norm', or which encourages homosexual experimentation by pupils. Indeed, encouraging or procuring homosexual acts by pupils who are under the age of consent is a criminal offence. It must also be recognised that for many people, including members of various religious faiths, homosexual practice is not morally acceptable, and deep offence may be caused to them if the subject is not handled with sensitivity by teachers if discussed in the classroom".[48]

This strenuous prohibition in the 1987 Circular may well have been a direct reaction to some highly adverse and perhaps inaccurate press coverage of some curricular initiatives which had been launched within a small number of LEAs, notably the Inner London Education Authority, at the time, as well as to a strong moralistic tendency within the Government to promote "traditional" values. The omission of this paragraph from the 1994 Circular *may* reflect a more accepting approach, but it remains noteworthy that the 1994 Circular did not expressly endorse the inclusion of the topic of homosexuality within the sex education syllabus, in contrast with contraception and abortion, and with the mandatory inclusion, at secondary school level, of AIDS, HIV and other sexually transmitted diseases. The 2000 Guidance similarly focuses on such issues as contraception and abortion and strongly endorses teaching about safer sex and sexually transmitted diseases. Unlike its predecessor, it does mention sexual orientation, emphasising the importance of tackling homophobic bullying (para. 1.32). It also emphasises that teachers should be able to deal honestly and sensitively with the issue of sexual orientation, although it stresses that "There should be no direct promotion of sexual orientation".[49]

---

[47] DFE Circular 5/94, para 11.
[48] Department of Education and Science Circular 11/87, *Sex Education at School*, para 22.
[49] Para 1.30.

The exclusion of specific mention of homosexuality in the 1994 Circular, and its extremely brief treatment in the 2000 Guidance along with the firm injunction against the "direct promotion of sexual orientation" may compound a reluctance by many governing bodies in devising their policies on sex education, and by teachers in presenting sex education classes, to raise the topic openly and freely, generated by the "chilling effect" of section 28 of the Local Government Act 1988.[50] Section 28 is addressed expressly to local authorities and, insofar as it relates specifically to maintained schools, prohibits local authorities from promoting the teaching of "the acceptability of homosexuality as a pretended family relationship".[51]

Insofar as it relates to schools, section 28 is almost certainly unenforceable in legal terms, given that it is addressed to LEAs which in law have no direct role in the formulation of sex education policies. Furthermore, the phraseology of the section is so obscure that it is arguably impossible to discern in it any rational meaning. It leaves singularly unclear what type of curricular initiative might offend against the provision; what level of active advocacy or positive portrayal of homosexuality might constitute "promotion"; what might be meant by the word "acceptability"; and, at a time when there are very many diverse forms of "family" within our pluralist multi-cultural society, it leaves quite unclear what might be meant by a "pretended family relationship".[52] Nonetheless, it may well have a significant practical impact in the light of its potential for inhibiting practising teachers from open and free discussion of the topic in the classroom for fear of adverse criticism from parents, headteachers and school governors, and, possibly, of disciplinary action. Even though those fears *may* be unfounded, their very existence may have a significant inhibitory or "chilling" effect on the substance or manner of presentation of issues relating to homosexuality in sex education classes, and very significantly, may also inhibit teachers when counselling pupils in relation to personal problems and sexuality.

We have focused above on some key areas of potential conflict over the sex education curriculum—first, conflict over whether the Government's advice to school governors in formulating their policies is sufficiently inclusive and pluralistic in its approach, or whether on the contrary, it seeks to promote a narrow, idealised view of "stable married family life" which may serve to alienate many children and fail to give them a genuine sense of worth; and secondly, we have focused on some more specific topics which either may or must be included within the sex education curriculum—contraception, abortion, homosexuality, and AIDS, HIV and other sexually transmitted diseases—indicating that there is extensive scope for conflict as to both the formulation and delivery of the curriculum in relation to each of these issues. School governors, indeed, face a delicate and unenviable task in formulating their sex education policies, and the

---

[50] S. 28 has now been repealed in Scotland by s. 34 of the Ethical Standards in Public Life, Etc. (Scotland) Act 2000.

[51] Local Government Act 1988, s. 28(1)(b).

[52] See P Meredith, *Government, Schools and the Law, op cit* n 3, pp 74–76.

probability of individual parents or children seeking to challenge the contents or mode of delivery of the sex education curriculum is not inconsiderable.

It would, however, be extremely difficult for any such parents or children to launch any form of legal challenge to a governing body's policy, or the delivery of sex education classes in a school, beyond the submission of a complaint under section 409 of the 1996 Act, which, as seen above, presents an avenue of redress offering no tangible remedy and without any significant likelihood of success. Given the breadth of the governing body's discretionary powers over formula-tion of their sex education policy,[53] judicial review of the policy as formulated would similarly be a remote prospect. This in effect is an aspect of discretionary decision-making beyond effective legal challenge, despite the fundamentality of its importance to the individual parent or child. In the case of parents, it could be argued that their claim may be met, at least in part, by the fact of parental representation on the school's governing body.[54] Arguably, their claim could, further, be met through exercise of the parents' absolute right to withdraw the child—in whole in or part—from sex education classes by virtue of section 405 of the Education Act 1996. Neither, however, could be said to provide full sat-isfaction: while the inclusion of parental representatives on the governing body is of crucial importance—and may indirectly offer an outlet for the interests of the children themselves—that representation is limited numerically and also, arguably, in terms of the extent of influence exerted by parents in relation to cur-ricular policy-making when faced with the educational expertise of other mem-bers of the governing body. Furthermore, the capacity of parents to withdraw their child from sex education classes affords, arguably, a highly undesirable remedy of last resort whose exercise could be seriously damaging to the child's interests, given the crucial importance that children should receive balanced, coherent and sensitively delivered education on sex and sexuality. Parents may thus be highly reluctant to exercise their right of withdrawal, despite having considerable misgivings about the content or presentation of sex education in the school concerned. It is also highly improbable that parental misgivings over sex education would be alleviated by the main operative provision in the educa-tional sphere of the European Convention on Human Rights—the second sen-tence of Article 2 of the First Protocol, requiring signatory states in exercising their functions relating to education and teaching to respect the right of parents to ensure such education and teaching in conformity with their own religious and philosophical convictions. This Article was acceded to by the UK Government subject to its compatibility with the provision of efficient instruc-tion and training and the avoidance of unreasonable public expenditure, a reser-vation expressly preserved by the UK Government in the Human Rights Act

[53] See Education Act 1996, s. 404(1)(a).
[54] See School Standards and Framework Act 1998, s. 36 and Schedule 9; The Education (School Government) (England) Regls, SI 2163, 1999.

1998 incorporating the European Convention into domestic law.[55] In a leading case, *Kjeldsen, Busk Madsen and Pedersen* v. *Denmark*,[56] parents of children attending Danish state primary schools sought to challenge the provision of compulsory sex education integrated into the teaching of other subjects within the curriculum on the basis that they objected both to its substantive content and to the fact that their children could not be withdrawn. The parental challenge in this case failed on the facts, but the case is of wide importance as the European Court of Human Rights sought to define the extent of the state's duty under the second sentence of Article 2:

> "The second sentence of Article 2 implies . . . that the State, in fulfilling the functions assumed by it in regard to education and teaching, must take care that information or knowledge included in the curriculum is conveyed in *an objective, critical and pluralistic manner*. The State is forbidden to pursue an aim of indoctrination that might be considered as not respecting parents' religious and philosophical convictions".[57]

This definition in practice leaves public authorities with a very wide discretion in the formulation of policies on sex education. Very significantly, the case also emphasises that the state is under no obligation to provide a parental right of withdrawal from sex education classes. Although, as discussed above, arguments relating to the narrow focus of the British Government's sex education legislation and guidance could be put, it is thought unlikely that any challenge on the ground that it was insufficiently pluralistic would succeed, given particularly that the 1994 Circular and 2000 Guidance do exhort teachers to recognise that children come from a diverse range of backgrounds, and that sensitivity is required to avoid causing offence.[58] It is thought similarly unlikely that parental challenges to the formulation or delivery of the sex education curriculum in respect of such controversial issues as contraception, abortion, homosexuality, AIDS, HIV or other sexually transmitted diseases would succeed, particularly given the inclusion in the Education Act 1996 of an unqualified parental right of withdrawal. The *Kjeldsen* case did not impose rigorous and restrictive conditions upon state authorities in the formulation and delivery of their sex education curricula but, on the contrary, left them very generous discretion which would be hard to challenge unless the state could be seen to be acting in an overtly indoctrinatory manner. In the improbable event of parents succeeding in establishing a breach of the state's obligation to respect their religious or philosophical convictions in this context, the public authorities would also almost certainly argue strenuously—and probably successfully—that the provision of segregated classes with a different emphasis or educational philosophy would

---

[55] Human Rights Act 1998, s. 15. By virtue of s. 17 of the Human Rights Act 1998, this reservation is subject to review every five years. The exact scope of the reservation is subject to some doubt: see *Campbell & Cosans* v. *UK.* (1982) Series A, No. 48.

[56] (1976) Series A, No. 23.

[57] *Ibid*, para 53. Emphasis added.

[58] DFE Circular 5/94, para 8; *Sex and Relationship Education Guidance*, DfEE D116/2000, Introduction, para 4.

fall foul of the UK Government's reservation to the second sentence of the Article as being incompatible with efficient instruction and training and the avoidance of unreasonable public expenditure.

The argument thus far in respect of challenges to the content or presentation of sex education has focused principally on parental challenges, based on the assumption that the parental and the children's interests coincide. This, however, is clearly a fallacious assumption in relation to many aspects of educational provision, and the fallacy is very clearly illustrated by sex education, and in particular by the absolute right of parental withdrawal. While the parental interest may well be satisfied—at least in part—by withdrawal of the child, the exercise of the parental right may serve to damage the child's interest: this is perhaps most graphically illustrated by the fact that such a child may receive no formal education relating to matters of sex and sexuality, yet if aged sixteen years or over may lawfully marry or engage in consensual intercourse. This may be of particular importance given that the topics of AIDS, HIV, other sexually transmitted diseases and all non-biological aspects of human sexual behaviour are expressly excluded from the Science National Curriculum by virtue of the Education Act 1996.[59] Children in such circumstances could thus clearly be placed in a potentially life-threatening situation by virtue of a legal structure which in this, as in so many other areas, accords a significantly higher priority to the realisation of the interests of parents than those of their children. Indeed, it is arguable that the provision by statute of an unqualified right of parents to withdraw their children from any or all sex education in maintained schools is seriously misconceived. Not only is the parental right absolute, but there is no obligation on parents to express any reasons for their decision to withdraw their child, nor to make any alternative satisfactory provision.[60] It is true that the Government's 1994 Circular on sex education did encourage a co-operative and collaborative approach by schools in the event of parents seeking to withdraw children, suggesting that parents be invited voluntarily to indicate their reasons for withdrawal and that schools should be ready to offer appropriate support and information—as by recommending written materials on aspects of sex education, including HIV, AIDS and other sexually transmitted diseases—to such parents.[61] The *Sex and Relationship Education Guidance 2000* exhorts schools to make alternative arrangements for children withdrawn from sex education classes, and offers schools a standard pack of information for parents who withdraw their children.[62] Nonetheless it remains open to the parents to refuse to offer any reasons and to resist all forms of support from the school. Whether parents may lawfully refuse to make any form of alternative provision for their children's education in relation to sex and sexuality, whether at home or

---

[59] S. 356(9).
[60] See DFE Circular 5/94, para 36.
[61] *Ibid*, para 37.
[62] Para 5.7.

otherwise, is an open question: it has been suggested[63] that parents of compulsory school age children who fail to do so could conceivably be in breach of their duty to ensure their children's "efficient full-time education" suitable in the light of their age, ability and aptitude.[64] Though many may sympathise with that view, it is thought unlikely that this would constitute a breach, given the wide diversity of opinion as to what constitutes appropriate sex education and the sensitivity of the issues in the light of individual conscience and convictions.

Children denied sex education by virtue of their parents' decision to withdraw them are afforded no remedy under domestic education legislation; nor do they even have a procedural right to be heard as part of the process of parental exercise of the statutory right of withdrawal. There simply are no mechanisms under education law for giving vent to the child's view, let alone permitting that view to prevail.[65] This important omission from education law exists despite Article 12 of the UN Convention on the Rights of the Child which requires that children should be heard in relation to all matters affecting them, due weight being given to their views in the light of their age and understanding. Furthermore, it is inadequate to defend the existence of this omission from education legislation by simply pointing to section 1(3) of the Children Act 1989, which imposes an obligation on the court in certain family proceedings to have regard to the child's ascertainable wishes and feelings; and to the existence of orders under section 8 of the 1989 Act, which may be made in a range of circumstances including disputes between parents (or those otherwise with responsibility for a child's upbringing) in respect of a child's education. While such proceedings under the Children Act are clearly important, their existence does not adequately compensate for the virtually total absence of procedural mechanisms upholding the interests of children under education legislation.

Not only does domestic education law fail children in this context, but it is very doubtful whether the European Convention on Human Rights would afford any protection either. As discussed above, the second sentence of Article 2 of the First Protocol to the Convention focuses entirely on the *parents'* religious and philosophical convictions. The first sentence, requiring that no person be denied the right to education, might be thought potentially to be of value to children withdrawn against their will from sex education classes. The European Convention, however, nowhere defines the substance or content of the education which may not be denied, and was held in the *Belgian Linguistics Case*[66] to impose no obligation on public authorities to provide education of any particular type or at any particular level. Furthermore, it is noteworthy that the first sentence of Article 2 is formulated in negative rather than positive terms, the

---

[63] See N Harris, "The Regulation and Control of Sex Education" in N Harris (ed), *Children, Sex Education and the Law, op cit* n 32, p 14.

[64] Education Act 1996, s. 7.

[65] But see now the Standards in Scotland's Schools, Etc. Act 2000, s. 2(2) which does impose a qualified obligation on education authorities in Scotland to consult children.

[66] (1968) Series A, No. 6.

negative formulation having been adopted perhaps in part in order to allay the fears of some states that positive phraseology might impose upon them obligations which they would find it impossible to meet.[67] The first sentence is accordingly unlikely to be of any significant value to the individual child, whether challenging the substance or delivery of sex education classes or the exercise by his or her parent of the right of withdrawal.

CONCLUSIONS

This chapter has focused in a highly selective way on the interests or rights of children in respect of the secular curriculum, and in particular on sex education as one of the most keenly controversial facets of the curriculum. There are very many other aspects of education, each raising fundamental questions in relation to children's rights which it has not been possible within a single chapter to examine, including the rights of children in the contexts of religious education, special educational needs, choice of school, school attendance, and the disciplinary process. Each could well form a chapter in its own right. As argued in the introduction, children's rights—whether procedural or substantive—are barely discernible within English education law, at least in the narrower sense of rights which are clearly defined in law and enforceable through some form of statutory process or by recourse to the courts. Insofar as any individual rights do exist, they tend to be vested in the parents rather than in the child, on the simplistic assumption that the interests of the parents and the child coincide. This assumption may be true of many parents and their children, but it is plainly fallacious in some cases, as exemplified most graphically in the context of the parental right to withdraw a child from sex education classes. A further dimension to this is also, of course, that the parents themselves may be at odds as to the child's best educational interests, in which case it may be necessary to have resort to proceedings under the Children Act 1989 under which it is true that the court will seek if appropriate to ascertain the child's wishes—a most important exception to the general proposition that the child's view goes unheard.

In the curricular context, it is tempting to conclude that, while one may say that children do have a right to education, the general body of children of compulsory school age have no more sophisticated right beyond the curricular provision provided within the "basic" school curriculum required by law for every maintained school as defined by section 352 of the Education Act 1996. This comprises provision of religious education and sex education in addition to the National Curriculum. A very important exception to this basic entitlement of the general body of children is the right of children with learning difficulties calling for special educational provision to be assessed by their LEA and, where

---

[67] See D J Harris, M O'Boyle and C Warbrick, *Law of the European Convention on Human Rights* (London, Butterworths, 1995), pp 540–1.

appropriate, to have a statement of their special needs drawn up specifying the special educational provision to be made for the purpose of meeting those needs.[68] In this context a whole complex of rights arises in the children concerned correlative to the duties imposed by the Education Act 1996 on LEAs; and a complex of rights of appeal to the Special Educational Needs Tribunal against a decision by the LEA not to make a statement of special needs or against the contents of such a statement rests in the child's parents.[69]

For the general body of pupils, however, the right is essentially limited to the basic provision envisaged in section 352. This right may be discerned from the terms of section 352 itself, and may also be seen as correlative to the duty of LEAs under the 1996 Act to secure sufficient primary, secondary and further education to meet the needs of the population of their area;[70] and also, in the case of children of compulsory school age, as correlative to their parents' duty to ensure that they receive efficient full-time education suitable to their age, ability and aptitude, whether by school attendance or otherwise.[71] The reality is that the curricular rights of children (other than those with special educational needs) go little further than this somewhat elementary proposition, with legal enforcement of these elementary rights a remote prospect.[72] It may be that, in large part, this is inevitable given the enormous scale of the provision of education in maintained schools and the economic and educational impracticality of fine-tuning that provision to individual preferences. The response of the state is to deny any right in children more sophisticated than that of basic provision, but to establish, principally through the School Inspections Act 1996 and the School Standards and Framework Act 1998 a huge edifice of quality assurance mechanisms from OFSTED inspections to the closure of failing schools and the issuing of directions to LEAs and hiving off some or all of their school functions to the private sector.[73]

Broadly this may be inevitable and appropriate, given the scale and the complexity of mass educational provision. But one must not lose sight of the fact that key issues in education do arise where it would be both practical and appropriate to recognise that children—particularly, but not necessarily exclusively, older adolescents—may have significant preferences in respect of matters which may profoundly affect their future: choice of school, the decision to withhold a child from school, provision of special educational needs, the decision to withhold a child from some or all sex education classes or from religious education or worship, and disciplinary processes, are some important examples. In particular,

---

[68] See Education Act 1996, ss. 312–24.

[69] *Ibid*, ss. 325–6. It is noteworthy that the right of appeal vests in the parent and not in the child.

[70] *Ibid*, s. 13.

[71] *Ibid*, s. 7.

[72] See R v. *Inner London Education Authority, ex parte Ali and Murshid, The Times,* 21 February 1990; P Meredith, *Government, Schools and the Law, op. cit.* n 3, pp 106–111; N Harris, "Education by Right: Breach of the Duty to Provide 'Sufficient Schools'" [1990] *MLR* 525.

[73] See P Meredith, "The Fall and Rise of Local Education Authorities" (1998) XX(1) *Liverpool Law Review* 41.

where a specific right in respect of the education of a child is vested in parents—as, for instance, the right to express a preference as to choice of school, or to educate a child other than at school, or withdraw a child from religious or sex education—there needs to be a very strong justification for failing to provide an express procedural mechanism in education law permitting the child in question to express his or her opinion on the matter, the weight attaching to that opinion being dependent upon the age, understanding and appreciation of the child. This would accord with the requirement of Article 12 of the UN Convention on the Rights of the Child that children should be heard in respect of all matters affecting them, "their views being given due weight in accordance with their age and understanding", as well as recognising that crucial educational decisions may fundamentally affect a child's future well-being and capacity for personal autonomy and that, by analogy with the *Gillick* case,[74] it is right that, at least in the case of more mature children, their voice should be heard.

---

[74] See n 4 *supra*.

13

Children and Social Security Law

NICK WIKELEY*

INTRODUCTION

THIS CHAPTER EXAMINES the position of children within the social security system and its analysis is characterised by two main themes. The first is the enduring nature of the principles underlying welfare provision for children and young persons, with much of the rhetoric of the Poor Law having resonance in contemporary discourse about the appropriate status of school-leavers in the modern benefits system. The second is the manner in which this ideological underpinning masks both paradoxes and conflicts in the law's treatment of children and young people as nascent full members of the community.

In broad terms modern social security law makes a distinction between children (those aged under sixteen) and young persons (those aged sixteen or seventeen). So far as the former group is concerned, the law typically perceives children under the age of sixteen as mere members of a family group, defined in relation to their parents or guardians. As such they are effectively incapacitated in social security legislation, not least because it is assumed that "they do not have the maturity required to order their own lives and participate in political life".[1] The consequence of this approach is that parents are accorded social security rights that they may exercise on behalf of their children, rather than children being granted an independent right to benefit. The sole exception to this broad approach is in relation to disability living allowance, the only benefit which is clearly available to a child under sixteen in her or his own right. Yet, as we shall see later in this chapter, this exception is in many ways more apparent than real, as children are required to act through an adult appointee.

The position of sixteen and seventeen-year-olds is in many ways still more problematic. For the purposes of child benefit, these young people remain categorised as children so long as they are in full-time education (up to but not beyond 'A' Level or equivalent). It follows that they are regarded as dependants of their parents under the various means-tested benefit schemes. In 1988 the normal minimum age for entitlement to income support was raised to eighteen.

---

* I am indebted to Philip Larkin both for discussing ideas on this chapter and for his research assistance.
[1] J Montgomery, "Children as Property?" (1998) 51 MLR 323 at 323.

Those sixteen and seventeen-year-olds who are still able to claim either income support or income-based jobseeker's allowance[2] are now very much the exception rather than the rule. It is in this area that the paradoxes and conflicts within prevailing ideologies come to the fore. Most notably, government policy, avowedly designed to promote independence, self-reliance and support for the family, has led to a significant reduction in the autonomy afforded to young people within the benefits system. As Harris has observed, "social security does not embrace a coherent policy in relation to the transition out of childhood and into adulthood".[3]

Social security benefits are conventionally categorised according to a three-fold typology of contributory benefits, non-contributory benefits and means-tested benefits. The most instructive way of arriving at a fuller understanding of the status of children and young persons respectively in social security law is to consider their place within each of these three main branches of the benefits system.

CHILDREN UNDER THE AGE OF SIXTEEN

Contributory benefits

A precondition of entitlement to contributory benefits, often described as national insurance benefits, is that the claimant has a satisfactory contributions record. However, contributions are not payable by those under the school leaving age of sixteen.[4] It necessarily follows that children are accorded no independent role within the national insurance scheme. Instead, the traditional status of children within the contributory benefits system is one of dependency upon their parents or guardians.

National insurance benefits (namely contribution-based jobseeker's allowance, incapacity benefit, maternity allowance, bereavement benefits[5] and retirement pensions) developed on the basis of paying a standard individual weekly rate of benefit for the contributor to which could be added dependency additions for adult or child dependants. The availability of such additions was radically

---

[2] For present purposes, the distinction between the two benefits depends on whether or not the claimant falls within one of the categories of people who are relieved of the obligation to "sign on". See further the discussion below at pp 238–240.

[3] N S Harris, *Social Security for Young People* (Aldershot, Avebury, 1989), p 4.

[4] Social Security Administration Act 1992, ss. 6(1)(a), 11(1) and 13(1) and Social Security (Contributions) Regulations 2001 (SI 2001 No. 1004), reg 93. The original national insurance scheme of 1911 did not cater for those under 16, even though the school leaving age at that time was 14. The Unemployment Act 1934 lowered the age of entry to the scheme to 14 but benefits were not payable until 16: Harris, *supra* n 3, pp 46 and 52.

[5] Formerly known as widow's benefits, the eligibility criteria have been made gender neutral by the Welfare Reform and Pensions Act 1999. Thus widow's payments, widow's pensions and widowed mother's allowance have become bereavement payments, bereavement allowances and widowed parent's allowance respectively.

reduced during the period of the Conservative governments between 1979 and 1997. Increases for child dependants can now only be paid with the higher rate of short-term incapacity benefit and with long-term incapacity benefit,[6] widowed parent's allowance and retirement pensions.[7] The qualifying criteria[8] are essentially that the claimant must also be entitled to child benefit for the child in question and that the child must live with the claimant.[9] In addition, the allowance is not payable if the earnings of the claimant's partner exceed a specified figure.[10] The increases themselves are paid at a standard weekly rate per child, irrespective of age.[11]

These child dependency additions are now of very limited significance within the overall national insurance budget, although they may of course be of considerable importance to individual claimants. The extent to which child dependency additions are in payment very much reflects the demographic composition of the client groups for the particular benefits involved. For example, there are nearly eleven million recipients of the state retirement pension, of whom just 10,400 receive increases for child dependants. Similarly, incapacity benefit is predominantly a benefit claimed by the over-fifties, and so only seven per cent of all incapacity benefit claimants receive additions for child dependants.[12] Not surprisingly, however, given the nature of the benefit, the clear majority of recipients of widowed parent's allowance receive child dependency additions.[13] Twenty years ago increases for children were a much more important feature of the national insurance scheme, as at that time they were paid as an addition to unemployment benefit. In 1984 123,000 unemployed claimants were receiving additions in respect of children[14] but the child dependency addition was abolished for unemployment benefit in the same year, with the curious exception of claimants who were over pensionable age. When jobseeker's allowance replaced unemployment benefit and income support for unemployed people in October 1996, even this concession disappeared.

---

[6] Child dependency additions can also be paid with the lower rate of short-term incapacity benefit but only if the claimant is over pensionable age.

[7] But not with Category D retirement pensions (but there are only 24,800 such pensions in payment in any event, as these are payable to people aged over 80 who do not qualify for a standard Category A or B state pension): DSS, *Social Security Statistics 1999* (Leeds, Corporate Document Services, 1999), Table B1.09, p 135.

[8] Social Security Contributions and Benefits Act (SSCBA) 1992, s. 80(4).

[9] Or the claimant is contributing to the cost of keeping the child at a weekly rate of not less than the amount of the increase, over and above any amount received by way of child benefit.

[10] For 2001–02, this limit is £150 per week for the first child and £20 per week per child thereafter.

[11] For 2001–02, the weekly rate is £11.35, which is reduced where the higher rate of child benefit for the only or eldest child is in payment.

[12] The highest rate is 18% of claimants, in the 35–39 age band: DSS (1999), *supra* n 7, Table D1.11, p 183. On pensioners, see *ibid*, Table B1.05, p 130.

[13] Some 44,800 women receive widowed mother's allowance with payments for child dependants, as against 3,300 who receive just WMA: *ibid*, Table G3.02, p 287. Statistics for the new gender-neutral widowed parent's allowance were not available at the time of writing but are unlikely to be appreciably different.

[14] DHSS, *Social Security Statistics 1987* (London, HMSO, 1987), Table 1.40, p 16.

The only benefit within the national insurance scheme which is, in its own right, specifically directed towards supporting the costs of raising children is the now obsolete child's special allowance.[15] Child's special allowance was introduced in 1957 to provide a degree of assistance to a woman who failed to qualify for widowed mother's allowance because she was divorced from her husband before he died. As such, the benefit was very much in the Beveridge tradition, premised on male breadwinners and nuclear families. Child's special allowance was abolished for new claimants by the Social Security Act 1986 on the ground that assistance for such lone parents was better targeted through one parent benefit[16] and the means-tested benefits. By 1998 there were just twelve families receiving the allowance.[17] Within a year or two the benefit will disappear altogether as these children reach maturity.

Non-contributory benefits

The various non-contributory benefits, most of which are also non-means-tested, have been developed in part to fill the gaps left by the inadequate coverage of the contributory benefits. These benefits fall into two main groups: those related to disability needs in one way or another (e.g. disability living allowance and invalid care allowance) and those which are specifically child-related benefits (child benefit and guardian's allowance). Child benefit is thus also a non-contributory benefit,[18] but is very much designed to provide assistance to parents with the costs of raising children, and is not a benefit *for* children as such. It should also be noted that working children under the age of sixteen have no access to the industrial injuries scheme in the event that they suffer an accident or contract a disease in the workplace: their only redress would be through the lottery of the law of tort.

Disability benefits

Disability living allowance

Disability living allowance (DLA) is unique in that it is the one benefit available to children under the age of sixteen in their own right. However, children can only act through an adult appointee, typically their parent, whose function it is to "receive and deal on [their] behalf with any sums payable by way of that

---

[15] SSCBA 1992, s. 56.

[16] Now also abolished; see further p 231 below.

[17] DSS (1999), *supra* n 7, Table G4.03, p 296.

[18] It does not appear in Part III of the SSCBA 1992, which is devoted to non-contributory benefits, because of its different statutory lineage; instead it appears separately in Part IX of the 1992 Act.

allowance".[19] DLA itself consists of two components, for mobility and care respectively.[20] The mobility component is paid at one of two rates and the care component at three rates, leading to a total of eleven different levels of weekly benefit, depending on the combination of components and rates involved. The two components have different age rules which can be traced back to their respective predecessor benefits, mobility allowance and attendance allowance.

The mobility component is paid at the higher rate to claimants who are unable or virtually unable to walk,[21] and at the lower rate to those who can walk but need guidance or assistance most of the time when walking out of doors on unfamiliar routes.[22] The higher rate mobility component is now available to children from the age of three, with an upper age limit for claiming of sixty-five. Until April 2001 the threshold for entitlement was the child's fifth birthday. The justification for the imposition of a such a minimum age limit had been that children under the age of five are not independently mobile and need constant supervision in any event,[23] but both the age restriction and the underlying reasoning have been subject to criticism over the years. A study conducted by Disability Alliance in 1994 of eighty-four families with a disabled child aged under five found that over half of the children could not walk at all, most of whom were over the age of two, i.e. at an age when even late developers would be walking.[24] Two-thirds of the children were unable to use public transport and 75 per cent of the families surveyed had frequent hospital visits. In November 1998 the Disability Living Allowance Advisory Board published a discussion paper on childhood mobility and DLA.[25] The Board concluded that by the age of two-and-a-half "the very great majority of normal children will be walking independently".[26] It was estimated that about 4,000 children

---

[19] Social Security (Claims and Payments) Regulations 1987 (SI 1987, No. 1968), reg. 43. A similar rule applied for mobility allowance, but actual entitlement to the former attendance allowance for children was vested in the mother, not the child (with a list of other adults in descending order of priority if she did not live with the child): Social Security (Attendance Allowance) (No. 2) Regulations 1975 (SI 1975 No. 598), reg. 6(4)), now repealed.

[20] DLA was created in 1992 by amalgamating the old mobility and attendance allowances; mobility allowance was abolished but attendance allowance remains as a benefit for those with care needs who claim for the first time after the age of 65.

[21] SSCBA 1992, s. 73(1)(a) and (11)(a). There are a very limited number of other qualifying routes for the higher rate of the DLA mobility component; see further N Wikeley, "Severe mental impairment and the higher rate mobility component of DLA" (1999) 6 *JSSL* 10.

[22] SSCBA 1992, ss. 73(1)(e) and (11)(b).

[23] A Ogus, E Barendt and N Wikeley, *The Law of Social Security* (London, Butterworths, 4th ed, 1995), p 195.

[24] M Howard, *Too Young to Count* (London, Disability Alliance, 1994).

[25] Disability Living Allowance Advisory Board, *Childhood Mobility and Disability Living Allowance* (London, DLAAB, 1998).

[26] *Ibid*, para 2.4. The evidential basis for the DLAAB's conclusion is somewhat unclear. The Board reports that in one major study "At 18 months, all but 4.3% of children were walking independently" (para 2.3), while also observing that "only about 15 children per 10,000 in the general populations [sic] (i.e. 0.15%) have failed to reach this milestone by [30 months]" (para 2.2). The Board does not explain why 99.85% (at 30 months) is "the very great majority" whereas 95.7% (at 18 months) is not.

would fail to walk between the age of thirty months and five years.[27] The majority of children who fail to make the transition to independent walking or unsupervised mobility fall into three categories of severe disability: severe learning disabilities, severe autism and severe cerebral palsy.[28] The publication of this report followed, but presumably had informed, the Government's decision to announce in the Green Paper, published the month before, that the higher rate mobility component of DLA would be extended to three and four-year-olds.[29] This proposal was subsequently embodied in the Welfare Reform and Pensions Act 1999 and finally took effect in April 2001.[30] Although welcome, this reform was one of relatively few measures in the 1999 Act that extended, rather than qualified or reduced, benefit entitlement. It is also of limited significance in terms of the overall cost of DLA.[31]

In principle the lower rate mobility component is available to children of any age. In practice it is extremely difficult for a disabled child to qualify as it must be shown that he or she "requires substantially more guidance or supervision" in walking outdoors than children of the same age in "normal physical and mental health".[32]

The eligibility conditions for the care component of DLA are highly complex and have been the subject of a series of test cases in the House of Lords.[33] A claimant must be severely mentally or physically disabled and have either personal care or supervision needs.[34] The degree of such needs determines whether the claimant receives the highest, middle or lowest rate care component. The highest rate is paid where a person has care or supervision needs by day *and* by night and the middle rate where those needs exist only by day *or* by night. The lowest rate is awarded where a person has more limited care or attendance needs: either that they require help with personal care functions "for a significant portion of the day" or because they are unable to prepare and cook a main meal for one person (the so-called "main meal test"). About nine out of ten awards of the lowest rate care component are paid on the basis of the main meal

---

[27] *Ibid*, para 4.2. A subsequent Parliamentary Answer indicated that about 8,000 children were expected to benefit in the first year: *Hansard*, HC Debs, Vol 319, col 500w (17 November 1998).

[28] DLAAB, *supra* n 25, para 4.1.

[29] DSS, *A new contract for welfare: Support for Disabled People*, Cm 4103, (London, The Stationery Office, 1998), pp 2 and 10

[30] Welfare Reform and Pensions Act 1999, s. 56(3), inserting SSCBA 1992, s. 73(1A).

[31] The total cost of DLA is more than £5 billion; the cost of extending the higher rate mobility component to 3 and 4-year-olds is estimated to be about £15 million. It is significant in this context that the House of Commons Select Committee on Social Security omitted to make any mention, let alone any recommendation, in this respect in its detailed *Fourth Report*, Disability Living Allowance, Session 1997–8, HC 641.

[32] SSCBA 1992, s. 73(4).

[33] See generally Ogus, Barendt and Wikeley, *supra* n 23, pp 187–208 and N Wikeley, "Social Security and Disability" in N Harris (ed), *Social Security Law in Context* (Oxford, OUP, 2000), ch 12.

[34] SSCBA 1992, s. 72(1). The test cases have centred on the meaning of "attention in connection with bodily functions", the statutory formulation for personal care needs. See further N Wikeley, "Benefits, Bodily Functions and Living with Disability" (1998) 61 *MLR* 551–60.

test.[35] However, children are excluded from qualifying on the latter basis as that test,[36] albeit hypothetical in the sense that it is not directly assessed, is clearly inappropriate for children. There is nonetheless some evidence that the introduction of the lower rates of DLA has brought into entitlement some younger children with disabilities who would not previously have qualified for attendance or mobility allowance.[37] In particular, the lowest rate care component is associated with children with asthma, eczema and diabetes.[38] There is, however, little to distinguish recipients of the lowest rate care component from unsuccessful claimants; indeed, the latter were found to be *more* severely disabled.[39]

Children under the age of sixteen are also subject to an extra qualifying condition that does not apply to adults claiming the DLA care component. As well as having attendance or supervision needs, it must be shown that the child's requirements are "substantially in excess of the normal requirements of persons of his age".[40] The rationale for this extra condition is that all children require a degree of care and supervision, varying according to their age, and so DLA should only be payable where those needs are out of the ordinary.

These requirements might suggest that children would face more difficulty in establishing entitlement to the care component of DLA. In fact, whereas children tend to fare less successfully than adults on claims for the mobility component, the position is reversed for the care component. Proportionately twice as many children as adults receive the highest rate care award,[41] whereas adults are three times as likely to receive the lowest rate care component.[42] Whether DLA actually meets the real costs associated with caring for a disabled child is another matter altogether.[43]

---

[35] K Swales, *A Study of Disability Living Allowance and Attendance Allowance Awards*, In-house report 41 (London, DSS, 1998) , p 48.

[36] SSCBA 1992, s. 72(6)(a).

[37] R Sainsbury, M Hirst and D Lawton, *Evaluation of Disability Living Allowance and Attendance Allowance*, DSS Research Report No. 41 (London, HMSO, 1995), p 95.

[38] *Ibid*, p 98. This also reflects the general finding that conditions causing disability in children are intrinsically different from those which affect adults, as problems such as arthritis, rheumatism and heart conditions tend to develop later in life: *ibid*, p 97. See further M Bone and H Meltzer, *The prevalence of disability among children*, OPCS Surveys of Disability in Great Britain, Report 3 (London, HMSO, 1989).

[39] Sainsbury, Hirst and Lawton, *supra* n 37, p 101. As the authors comment, "perhaps the absence of the 'meals test' makes adjudication on this boundary particularly difficult"; *ibid*, p 105.

[40] SSCBA 1992, s. 72(6)(b)(i). The alternative formulation is that the child has requirements "which younger persons in normal physical and mental health may also have but which persons of his age and in normal physical and mental health would not have"; *ibid*, s. 72(6)(b)(ii). An analogous additional requirement applies to the lower rate mobility component: *ibid*, s. 73(4).

[41] 41% of children as against 20% of adults: Swales, *supra* n 35, p 57.

[42] This is largely because children are not eligible to claim on the basis of the "main meals test".

[43] See for example, B Dobson and S Middleton, *Paying to Care: The cost of childhood disability* (York, Joseph Rowntree Foundation, 1998), suggesting that it costs at least three times as much to bring up a severely disabled child as a child who is not disabled. See also J Cavet, *People Don't Understand: Children, young people and their families living with a hidden disability* (London, National Children's Bureau, 1998).

Invalid care allowance

Invalid care allowance is the carer's benefit, payable to those who provide regular and substantial care for a person who receives either attendance allowance or the highest or middle rate of the DLA care component.[44] It is intended as an earnings replacement benefit and so is not payable to those under the age of sixteen or who are receiving full-time education,[45] and entitlement ceases on attaining pensionable age.[46] It is therefore not payable to school age children who may carry the burden of caring for a disabled parent or other relative.

Child-related benefits

Child benefit

Child benefit was introduced in 1975 as an amalgamation of the former family allowance[47] and child tax allowance.[48] It is a universal non-means tested benefit representing a (limited) contribution by the community to the expenses of child rearing within the confines of the family. The principal statutory requirement for receipt of the benefit is relatively straightforward: the claimant must be responsible for one or more children, defined as a person either under sixteen, or under eighteen and not in full-time education but who satisfies prescribed conditions, or under nineteen and still in full-time education.[49] There is no minimum qualifying age for child benefit, and so a fifteen-year-old mother could qualify for child benefit.

The very simplicity and universality of child benefit mean that it enjoys a very high take-up rate of 98 per cent, far in excess of any means-tested benefit,[50] reflecting its popularity among the public. It is, nonetheless, clearly designed as a benefit for *adults*, who are left to apply it, in their discretion, to the best interests of their children.[51] There is clearly an argument that child benefit should be

---

[44] SSCBA 1992, s. 70 and Social Security (Invalid Care Allowance) Regulations 1976 (SI 1976 No. 409).

[45] SSCBA 1992, s. 70(3).

[46] *Ibid*, s. 70(5).

[47] On the history of which, see J Macnicol, *The Movement for Family Allowances 1918–45: A Study in Social Development* (London, Heinemann, 1980).

[48] On the background to this reform, see M A McCarthy, "Trade Unions, the Family Lobby and the Callaghan Government" 11 *Policy and Politics* 461 and generally M McCarthy, *Campaigning for the Poor* (London, Croom Helm, 1986).

[49] SSCBA 1992, ss. 141 and 142; on the position of 16 and 17-year-olds, see further below.

[50] Commission on Social Justice, *Social Justice: Strategies for National Renewal* (London, Vintage Press, 1994), p 314.

[51] See further R Walker, S Middleton and M Thomas, "How mothers use child benefit" in S Middleton, K Ashworth and R Walker, *Family Fortunes* (London, CPAG, 1994), ch 10 and the comprehensive review of the research evidence by J Bradshaw and C Stimson, *Using Child Benefit in the Family Budget* (York, SPRU, 1997).

paid direct to those children who satisfy the "mature minor" test under *Gillick*[52] but this has never attracted widespread support.[53] Rather the primary focus of the debate in recent years has centred on whether it is indeed appropriate to retain child benefit as a universal benefit, or to subject it to means-testing or taxation.[54]

The commitment of successive Conservative administrations since 1979 to the principle of universal child benefit was by no means clear, not least given the failure to maintain the value of the benefit in line with inflation.[55] In 1991, however, a higher rate of child benefit was introduced for the only or eldest child in the family. In 1995 the then Conservative Secretary of State for Social Security, Peter Lilley, announced the Government's intention to withdraw gradually the special rates of benefits paid to lone parents. Accordingly the rate of one-parent benefit, a supplement to child benefit, was not increased in line with inflation in the April 1996 up-rating exercise.[56] In the following year one-parent benefit was integrated as a special rate of child benefit for lone parent families. This policy was carried through by the Labour Government, following its election in May 1997, with a provision in the Social Security Act 1998 which prompted the first significant backbench rebellion in its first term of office. Section 72 enabled one-parent benefit to be abolished for new claimants with effect from July 1998.[57]

The Government justified its approach on the basis that "additional support should be provided for children in poorer families on the basis of the identifiable needs of children, not on whether there happens to be one parent or two".[58] Although the Government's decision generated considerable difficulties with its own backbenchers, the basic strategy would seem to be consistent with public opinion, which apparently does not prioritise benefits for lone parents.[59] Nevertheless, the Government subsequently announced in the 1998 Budget that child benefit was to be increased by £2.50 per week for the eldest child for all families and that the income support scale rates for children under eleven were

---

[52] *Gillick* v. *West Norfolk and Wisbech Area Health Authority* [1986] AC 112; see further the discussion by Michael Freeman, ch 11 above.

[53] See N Harris, "Social security and the UN Convention on the Rights of the Child in Great Britain" 7 *JSSL* 9 at 19.

[54] A useful discussion of the options is contained in P Hewitt and P Leach, *Social Justice, Children and Families*, Commission on Social Justice Issue Paper 4 (London, IPPR, 1993), pp 31–41.

[55] See N Wikeley, "Training, Targeting and Tidying Up: The Social Security Act 1988" [1989] *JSWFL* 277 at 285–7.

[56] On one-parent benefit, see Ogus, Barendt and Wikeley, *supra* n 23, p 449. The lone parent premium in respect of means-tested benefits was also frozen.

[57] See Child Benefit and Social Security (Fixing and Adjustment of Rates) (Amendment) Regulations 1998 (SI 1998 No. 1581).

[58] DSS, *New ambitions for our country: A new contract for welfare*, Cm 3805 (London, The Stationery Office, 1998), ch 7, para 2.

[59] In the British Social Attitudes Survey, benefits for single parents received a low priority: only 12% regarded benefits for lone parents as their top priority for extra public spending on social security benefits. In contrast, 71% rated retirement pensions as their first priority (notwithstanding the fact that they go to many people who are not in poverty): *Social Trends 1998* (London, The Stationery Office, 1998), p 141.

to be increased over and above the rate of inflation. The Labour Government's broader strategy for tackling child poverty is considered further in the conclusion below.

Guardian's allowance

Guardian's allowance was introduced in 1946 to replace the orphan's pension first established in 1925. The name of the benefit is somewhat misleading, as the recipient need not be the child's legal guardian under the Children Act 1989. Guardian's allowance is paid (in addition to child benefit) to someone who is bringing up a child or children whose own parents have died and is very much a minority benefit.[60] In very exceptional circumstances it can be paid when only one parent is dead, such as where the other parent is in prison or is missing and cannot be found.[61]

Means-tested benefits

Children under the age of sixteen are almost exclusively regarded as dependants of their parents or guardians, and denied any autonomous rights to means-tested benefits. As we shall see below, entitlement to income-based jobseeker's allowance (JSA) does not normally start until a young person reaches eighteen; although income support may be paid from the age of sixteen, this benefit is now paid only to those categories of claimant who do not have to be available for work.[62] Indeed, the very structure of these benefits assumes dependency. Thus a person's income support or income-based JSA entitlement is calculated by comparing their income with their "applicable amount";[63] the latter figure comprises a personal allowance for the claimant (and, where applicable, their partner and any children) together with any relevant premiums and housing costs.[64] For some years the personal allowances were grouped in three bands, according to the age of the children, with different (and increasing) rates for under eleven-year-olds, eleven to sixteen-year-olds and seventeen to eighteen-year-olds.[65] However, with effect from April 2000 the higher 11–16 rate was extended to all children below the age of sixteen.[66] The assumption of dependency is also inherent to the system

[60] SSCBA 1992, s. 77. In 1998 there were 2,329 families receiving guardian's allowance in respect of 2,944 children: DSS (1999), *supra* n 7, Tables G4.01 and G4.02, pp 295–6.
[61] See Ogus, Barendt and Wikeley, *supra* n 23, pp 287–92.
[62] Thus a young person who leaves school before their sixteenth birthday and lives away from their parents will have to rely on assistance from social services, using their powers under the Children Act 1989.
[63] SSCBA 1992, s. 124(4).
[64] In this context this refers to mortgage interest payments; assistance for liability for rent is provided through the housing benefit scheme.
[65] Income Support (General) Regulations 1987 (SI 9187 No. 1967), Sched 2, para 2.
[66] Social Security Amendment (Personal Allowances for Children and Young Persons) Regulations 1999 (SI 1999 No. 2555).

of premiums: these include the family premium, payable where a claimant is responsible for a child or young person,[67] and the disabled child premium, payable where such a child or young person receives DLA or is blind.[68] The same basic principles apply to the calculation of entitlement to housing benefit and council tax benefit.[69]

Children under the age of sixteen also have no right of direct access to the social fund, the system of grants and repayable loans that was introduced in 1988 by the Social Security Act 1986. The social fund replaced the former arrangements for single payments for one-off needs under the supplementary benefits scheme.[70] Applicants for budgeting loans and community care grants must themselves be in receipt of a qualifying benefit, namely income support or income-based jobseeker's allowance.[71] An applicant for a crisis loan need not be claiming a qualifying benefit but must be aged sixteen or over.[72]

YOUNG PEOPLE AGED SIXTEEN OR SEVENTEEN

The discussion above has demonstrated that children under the age of sixteen have very little autonomy within the social security system. In the following section the status of sixteen and seventeen-year-olds are considered; in particular, do they have any independent right to benefit? Before doing so, it needs to be understood that many sixteen and seventeen-year-olds, *and indeed some eighteen-year-olds*, will still be seen by the benefits system as dependent on their parents. We have already seen that young people under the age of nineteen who are still in full-time education are regarded as children for the purposes of child benefit. Moreover, means-tested benefits are assessed and paid according to family units; and a "family" is defined as a married or unmarried couple, or a lone parent, together with a member of the same household for whom they are responsible "and who is a child or a person of a prescribed description".[73] For these purposes a "child" is defined as a person under the age of sixteen,[74] while regulations define a person of a prescribed description as "a person aged 16 or over but under 19 who is treated as a child" for the purposes of child benefit; these sixteen, seventeen and eighteen-year-olds are known as "young persons",[75] although, as Harris observes, "this change is cosmetic, and offers no additional rights or improved status to young people".[76]

---

[67] Income Support (General) Regulations 1987 (SI 9187 No. 1967), Sched 2, para 4.

[68] *Ibid*, para 14.

[69] The rare situation in which an under 16-year-old can claim housing benefit is considered below.

[70] See generally T Buck, *The Social Fund: Law and Practice* (London, Sweet & Maxwell, 2nd ed, 2000).

[71] Social Fund Directions 8 and 25.

[72] Social Fund Direction 14.

[73] SSCBA 1992, s. 137(1).

[74] *Loc. cit.*

[75] See for example, Income Support (General) Regulations 1987 (SI 1987 No. 1967), reg. 14.

[76] N Harris, "Youth, Citizenship and Welfare" [1992] *JSWFL* 175 at 186.

Contributory benefits

Contributory benefits were first established by the National Insurance Act 1911 and the basis for the modern scheme remains Beveridge's later reforms, as implemented in the National Insurance Act 1946.[77] The prime purpose of contributory benefits is to provide an alternative source of income, where the claimant's normal means of support has been lost owing to the occurrence of one of the specific social risks recognised by the Beveridge scheme, e.g. bereavement, illness, maternity, retirement or unemployment. They are therefore fundamentally earnings-replacement benefits and are paid out of the National Insurance Fund, which in turn is funded by contributions levied on both employers and employees. The working assumption of the scheme is still that contributions will be paid during a normal adult working life, as a result of which the claimant will build up the necessary contributions record. Yet the scheme operates on a pay-as-you-go basis, so today's contributors are paying for today's claimants. There is, therefore, no direct actuarial link between the contributions paid in by individuals and any benefits that they may receive in the future.

In principle young people aged sixteen or seventeen enjoy an independent right to national insurance benefits. The contributory benefits, with the major exception of the state retirement pension, do not impose any qualifying age limit (e.g. eighteen) for their receipt. In practice, however, the fundamental difficulty is precisely that these benefits are paid on the basis of contributions records. There are separate contribution conditions for each of the various benefits, the effect of which is that it is unlikely that young people will be able to claim a contributory benefit before the age of eighteen, given the need to build up a contributions record in the first place. Assuming a young person had started work immediately on leaving school at sixteen, it would not be possible for him or her to have built up a contributions record in order to claim, for example, incapacity benefit when nearing eighteen. For this reason a comprehensive practitioner's guide to young people's benefits rights, produced by Youthaid, simply ignores contributory benefits altogether.[78] There is nothing new about this exclusion of young people from contributory benefits.[79]

However, as a result of reforms introduced by the Welfare Reform and Pensions Act 1999, some very severely disabled young people may now be eligible

[77] See now SSCBA 1992, Part II.

[78] B Chatrik, *Guide to Training & Benefits for Young People* (London, Unemployment Unit & Youthaid, 5th ed, 1999), p 28.

[79] As one study of the inter-war years has commented, "Juveniles, however, had access to much less generous benefits, could collect them for a much shorter period of time, and were subject to what amounted to stiffer contributory requirements before becoming eligible at all": D K Benjamin and L A Kochin, "What went Right with Juvenile Unemployment Policy between the Wars: A Comment" 32 *Economic History Review* 523 at 525; see also W R Garside, "Juvenile Unemployment and Public Policy between the Wars" 30 *Economic History Review* 322 and "Juvenile Unemployment between the Wars: A Rejoinder" 32 *Economic History Review* 529.

for incapacity benefit notwithstanding the absence of an adequate contributions record.[80] This undoubted improvement in benefit rights for young people has to be seen in a broader context. The 1999 Act abolished severe disablement allowance (SDA), a benefit which itself was only introduced in 1984, which had in turn replaced the former non-contributory invalidity pension and housewives' non-contributory invalidity pension. SDA was essentially a benefit for people who were incapable of work but who failed the contributions test for incapacity benefit. Reflecting its status as a non-contributory benefit, it was paid at a much lower rate.[81] As an earnings replacement benefit, it was not payable to those aged under sixteen or who were in full-time education.[82] Moreover, SDA claimants had to be aged between sixteen and sixty-five when they claimed and must have *either* been incapable of work for at least twenty-eight weeks beginning on or before the claimant's twentieth birthday *or* been assessed as being at least 80 per cent[83] disabled for a minimum of twenty-eight weeks. The effect of the 1999 Act has been to transfer the former group, those incapacitated in their youth, to the more generous incapacity benefit, but to withdraw entitlement altogether from new claimants in the latter group, over the age of twenty-five,[84] who would previously have satisfied the 80 per cent disablement test.[85] The incorporation within the mainstream incapacity benefit of those incapacitated in their youth implements a proposal first made by the Social Security Advisory Committee in 1988.[86]

Non-contributory benefits

Young people who are sixteen or seventeen may qualify for industrial disablement benefit if they are injured in an accident at work or contract an industrial disease. The eligibility rules are the same as for adults, and do not require the payment of contributions. There is, however, a reduced rate of industrial disablement benefit paid to this group,[87] reflecting a similar policy which operated historically for national insurance benefits. Young people aged sixteen and seventeen are also entitled to disability living allowance in the same way as adults.

---

[80] S. 53, amending SSCBA 1992, s. 30A.

[81] In 2001–02 the long-term rate of incapacity benefit was £69.75 a week compared with £42.15 for SDA.

[82] SSCBA 1992, s. 68(4).

[83] The principles governing the percentage assessment of disablement were the same as those applying under the industrial injuries scheme.

[84] The original proposal was to retain the SDA age limit of 20, but this was raised to 25 following lobbying during the passage of the Act.

[85] Those aged 20 and over who were in receipt of SDA on the basis of an 80% assessment continue to receive the benefit, but new claims have not been accepted from the point of change: WRPA 1999, s. 70.

[86] SSAC, *Benefits for Disabled People: A Strategy for Change* (London, HMSO, 1988), para 11.20. See further N Wikeley, *supra* n 33.

[87] SSCBA 1992, Sched 4, Part V.

The additional requirement that the claimant's needs are "substantially" more than those of other children ceases once the claimant reaches the age of sixteen.[88] If the young person is a carer, and provided she is not in full-time education, she can claim invalid care allowance.[89] Where a sixteen or seventeen-year-old (and indeed an eighteen-year-old) continues to be in full-time non-advanced education,[90] their parent may continue to claim child benefit for them.[91] In 1996 Gordon Brown, then Shadow Chancellor, proposed that child benefit should be abolished for sixteen to eighteen-year-olds who were still in education and the resources invested in a training scheme for school leavers. The argument in part was one of targeting: why should the parents of Etonians studying for 'A' Levels receive child benefit while those young people on training schemes were denied adequate support? This proposal now appears to have been dropped, at least for the time being.[92]

Means-tested benefits

Means-tested benefits exist as the safety net of the welfare state. Income support and income-based jobseeker's allowance (JSA) are the direct lineal descendants of the Poor Law and it is in this context that the position of sixteen and seventeen-year-old young people becomes most acute. Indeed, there are significant historical continuities in the state's treatment of young people who are of an age to work (howsoever that has been defined at different stages) but who are not gainfully employed. Hendrick has argued that "social policy for deprived children began seriously in the sixteenth century with the inauguration of the 'boarding-out' system whereby Poor Law children were apprenticed to whomsoever would take them".[93] Thus, from the earliest days of the Poor Law the philosophy was that children—at much younger ages than sixteen and seventeen—who were not supported by their families should be instructed in

---

[88]   SSCBA 1992, ss. 72(6) and 73(4).

[89]   However, "entitlement is often missed for under 18s who have no other benefit entitlement": J Barlow and P Lamb, "Age limits and benefits" *Legal Action*, November 1990, 14 at 17.

[90]   Essentially defined to mean a course of at least 12 hours' supervised study a week at a level up to and including 'A' Level: SSCBA 1992, s. 142 and Child Benefit (General) Regulations 1976 (SI 1976 No. 965).

[91]   This continues until the "terminal date", i.e. the end of the holiday after the term in which the young person leave education. For a helpful guide to the practical issues involved, see Chatrik, *supra* n 78, pp 8–13.

[92]   As Bradshaw and Stimson comment (*supra* n 51, p 58), "if the aim is to fund a decent training programme, it would be better to raise the revenue by taxing better-off parents (including old Etonians but, more importantly, the single and the childless) rather than taking Child Benefit from the many already hard-pressed families supporting children in education beyond the statutory school leaving age". On education maintenance allowances, introduced on a pilot basis in 1999, see N Harris, "Social security and education", ch 11 in N Harris (ed), *supra* n 33, p 356.

[93]   H Hendrick, *Child Welfare: England 1872–1989* (London, Routledge, 1994), p 74.

appropriate trades, rather than receive unconditional relief.[94] Apprenticeship and training were thus seen as the means by which children should become self-supporting and so avoid the fate of child vagrancy, with all the associated public order problems which that involved.[95] After the Poor Law Amendment Act 1834 outside apprenticeships were abandoned in favour of industrial training and education in buildings separate from the workhouse, so as to avoid the contamination of pauperism.[96] The treatment of unemployed young people, or juveniles, continued to be a matter of concern to policy-makers throughout the Victorian era and into the twentieth century, but principally during periods of high unemployment. As Harris observes, the period from 1911 to 1980 appears to be marked "by complacency or indifference towards the position of young people under the benefits system. Intervention only occurred when there was a threat to social order, a massive drain on the insurance fund, or suspected 'idleness' on the part of the unemployed".[97]

In the 1980s government policy towards unemployed young people, manifested in a succession of training schemes and the withdrawal of benefit rights,[98] resulted in a process of marginalisation and social exclusion.[99] Indeed, as Berthoud notes in the context of the safety net of income support, "the two biggest categories of excluded people, which overlap considerably, are the homeless and young people under 18".[100] For those young people who stay at home, the consequence is that their dependence on their families is prolonged, at a time both when young people are seeking to assert their independence and successive governments have adopted the rhetoric of self-reliance.[101] The result, according to Harris, is that "the social security system does not reveal a commitment by society to the citizenship needs of young people. Moreover, it fails to provide the support needed for the transition to adult independence".[102]

Means-tested benefits are paid to those citizens who meet the prescribed conditions of entitlement and whose income from other sources (including other social

[94] See for example, W P Quigley, "Five Hundred Years of English Poor Laws, 1349–1834: Regulating the Working and Nonworking Poor" (1986) 30 *Akron Law Review* 73. For an invaluable summary of the legal position, see R Cranston, *Legal Foundations of the Welfare State* (London, Weidenfeld & Nicolson, 1985), n 36, pp 343–4.

[95] Indeed, poor law legislation of 1547 provided for the children of beggars to be apprenticed, while if they ran away servitude could be imposed: W K Jordan, *Philanthropy in England 1480–1660* (London, George Allen & Unwin Ltd, 1959), p 86.

[96] Hendrick, *supra* n 93, p 74. See further on Poor Law education, U R Q Henriques, *Before the Welfare State* (London, Longman, 1979), pp 210–15 and M A Crowther, *The Workhouse System 1834–1929* (Athens, University of Georgia Press, 1982), pp 201–07.

[97] Harris, *supra* n 3, p 66.

[98] See further N Wikeley, "Training for Employment in the 1990s" (1990) 53 *MLR* 354.

[99] T Chapman and J Cook, "Marginality, youth and government policy in the 1980s" (1988) 22 *Critical Social Policy* 41.

[100] R Berthoud, "Income protection, inclusion and exclusion in the UK" in D Hirsch (ed), *Social protection and inclusion: European challenges for the United Kingdom* (York, York Publishing Services, Joseph Rowntree Foundation, 1997) ch 8, p 75.

[101] N Harris, "Social Security and the Transition to Adulthood" (1988) 17 *Journal of Social Policy* 501 at 502 and 518.

[102] *Ibid* at 512.

security benefits) is insufficient to reach whatever level of income is effectively defined as the state's poverty line. The principal means-tested benefits are income support, income-based JSA, housing benefit and council tax benefit.[103] We have seen that young people aged sixteen, seventeen or eighteen who are still in full-time education, and for whom child benefit is payable, will be treated as dependent upon their parents in the event that their parents claim a means-tested benefit. But what is the position of young people in this age group who have left full-time education? The lower age limit for income support is sixteen and, for income-based JSA normally eighteen[104] although, as shall be seen below, very few sixteen and seventeen-year-olds will in fact qualify for either benefit. This inevitably has consequences in terms of access to the social fund, for which receipt of a qualifying benefit is a precondition for budgeting loans and community care grants.

Income support

Entitlement to the main means-tested benefit has not always been tied into the school leaving age. The minimum age for receipt of national assistance was sixteen, at a time when the school leaving age was fourteen. This age limit was carried over into the supplementary benefit scheme in 1966. The Social Security Act 1986, introducing income support, likewise specified sixteen as the lower age limit.[105] However, Mrs Thatcher had made clear her antipathy to the concept of school-leavers having an automatic right to benefit some years earlier: "It's too easy for some of them, straight out of school, to go on to social security at the age of 16".[106] The Social Security Act 1988 accordingly raised the normal minimum age of entitlement to income support to eighteen years, with sixteen and seventeen-year-olds only being entitled in exceptional circumstances.[107]

A consequence of the introduction of JSA in 1996 was the reduction in the lower age limit for income support to sixteen again. Thus sixteen and seventeen-year-olds can claim income support but only, as with adults, if they fall within the "prescribed groups of persons".[108] These include lone parents, pregnant women, carers, blind people and a limited range of pupils in education, including parents, severely handicapped persons, orphans and persons estranged from their parents or guardian. The common thread between all these diverse groups is that they are all relieved of the obligation to be available for and actively seeking work or, in common parlance, to "sign on".

---

[103] SSCBA 1992, s. 123(1). For a practical guide, see Chatrik, *supra* n 78.

[104] SSCBA 1992, s. 124(1)(a) and Jobseekers Act 1995, s. 3(1)(f).

[105] Social Security Act 1996, s. 20. Indeed, the Fowler Review Green Paper declared: "no changes are proposed to the eligibility of young unemployed people to benefit" (*Reform of Social Security*, Cmnd 9517 (London, HMSO, 1985), Vol 1, para 9.27, p 36.

[106] *Daily Express*, 15 June 1983, quoted in J Allbeson, "Seen but not heard: young people", ch 7 in S Ward (ed), *DHSS in Crisis* (London, CPAG, 1985), p 90.

[107] See N Harris, "Raising the Minimum Age of Entitlement to Income Support: Social Security Act 1988" (1988) *JLS* 201 and Wikeley, *supra* n 55. These rules have now been carried over into income-based JSA, which replaced income support for unemployed people in October 1996.

[108] SI 1987 No. 1967, reg. 4ZA and Sched 1B.

Income-based jobseeker's allowance

In 1996 income-based JSA replaced income support for all unemployed people of working age who are expected to "sign on". The rules that governed the (very limited) entitlement of sixteen and seventeen-year-olds to income support before the introduction of JSA have been carried forward (with some amendments to the details) into the arrangements for income-based JSA. Young people in this age group may only qualify for income-based JSA if they fall within one of four categories.

The first group comprises those who are able to claim such benefit without restriction, i.e. at any time and for any period when they are sixteen or seventeen. This includes those with a partner and who have a child.[109] The second category consists of young people who may claim during the child benefit extension period, a period of twelve weeks after the terminal date for a normal child benefit claim once a young person leaves full-time education. A range of young people who might be considered "at risk" are included under this heading,[110] but they must also register for a youth training place as a condition of eligibility. Thirdly, some young people leaving care or custody and living independently may qualify for a maximum of eight weeks after the expiry of the child benefit extension period.[111] Finally, where a young person does not fall within any of the categories outlined above, she may claim income-based JSA if "severe hardship" will result if benefit is not paid. There is no legislative definition of "severe hardship", nor any officially published rules.[112] However, relevant factors include the young person's means of support, health and vulnerability and the risk of losing accommodation.[113] These narrow eligibility conditions, when combined with the complexity of the administrative arrangements, have led to real hardship and social exclusion for many 16 to 18 year olds.[114] According to one official estimate, there are around 161,000 young people aged sixteen to eighteen (about 9 per cent of the age group) in the United Kingdom who are not in any form of education, employment or training,[115] although this figure

---

[109] Jobseeker's Allowance Regulations 1996 (SI 1996 No. 207), reg. 61. If the claimant is a lone parent, she can claim income support. She could, alternatively, claim income-based JSA, but would face the risk of sanctions for non-compliance with the labour market conditions.

[110] *Ibid*, reg. 57(2).

[111] *Ibid*, reg. 60.

[112] For an analysis of the operational issues involved, see B Stafford, B Dobson and J Vincent, *Delivering Benefits to Unemployed 16 and 17 Year Olds*, DSS Research Report No. 70 (London, The Stationery Office, 1997).

[113] Chatrik, *supra* n 78, pp 31 and 35–44.

[114] For evidence, see D Kirk, S Nelson, A Sinfield and D Sinfield, *Excluding Youth* (Edinburgh, Bridges Project and Edinburgh Centre for Social Welfare Research, 1991); I Maclagan, *A Broken Promise* (London, Youthaid and The Children's Society, 1992); NACAB, *Severe hardship* (London, NACAB, 1992 (E/3/92)); I Maclagan, *Four Years' Severe Hardship* (London, Youthaid and Barnardos, 1993). Specifically on health consequences, see A Dennehy, L Smith and P Harker, *Not to be ignored: young people, poverty and health* (London, CPAG, 1997).

[115] Social Exclusion Unit, *Bridging the Gap: New Opportunities for 16–18 Year Olds not in Education, Employment or Training* Cm 4405 (London, The Stationery Office, 1999), p 15.

probably underestimates the scale of the problem.[116] The two main sets of factors associated with non-participation at sixteen to eighteen are educational underachievement and disaffection together with family disadvantage and poverty.[117]

Housing benefit and council tax benefit

There is no statutory minimum age for entitlement to housing benefit. A sixteen or seventeen-year-old tenant may therefore qualify for housing benefit, and it is conceivable that a child under the age of sixteen may also qualify. The potential difficulty is whether it can be demonstrated that such a child has a legally enforceable liability for the rent.[118] As a person has to be at least eighteen in order to be liable for council tax,[119] council tax benefit is only available to adults.

Working families' tax credit and disabled person's tax credit

The former family credit and disability working allowance, both of which were in-work benefits for people working at least sixteen hours a week, were replaced by working families' tax credit and disabled person's tax credit in October 1999. There was no minimum age limit for family credit and so it was possible, in quite exceptional circumstances, for a child under sixteen to claim family credit.[120] Disability working allowance, on the other hand, was subject to a minimum age requirement of sixteen.[121] There was no change to this position in the primary legislation governing tax credits, the Tax Credits Act 1999, but the whole system is premised on an individual receiving wages from an employer. In a similar (but not identical) way to income support, a claimant's working families' tax credit entitlement is calculated by reference to the number of dependent children.

---

[116] Social Exclusion Unit, *Bridging the Gap: New Opportunities for 16–18 Year Olds not in Education, Employment or Training* Cm 4405 (London, The Stationery Office, 1999), p 21.

[117] *Ibid*, p 24.

[118] Housing Benefit (General) Regulations 1987 (SI 1987 No. 1971), reg. 6. See also the discussion in L Findlay et al, *Housing Benefit and Council Tax Benefit Legislation* (London, CPAG, 11th ed, 1999), pp 117–18. A child can succeed to a secure tenancy under the Housing Act 1985: see *Kingston-upon-Thames* v. *Prince* [1999] 1 FLR 593 and the discussion by David Cowan, ch 10 above.

[119] Local Government Finance Act 1992, s. 6(5).

[120] See the discussion in C George et al, *Welfare Benefits Handbook*, Vol 1 (London, CPAG, 1st ed, 1999), p 461. In practice the requirements of remunerative work for at least 16 hours a week and responsibility for a dependent child or young person excluded almost all under-16s: see J Mesher and P Wood, *Income Related Benefits: The Legislation 1999* (London, Sweet & Maxwell, 1999), p 13.

[121] SSCBA 1992, s. 129(1).

CONCLUSION

The immediate post-war perception of the success of the welfare state was followed by the "rediscovery" of poverty, and especially child poverty, in the 1960s. The late 1960s and the 1970s witnessed a series of social security reforms which were designed to tackle these problems, such as the introduction of child benefit as a universal benefit and of family income supplement (later family credit and now working families' tax credit), as a top-up to low earnings. Since then child benefit has not been consistently up-rated with inflation and family credit has suffered take-up difficulties, as with any means-tested benefit. Nearly two decades of Conservative rule have resulted in significant increases in inequality and a rising proportion of children living in poverty.[122] In 1979 there were 923,000 children under the age of sixteen in Great Britain who were living in families reliant on supplementary benefit, representing 7.3 per cent of the child population. By 1998 the number of children dependent on income support had risen to 2.2 million, or one in five children in this age group.[123] Moreover, the inadequacy of basic income support levels has been comprehensively detailed by the Family Budget Unit, whose research demonstrates that the gap between a low cost but acceptable budget and income support for a two-parent family was between £32 and £39 a week at January 1998 rates, and between £24 and £27 for a lone parent.[124] As the study concludes, "For families with children, income support is unsustainable except in the short term".[125]

In 1999 Tony Blair declared that the "historic aim" of the Labour Government was to end child poverty forever within a generation: "It is a 20 year mission but I believe it can be done".[126] The Green Paper on welfare reform, published the previous year, had made it clear that the centrepiece of this strategy was not going to be one of increasing mainstream social security benefits directed towards children. This impression was reinforced by the announcement in the 1999 Budget that child tax allowances would be introduced from April 2001. True, the rate of child benefit for the eldest child and the income support personal allowances for children under eleven were to be increased above the rate of inflation and the latter were subsequently aligned with the eleven to sixteen rate. Yet this was in large part a response to the political difficulties generated by the decision to carry through the Conservative administration's decision to abolish one-parent benefit.[127] The focus of the

---

[122] J Hills, *Income and Wealth: The Latest Evidence* (York, Joseph Rowntree Foundation, 1998).

[123] *Hansard*, HC Debs, Vol 319, col 160w, 10 November 1998. If housing benefit, family credit and disability working allowance were also included, one third of all British children lived in families dependent on means-tested benefits: L Adelman and J Bradshaw, "Children in Poverty in Britain: An Analysis of the F.R.S. 1994/95", SPRU paper, University of York, 1999, p 2.

[124] H Parker (ed), *Low Cost but Acceptable* (London, Policy Press, 1998), p 68.

[125] *Ibid*, p 89.

[126] Rt Hon Tony Blair, *Beveridge Lecture*, Toynbee Hall, London, March 18, 1999.

[127] See p 231. This alignment, with a single rate for children under 16, will also presumably entail administrative savings.

Green Paper was rather on making work pay; the introduction of the more generous working families' tax credit to replace family credit is a key component of this approach. This work-centred policy is also reflected in the New Deal for Lone Parents and the proposed reforms to the child support scheme.[128] The prospects of success for this strategy are closely bound up with the general state of the economy. A significant collapse in the demand for labour will necessarily increase reliance on out-of-work benefits, which will again focus attention on the inadequacy of the basic rates of income support and income-based jobseeker's allowance. As Adelman and Bradshaw conclude:

> "In *A New Contract for Welfare* the answer to poverty is 'work for those who can'. The alternative is 'security for those who cannot'. It is worrying, though, that there is no strategy in the Green Paper to ensure that there is indeed this security. This study has shown that children whose parents receive Income Support have far higher poverty measures than those that do not . . . If the scourge of child poverty is to be tackled then there must be further real increases in the Income Support scale rates for children."[129]

This is, above all, a political question. Other contributions to this volume have emphasised the importance of children's rights. The reality is that the development of human rights norms at supra-national level with a view to improving the position of children has had very little impact on domestic UK social security provision. The focus of the European Convention on Human Rights is on civil and political rights.[130] More promisingly, the UN Convention on the Rights of the Child expressly addresses social and economic rights, and Article 26 declares that children have "the right to benefit from social security, including social insurance". There is, however, no minimal international standard; instead, Article 26 requires contracting states to achieve the full realisation of this right "in accordance with national law".[131] UK social security law has traditionally seen children's social security entitlements as parasitical on those of their parents, an approach acknowledged by Article 26(2). Moreover, the limited nature of the Convention is underlined by Article 27. Thus although Article 27(1) requires contracting states to recognise "the right of every child to a standard of living adequate for the child's physical, mental, spiritual, moral and social development", Article 27(2) then specifies that the child's parents (or others responsible for the child) "have the primary responsibility to secure, within

---

[128] DSS, *A new contract for welfare: children's rights and parents' responsibilities*, Cm 4349 (London, The Stationery Office, 1999).

[129] *Supra* n 123, p 28.

[130] See further J Fortin, "Rights Brought Home for Children" (1999) 62 *MLR* 350.

[131] G Van Bueren, *The International Law on the Rights of the Child* (Dordrecht, Martinus Nijhoff, 1995), p 318. It is perhaps symptomatic that this comprehensive study devotes two pages to the rights of the child to an adequate standard of living in a text of over 400 pages. For a complacent account of the previous government's record under Arts. 26 and 27, see *The UK's First Report to the UN Committee on the Rights of the Child* (London, HMSO, 1994), pp 90–3. See now *Second Report to the U.N. Committee on the Rights of the Child by the United Kingdom* (London, The Stationery Office, 1999), pp 109–10 and the invaluable analysis by Harris, *supra* n 53.

their abilities and financial capacities, the conditions of living necessary for the child's development". Thus where particular groups within the community—for example, asylum seekers—are identified as appropriate targets for benefit cuts, their children are especially vulnerable.[132] Similarly, changes to the eligibility rules for sixteen and seventeen-year-olds have served only to reinforce this assumption of dependency and to increase the risk of social exclusion. In the absence of effective international norms, the status of children within the social security system necessarily reflects national trends and preoccupations. As this chapter has sought to demonstrate, this is apparent in the treatment of both children and young people for the purposes of welfare benefits.

---

[132] See for example, *R* v. *Adjudication Officer, ex parte Velasquez, The Times*, 30 April 1999, discussed by Thomas (1999) 6 *JSSL* 176 and see now Immigration and Asylum Act 1999, s. 115.

Index